Virtuality and the Art of Exhibition

Virtuality and the Art of Exhibition

Curatorial Design for the Multimedial Museum

Vince Dziekan

intellect Bristol, UK / Chicago, USA

First published in the UK in 2012 by
Intellect, The Mill, Parnall Road, Fishponds, Bristol, BS16 3JG, UK

First published in the USA in 2012 by
Intellect, The University of Chicago Press, 1427 E. 60th Street,
Chicago, IL 60637, USA

Copyright © 2012 Intellect Ltd

All rights reserved. No part of this publication may be reproduced,
stored in a retrieval system, or transmitted, in any form or by
any means, electronic, mechanical, photocopying, recording, or
otherwise, without written permission.

A catalogue record for this book is available from the
British Library.

Cover designer: Holly Rose
Copy-editor: Ed Hatton
Typesetting: Mac Style, Beverley, E. Yorkshire

ISBN 978-1-84150-476-6

Printed and bound in Great Britain by 4edge Ltd, Hockley. www.4edge.co.uk

Contents

Foreword

The museum plays an instrumental role in determining the contours of creative practices associated with artistic production and curation. The art object, the gallery's cubic environment and the museum's institutional apparatus are powerful manifestations that shape our perceptions and understanding, as well as the expectations that we place on art. The influence of such conventional structures on the forms – and resulting conformity – of artistic and curatorial practice cannot be overstated. Revealed in the light of new technologies, the physical structure traditionally associated with the museum is reconceived as a matrix of differently constituted but interrelated spaces. The impact of digital processes has begun to transform art's *exhibition complex* composed as it is from the interrelationship between artefact, gallery space and museum.

This book engages artistic production and its modes of exhibition under emerging contemporary conditions. The primary objective of its collected interdisciplinary investigations is directed at developing a conceptual framework for digitally informed creative production of exhibitions exemplified by applied *curatorial design*. The term *curatorial design* will be used across this text to encompass contemporary curating practices that influence aesthetic experience associated with the art of exhibition. The curatorial design project proposes a critically informed approach to creative curation, particularly as this relates to the production of exhibition-making that integrates digital mediation with spatial practice.

By focusing on emerging models of the multimedial museum and curatorial design, this book brings together critical and creative investigations that respond to the current state of adaptation and integration of digital media within museum-based cultural practices in order to speculate upon the interrelationship of digital mediation with spatial practice. In order to do so, its structure and contents have been designed to encompass a set of interdisciplinary investigations relating to virtuality and the art of exhibition. Undertaking such an inquiry at this particular cultural moment is both topical and necessary, as over the past decade issues associated with digital technologies have exerted a significant influence upon artistic practice, the institutions that support it, as well as the practice of curation. Illustratively, the exhibition *010101: Art in Technological Times* at the San Francisco Museum of Modern Art (SFMOMA) heralds such a state of affairs and announces a number of themes that have inspired this book's scope of enquiry. Ahead of the launch of the exhibition in March 2001, its stated objective was to chart new developments in contemporary art, architecture and design influenced by the increasing presence of digital media and technology. In conjunction with the exhibition, a special website was created to support and extend the exhibition both onsite in the museum's galleries and online through the Internet. Marking the start of the new millennium, the exhibition's online presence was launched on 1 January 2001 and was introduced with the following pronouncement:

> Over the past decade, the world of contemporary art has experienced the beginnings of a tectonic shift: digital technology has arrived as a component of everyday life and contemporary art on a global scale. Artists are adopting new technologies in the studio, deploying them in the gallery, inhabiting them through the Internet and making artwork that reflects our technology-saturated society in a stunning range of ways … Museums struggle to keep up, as audiences too are changed by the presence of technology in their lives. Distances shrink under the pressure of the Internet, cell phones, and e-mail. Attention spans flit nervously from message to message, channel to channel and site to site. Neither art nor those who make it, show it and look at it can ever be the same again![1]

Besides hosting a series of interactive public programs, including online discussion forums and providing interpretive materials giving background information on the artists included in the exhibition and investigating key concepts in their work, the site also featured a collection of specially commissioned online projects by digital artists and designers.[2] Manifested through a combination of online and installation forms, this particular exhibition project anticipated a number of interests and issues identified in this book that have been pursued here through a combination of practice-based and more conventional scholarly forms of interrogation and exploration.

Together, the critique and creative production documented in this book respond to the production and consumption models of forms of contemporary art directly influenced by the increasing integration of the digital with the practices of making and exhibiting contemporary media art. While the influence of digitization is relatively easy to recognise on the surface (artworks made with digital media tools and techniques, works distributed via digital channels such as the Internet), my curiosity has become directed more fundamentally towards how artistic and curatorial practices are transformed by *virtuality* and how aesthetic experience is mediated under these conditions. Throughout this text, the term *virtuality* will be used to describe the characteristic quality of aesthetic experience under contemporary conditions; conditions that are influenced, in part, by digital mediation, with the multimedial nature of the museum being so identified as the cultural form through which virtuality is expressed. This approach is empathetic to an interdisciplinary cultural analysis of new media (digital media, multimedia communication, virtual spaces), cultural production (exhibition-making) and digital aesthetics (exploration of forms of interaction, connectivity and systems). Common to all of these domains is the emancipation from fixed, rigid boundaries. Framing these investigations as an interdisciplinary project facilitates engaging with the concept of virtuality by moving the discourse around digital technologies and their challenge to contemporary creative practice beyond their consignment to the narrow margins of Electronic Art *per se*. By concentrating on the exhibition form itself, the increasingly complex relationship between culture, technology and space can be explored most directly.

In order to negotiate the influence of digital technologies on artistic practice and mediated aesthetic experience as these become increasingly integrated, the underlying approach I've taken to engage with this evolving situation is allied with Mieke Bal's appeal for interdisciplinary method to be applied to the cultural analysis of exposition that occurs through the museum. In *Double Exposures: the subject of cultural analysis*, she pronounces that 'museums are ideally suited to this new kind of integrative and self-critical analysis because they are multimedial' (Bal 1996a, p. 3). She continues: 'They appeal to those interested in challenging the artificial boundaries between media-based disciplines'. This appeal – proffered by the notion of the multimedial museum – motivates the overarching ambitions of this project.

By engaging with the topic of virtuality and the art of exhibition through the combination of both critical, contextual study and applied practice-based exploration, I have tried to develop a fuller understanding of art's contemporary aesthetic conditions through an investigative programme conceived as an 'heuretic' project. Gregory L. Ulmer describes heuretics as the branch of logic that treats the arts of discovery or invention. By seeking to traverse discourses of both art practice and theory, an heuretic approach contributes critically informed praxis to the broader deconstructive assignment. As such, it is appropriate that practice-based research be employed in order to 'to transform an institution while using it, not to reproduce reality but to experimentally rearrange reality (our reality being extant representations) for critical effect' (Ulmer 1994, pp. 81–2). The contents of this resulting book aim to contribute both theoretical framings and practical insights across inter-related discourses between art, design, media and museology. As Bal asserts: 'by selecting an object, you question a field' (2002, p. 4). In so doing, practices and techniques operating within given domains are themselves subjected to investigation: 'Nor are its methods sitting in a toolbox waiting to be applied; they too are part of the exploration'. As a result, an investigation conducted in an interdisciplinary way means that:

> You don't apply one method; you conduct a meeting between several, a meeting in which the object participates, so that, together, object and methods can become a new, not firmly delineated field (Bal 2002, p. 4).

Given the range of themes that fall within the scope of these interests, the resulting texts and documented exhibition projects precipitate encounters across different positions: artistic and curatorial, critical and speculative. Characteristically then, the investigations covered in this book set out to analyse the themes of virtuality and the art of exhibition, along with topics relating to digital mediation, spatial practice, the multimedial museum and curatorial design, and to 'transform', to 'experimentally rearrange' them in and through practice, as much as theoretically.

In response to this challenge, the contents of the book have been organized to accommodate a relatively flexible, exploratory approach to its reading and to invite the reader to build their understanding of this project's overarching motivations in an accumulative manner. Conceived as a 'constellation' of interrelating concerns, it is perhaps inevitable, then, that the structure of the resulting form that this publication takes can be viewed as an attempt to find a balance between the non-linearity of the programme (reflected by the episodic yet linked character of the relatively wide-ranging investigations) and the linearity expected of its narrative and exegetical unfolding (offering the reader a predetermined and sequential development of its main propositions). Unavoidably, the reader will find him- or herself at the intersection of these contradictory gravitational pulls.

The presentation of contextual and speculative critical writings is intended to work in tandem with the conceptual application of related ideas leading towards the creation of documented exhibition-based outcomes. As the primary practice-based aspects are focused upon curatorial design, the representation of this process is only possible in retrospect through reference and illustrative documentation of the creative outcomes. The discussion of the production of the four exhibition projects that form the basis of this creative investigation is supported (in specific cases) by original curator's essays, with subsequent reflective analyses providing critical expansions on curatorial philosophy and exhibition development. Further, supplementary writings have been included that address my artistic strategy of creating associated artworks designed to play specific roles in each of these exhibition. Each of the individual exhibition projects is capable of being read as a self-contained portfolio that, by extension, illuminates the central themes broached in the expository writings that precede them.

Structurally then, the book combines critical writings along with a body of creative work that is focused by a series of curatorial exhibitions and their associated production of artworks. The **Expositions** section contains a series of chapters that present the intersecting themes of virtuality and the art of exhibition, along with topics relating to digital mediation, spatial practice, the multimedial museum and curatorial design. By collecting these inter-connected contextual studies together in this section, it is intended that the set of investigative writings will establish a high degree of critical engagement with digital aesthetics, particularly as this relates to contemporary cultural production through curatorial design and the operations of the multimedial museum. The exposition of these inter-related themes over this set of chapters has been designed to complement the practice-based application of curatorial design. Related ideas drawn from these discussions were conceptually processed and applied towards the creation of original art and exhibition outcomes that are documented and reflectively analysed in the accompanying **Exhibitions** section. Formed in such a way, theory is applied to praxis (as demonstrated primarily through my curation of exhibitions and supplementary artworks); and in turn, praxis informs theory (as case studies offering creative perspectives for critical elaboration).

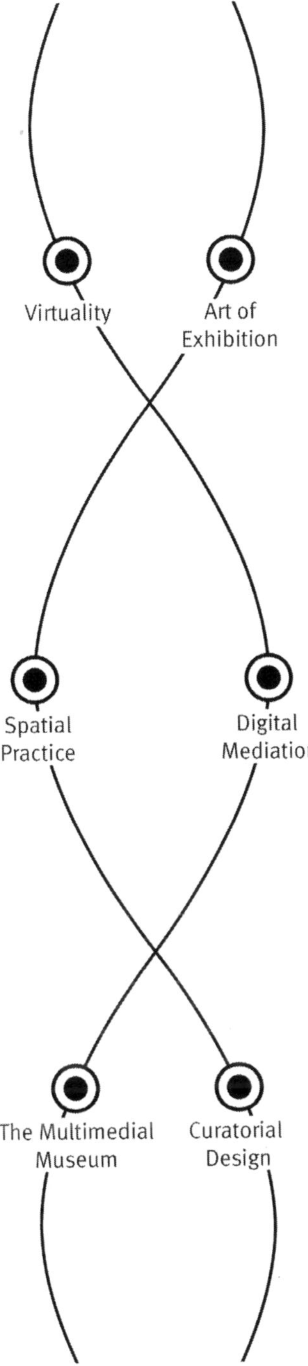

Virtuality
Art of
Exhibition
Spatial
Practice
Digital
Mediation
The Multimedial
Museum
Curatorial
Design

The **Exhibitions** section documents three distinct curatorial projects. Starting with *The Synthetic Image: Digital Technologies and the Image* from 2002 and followed closely thereafter by *Small Worlds: A Romance* produced one year later, this series of exhibitions culminates with *Remote* in 2005. The curatorial premise of *The Synthetic Image* focused on the character of the digital image through surveying imaging practices drawn from an Australian context that exemplify the crossover between a variety of digital and interactive media informed by remediation and individual positions on the role of the image in representing, simulating or creating realities. For its part, the curatorial premise of *Small Worlds: A Romance* explored the relationship between the real and the virtual, new media and other artistic traditions, while the curatorial design of *Remote* challenges the exhibition form itself by proposing a hybrid model that interconnects multimedia spaces with the physical qualities of the gallery and non-gallery environments. Reflecting the nature of the creative investigation that characterises my ongoing interests in fusing artistic and curatorial practices, each exhibition project was also elaborated by the studio production of an accompanying artwork.[3]

Exemplifying this aspect of my creative practice, I produced one particular work with a view towards demonstrating how the art object is modulated at the intersection of the exhibition. Resulting from a research residency hosted by the Slade School of Fine Art, London, in 2008 and subsequently exhibited as part of the International Symposium of Electronic Arts (ISEA) in Belfast in 2009, *The Ammonite Order, or Objectiles for an (Un) Natural History* promotes a non-deterministic approach that defamiliarises the relationship between digital mediation and spatial practice. By exercising the liberty afforded its conceptualisation as an exhibition/artwork that blurs the distinction between fact and fiction, the resulting exhibition demonstrates that the integration of real and virtual through the art of exhibition offers a proposition for how the nature of aesthetic experience associated with the multimedial museum might take shape.

It is a central contention of the interdisciplinary investigations brought together in this book that curation – and, more broadly, approaches to the art of exhibition – is being influenced by virtuality. The character of aesthetic experience under contemporary conditions appears to be leading towards a hybridised species of art that is occurring within a new context: the *multimedial museum*. Through recognising how the relationship between artwork and museum has become increasingly integrated, the exhibition form announces itself as the interface that actively mediates between physical and invisible realities. Crucially, I submit that any subsequent elaboration of digital aesthetics within the broader ecology of contemporary aesthetic production hinges on the pivotal issue of the intersection of new technologies with exhibition space. Today, art's spatial realisation is no longer accommodated exclusively through physical architectural settings. Increasingly influential is the way that the synthesis of exhibition-based spatial practice with digital mediation structures new creative practices, viewer experience and forms of engagement with art. What the thesis of this book refers to as *curatorial design* offers a programme for how art forms and aesthetic experience might operate across social, technological and physical architectures. Understanding the exhibition as the platform which brings this fluid and distributed set of relations together enables it to be viewed as an articulation of the virtual.

At this point, I wish to acknowledge the assistance of the following people, without whom the scope of the overall project would have been impossible to realise. To all of the contributing artists who have inspired the three curatorial projects that are documented herein: Marcus Bunyan, Megan Evans, Marcus Fajl, Phil George, Troy Innocent, Murray McKeich, Gerard Minogue, Matthew Perkins, Patricia Piccinini, Lynne Roberts-Goodwin, Daniel von Sturmer, Trinh Vu (*The Synthetic Image*), Richard Brown, Bruce Mowson, Csaba Szamosy and Joel Zika (*Small Worlds: A Romance*), and Susan Collins, Pete Gomes, Derek Hart, Nancy Mauro-Flude and Martin Walch (*Remote*). To the individuals at the participating galleries who have enabled me to realise the ambition of these exhibitions, in particular: Malcom Bywaters and Anu Jegadeva (Faculty Gallery); Tania Creighton and Tara d'Cruz-Noble (UTS Gallery); Pat Brassington and Paul Zika (Plimsoll Gallery). To Anne Marsh and Scot Cotterell for their insightful contributing essays (to *The Synthetic Image* and *Remote* respectively), along with the designers who have collaborated on the associated publications.

In the case of my demonstration exhibition, *The Ammonite Order*, I wish to acknowledge the cooperation and support of the following people and organizations: Natasha McEnroe (Museum Manager, The Grant Museum of Zoology); the International Organizing Committee of ISEA2009, Kathy Rae Huffman (Curator), Kerstin May and Cherie Driver (University of Ulster); Feargal O'Malley (Exhibition Officer, Ormeau Baths Gallery); Apple UK; Chris Feil (Apple Australia); and the production assistance of Warren Fithie, Joel Collins and Mario Milici from the Faculty of Art & Design, Monash University.

Over the course of this evolving project, I have been able to gain significant insights as a by-product of having numerous preliminary texts published in a variety of scholarly contexts. I would like to recognise these respective scientific committees, conference convenors, journal editors and reviewers. In particular, I'd like to single out: Kelli Dipple for inviting me to participate as panellist in Tate Online's *Liquid Architectures* forum, and Dagny Steudahl for approaching me to present a keynote at Nordic Digital Excellence in Museums (NODEM) 2006. I would also like to acknowledge the access provided by curatorial and other support staff at the Australian Centre for the Moving Image and the National Gallery of Victoria in Melbourne who have assisted me in pursuing particular lines of enquiry.

Importantly, I wish to express my indebtedness to the Faculty of Art & Design, Monash University, which extends to acknowledging the inspiration I have gained from all of my colleagues and members of the Faculty's research community. In particular I would like to acknowledge: Prof. Bernard Hoffert, Dr. Daniel Palmer and Dr. Peter Maddock for their invaluable counsel and input; Prof. Anne Marsh for her sage advice and guidance throughout; and Michelle Neal for her research assistance with preparations for this publication. I wish to recognise the support received from the faculty and university that has enabled me to realise my ambitions for this book. I would also like to give special thanks to Dr. Susan Collins for facilitating my Visiting Research Fellowship with the Slade Centre for Electronic Media in Fine Art (SCEMFA) in London during my research sabbatical in 2008. Additionally, I would like to acknowledge Mike Stubbs, Director of the Foundation for Art and Creative Technology (FACT) in Liverpool, for providing me with opportunities to test some of the propositions developed here as part of our research association.

Finally, to my family for their love, support and understanding.

Notes

1. This extract (along with the earlier cited reference) is drawn originally from the exhibition's online resource: http://010101.sfmoma.org/start.html.
2. Online projects were commissioned from Erik Adigard, Entropy8Zuper!, Mark Napier, Matthew Ritchie, and Thomson & Craighead.
3. While defined for simplicity as studio production, my personal approach to artistic practice has incrementally over time become less reliant on studio-based methodologies, demonstrating what more accurately could be described as a non-studio practice. I addressed this changing nature of my artistic production through a research thesis: V. Dziekan, 1997, Work-in-progress: the influence of photography on the production of representation in the age of mechanical reproduction (1912–1928), with a view towards the development of post-photographic practice and critique, thesis (MA), Monash University.

PART I: EXPOSITIONS

Chapter 1

Virtuality

Synopsis

Used routinely in discourse around digital media, virtuality describes the character of aesthetic experience influenced by contemporary technologised conditions. This cultural concept is represented by a paradigm shift away from consolidated objects to fluid relationships between objectiles. Enabled to a significant degree by digitisation, the experience of virtuality is tied to viewing conditions in physical space. The exhibition plays an influential role in mediating the interaction between cultural production and viewer experience.

Virtual is a term used routinely to describe digital media art. However, to convolute virtual with digital might significantly narrow the scope of its subsequent investigation. The interests that I will be exploring over the remainder of this book align more closely with an overarching conception of how virtuality might describe the characteristic quality of aesthetic experience under contemporary conditions exemplified by the multimedial museum. In its practice-based application, virtuality opens onto an exploration of the nature of the artwork (as an open 'aesthetic system') and the exhibition (as the zone where augmented realities arising from the interconnection between materiality and information overlap).[1]

It is undeniable that digital media practices have begun to impact on the broader art system, as it is constituted by the interrelationships between artefact, gallery and museum, and mediated by the exhibition. Digitally informed artistic and curatorial practices are ideally situated to explore the relationship between the virtual and real dialectically and dialogically, and there is arguably no better place for this investigation to play out than through the museum. As the museum itself adapts – becoming increasingly multimedial as a result – the nature of the ecology of which it is a part is transformed.

Rather than constraining the notion of the 'virtual museum' to a particularly narrow view of artistic activity conducted on the web, a more expansive notion of the multimedial museum opens the exploration of the art of exhibition to a wider range of encounters. As Erkki Huhtamo recognised, the notion of the virtual museum gained credence in cybercultural discourse as a result of the emergence of the World Wide Web (coinciding with its transformation into a multimedia environment with the introduction of the Mosaic browser in 1993). While influenced by the introduction of new software and media, the development of the concept was grounded in then current cultural discourses drawing on the critique of the museum institution. The main claim of Huhtamo's article, however, proposes that the origins of the virtual museum can be historically traced much further back to the emergence of exhibition design as a new medium within the avant-garde art movements of the early twentieth century (citing exemplars like László Moholy-Nagy, El Lissitzky, Herbert Bayer and Frederick Kiesler as pioneers). Citing how examples of their work 'often raise issues like storage and erasure, memory and forgetting, revealing and hiding, the physical and the virtual' (Huhtamo 2002, p. 4), Huhtamo concluded with a cautionary note:

However, solving problems of routing and data-transfer is not everything. Our modes and routines of communicating and interfacing with multimedia databases are cultural, historical and ideological issues as well. Considering precedents from the non-digital eras – covering most of the history of mankind so far – should not be neglected. (p. 14)

Ultimately, the implications of the investigation I wish to embark upon here in this book leads inexorably to a reassessment of the 'reality' of the artistic enterprise itself, challenging conceptions of art-as-object, gallery-as-space and museum-as-institution by reformulating them as contributing parts of an integrative art apparatus or complex. As philosopher Henri Lefebvre, whose critique was instrumental to the revolutionary cultural politics of the late 1960s, wrote:

> A reflection upon the virtual is what guides our understanding of the real (or actual), while also retroactively affecting – and hence illuminating – the antecedents and the necessary preconditions of that reality. (Lefebvre 1991, p. 219)

While it may seem paradoxical, do the underlying ideological foundations that support art and its institutions become more openly exposed to scrutiny under the challenge posed by digitisation? Through the fissures that open up, is it an inherent virtual reality, an absence (a smokescreen), that is revealed underpinning these structures? Following on from this last thought, does the encounter with the digital make the abstractions that reinforce any of a number of art's entrenched institutional precepts more apparent, their influence more pronounced and their agendas more obvious? Is this apperception ultimately the more challenging intervention that new technologies pose to the art of exhibition?

In March 2006, the Tate Gallery in London through its Tate Media programming instigated a forum focusing upon 'Liquid Architectures'. I was invited along with an international and interdisciplinary group of theorists and practitioners by Kelli Dipple (Tate Media's convenor of online events) to debate 'the future of the artefact, and the institutions which steward their exhibition, collection and preservation'. This contention raised a host of questions relevant to what methods and models might come to the fore in museum and gallery culture in the near future and what 'social, technological and physical architectures will become relevant to evolving artistic practice'. Over the course of the online forum a significant amount of discussion was directed at the kind of overlaps that exist between real and virtual dimensions of actualisation.[2] During the online discussion, architect Celine Condorelli observed that the artificial separation of the real from the virtual is not as interesting as their similarities and overlaps that might 'one day render obsolete these terms in their current limitations towards processes of actualisation, taking place regardless of the tools or forms at hand'. Drawing upon the recurrent metaphor of liquid architecture, she noted that 'architecture includes and inhabits invisible layers of spatial relationships as well as very material ones and always has done'. In turn, design theorist Ken Friedman reinforced this observation by making the point that the relation between virtual spaces and the larger physical world is not a duality between a 'virtual' world and a 'real' world: rather, human activity takes part in both. Observing that cyberspace takes on meaning only because it is linked with the physical world, he stated: 'It is embedded in the physical world, and it is important precisely because of the linkages that give physical meaning to virtual activities and the flow of information through cyberspace.'

Addressing the network of relations that support art under technologised conditions necessitates a digital aesthetics. The negotiation of the digital as an aesthetic extends beyond the technical deployment of digital media for artistic production and redirects focus to new modes of production and viewing experience that arise from social, cultural and technological arrangements.[3] According to media philosopher Brian Massumi (2002), digital media have a very limited link to the virtual: 'Nothing is more destructive to the thinking and imaging of the virtual than equating it with the digital' (p. 137).

In relation to the enquiry being embarked upon here, the investigation of the virtual has not been delimited by the technological capacity of digital technologies to produce new, artistic forms of illusionism. Rather, virtuality is understood as being determined by its situation in the real world and the capacity of social space to produce protocols for viewing and routines of audience engagement.

As a cultural concept, the virtual – from *virtus*, meaning essence or force – is representative of a generalised paradigm shift away from distinct, consolidated entities (objects) to the potential of relationships existing between events (instances of objects and their interactions). This description is sympathetic to the definition offered by curator and art critic Nicolas Bourriaud (2002) in the entry he provides for 'art' in the glossary found in his influential *Relational Aesthetics*:

Art.

1. General term describing a set of objects presented as part of a narrative known as art history. This narrative draws up the critical genealogy and discusses the issues raised by these objects, by way of three sub-sets: painting, sculpture, architecture.
2. Nowadays, the word 'art' seems to be no more than a semantic leftover of this narrative, whose more accurate definition would read as follows: Art is an activity consisting in producing relationships with the world with the help of signs, forms, actions and objects. (p. 107)

For his part, architect and philosopher Bernard Cache (1995) has called such virtual objects as *objectiles*.[4] Conceived in recognition of the generative potential of computationally based processes for designing architectural forms, an objectile is a technological object that is no longer defined by its essential form. Instead an objectile is described through its functions and is determined by parameters.

Is it possible to similarly reconceive of art as operating across an expanded bandwidth – in a way analogous to how infrared and ultraviolet ranges of light waves fall beyond the sensitivity of human seeing but are no less real or persistent? Amplified by the process of digitisation, the credibility of the artefact – and the methods of creative production that institutionalise this stabilising and condensing 'moment' (frozen at the juncture of artistic intention, concentrated in the artist's studio, fixed to the gallery wall, sealed in a vitrine) – is deflected and horizons open up that extend its spatio-temporal actualisation.

In his broader theorisation of the cultural implications of virtuality, Massumi (2002) asserts that the virtual is a 'transitional fringing' of the actual and is a property common to all emergent forms. Complementing this observation, Ian Burn's *Mirror Piece* from 1967 provides an illustrative example offering a quintessential conceptualist response. Selected as part of my contribution to the *Extra-Aesthetic* exhibition project (Delany & Hammond 2005), this seminal piece of conceptual art is comprised of a single framed mirror and a series of small frames containing typewritten notes and diagrams detailing the artistic conception involved and the physics – the 'physical' processes – involved in the viewing of the mirror as distinct from its reflected image. In effect, the work draws attention to how the mirror image is always provisional in the way that (paraphrasing from the artist's accompanying text) during observation an event (recognised in the phenomenon of the mirror reflex) subordinates the actual work. With mischievous simplicity, this work reminds us that art is an interactive, collective and always unfinished enterprise. Artworks continue to resonate by being refreshed, reiterated, reconceived through their circulation in real and virtual spaces (the exhibition and museum being such productive spaces). Recognised as a node within a field of fluid, interlacing spatial and temporal vectors, the artwork is a bit like an iceberg, in that it reveals substantially less than what is really there.

Writing in *The Production of Space*, Henri Lefebvre recognised: 'The distinction between infra and supra, between "short of" and "beyond", is just as important as that between "micro" and "macro" levels' (1991, p. 415). Anticipatory (infra) and extended (supra) states expose art to continued evolution, transformation and transience (before/during/after, anticipatory/actual/archival states). Through the operations outlined by Andre Malraux for his 'museum without walls', the artwork continues to resonate experientially beyond its immediate physically constituted presence. Artefactuality is thus understood as a node within the spectrum of active, intersecting spatial and temporal vectors. The artwork is revealed as an active, non-fixed means, not an apotheosised, museum-destined end.

While virtuality is enabled to a significant degree by digitisation, it is crucial to recognise that virtuality is also intimately tied to conditions of space. The visual experience of virtual forms and spaces is premised on the accompanying denial of our real spatial situation. According to art historian David Summers (2003), who traces the role of virtuality across the history of Western art in his imposing text, *Real Spaces*, illusionism in art is not based solely on the success, or otherwise, of artistic dexterity or technique supporting the depiction of realistic images and their representational verisimilitude. The artistic achievement of illusion is also intimately linked to the conditions of viewing and the exhibition space of its encounter. Illusionism conjures up access to another space or event that by definition has occurred elsewhere. For this to happen the viewer must also be induced to imaginatively pass to the 'other side' of the image that is presented before their eyes; they must be prepared to step out from the bounds of their present placement (in front of the image) and location (in the 'here' and 'now'). A significant part of the resulting success of illusionistic representation is premised upon 'over-looking' the basic fact that the act of looking 'into' a virtual space necessarily occurs in, or from the 'stand-point' of a real space. Viewing conditions establish new meanings and uses of virtual images, as well as offering alternative constructions of the social space of their exposition. This situation becomes increasingly complex in contemporary media art installations.

As Summers (2003, p. 431) points out: 'Virtual forms and spaces are for observers in one way or another presumed to be viewers or seers; they seem to describe the visible in terms of the surface or format, which in turn is always a determinate social space'. Places designed explicitly for exposition (from Çatal Hüyük in the Neolithic period – whose interior walls contain the earliest recorded paintings on a man-made surface – to customisable media environments like those found in new media and mixed-art form venues such as the Australian Centre for the Moving Image (ACMI) in Melbourne or the Foundation for Art & Creative Technology (FACT) in Liverpool) are domains established at a remove, a self-imposed distance from the 'real world' in order to instil a suspension of disbelief. [*Figure 1*] These are places where it is

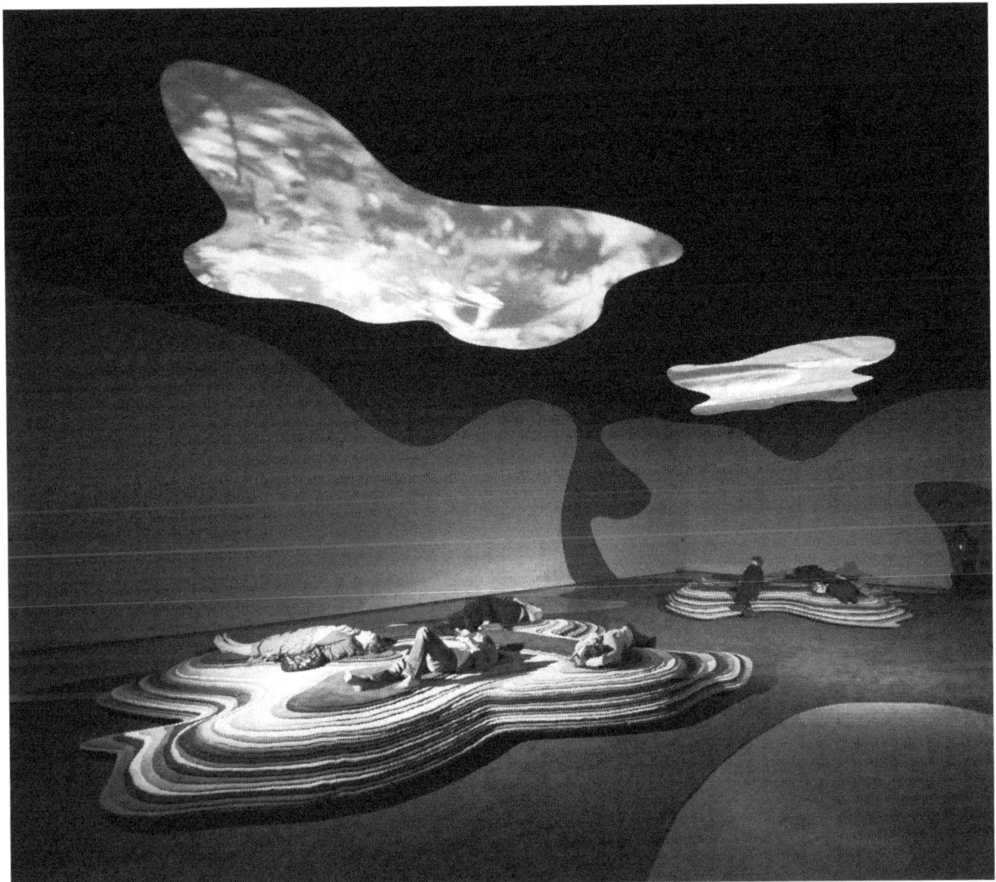

Figure 1: Installation view of Pipilotti Rist, *Gravity Be My Friend* (2007). Audio video installation (FACT: Liverpool, 2008).

'permitted to accept the apparent' (p. 432). Throughout the history of world art, visual and narrative cogency have been achieved with the support of architectural spaces that offer homogenous, unchanging viewing conditions. Adopted consistently since the Renaissance, spatial planarity, for example, establishes a controlled relationship between a spectator and the image realised with the representational technique of *perspectiva* (the application of geometric optics to the 'artificial perspective' of painting). Together with techniques of framing, planar surfaces provide a means of structuring the content represented within to the visual field of the image, and in turn, the relation of this virtual image to the viewer, corroborating their specific 'cardinality' and coordination on the floor plane.

The relationship between images and spatial conditions goes beyond the purely architectural to an engagement with the cultural positioning of interior spaces.[5] For example, the *camera obscura*, as an imaging technology that is indispensable to 'Cartesian perspectivalism' (the dominant 'scopic regime' that underpins much of Western art), models the viewing experience of a solitary subject and constructs a one-point perspective by organising the subject/spectator in a pivotal, central position. Conventionally, the *camera obscura* is viewed as contributing to the overarching quest of physical optics towards a 'natural' vision and the accurate 'real' representation of the physical world. However, a more radical appraisal of its wider socio-cultural influence accounts for it as a 'single, enduring apparatus of political and social power, elaborated over several centuries, that continues to discipline and regulate the status of an observer' (Crary 1990, p. 26). As outlined by Jonathan Crary, the *camera obscura*, as a manifestation of an ideology of representation and its transcendental subject, was 'embedded in a larger and denser organisation of knowledge and of the observing subject' (p. 27). More than a technical device, it acts as a philosophical metaphor and a model in both science and cultural pursuits (artistic practice, popular entertainment).

As demonstrated by any of a number of interactive installations, such a spatial arrangement continues to exert a powerful influence as an organising principle on the formation of 'black box' virtual environments that, as described by new media historian Oliver Grau (2003), 'reduce the observer to a disembodied state within a Cartesian space that is clear for miles around and quite often empty' (p. 193). For example, works by Jeffrey Shaw that employ the Advanced Visualisation and Interaction Environment (AVIE) exhibition platform are staged in an arena built to exacting specifications. The viewer's full sensory immersion with the artwork's virtual spaces is reinforced by the enveloping enclosure. Interiority is a prerequisite condition demanded to consolidate the work's totalising virtual reality effect.

Moving from interventions in physical space to the manipulation of virtuality, display can itself no longer be understood as a retrospective operation (happening 'after the fact', reactivating some essential artistic act or moment). As Nicolas Bourriaud comments:

Art is a space of images, objects, and human beings. Relational aesthetics is a way of considering the productive existence of the viewer of art, the space of participation that art can offer. (2001, p. 48)

The museum apparatus frames art and structures its various practices of production and distribution. Historically, the pronounced de-aestheticisation of the artwork can be shown to coincide with the dematerialisation of its primary site (the museum) leading to a blurring of the division between art and non-art. In tracking the genealogy of site-specific practices, Miwon Kwon (1997, p. 93) recognised a 'correspondence to the pattern of movement in electronic spaces of the Internet' in the slippage that inevitably results between site and content. Whether partly in response to this challenge, or as a result of an increased virtualisation of the museum, the overly narrow correlation of site-specificity with physical site has subsequently been reinvented: 'Beyond the museum, the site comes to encompass a relay of several interrelated but different spaces and economies' (p. 88). The ability to reconceive art's site as a cultural framework or eco-system is crucial to conceptualising art under contemporary aesthetic conditions.

The exhibition itself is a crucial component of the infrastructure that upholds this enterprise. Approaching the exhibition as a form of 'event-structure' enables it to be discerned as an articulation of the virtual. The exposition of art no longer solely privileges the spatial realisation of architectural spaces. Increasingly influential is the way that the design of an extended typology of spaces, including the networked and distributed ones, structure creative practices, viewer experiences and their subsequent interactions. Therefore, the concept of the virtual museum needs to evolve, from its narrow categorisation and over-simplification as a space initially consigned to presenting artworks exclusively on the Internet, to an extended application that exercises it as a conceptual strategy that accentuates the interrelationship of art's conceptually abstract and material natures. Reconceived as an infrastructure of propositions (related to the increasingly complex meshing of art, exhibition design and curatorial practice with digital technology and multimedia in museums), this emergent multimedial museum functions as a network of unanchored flows, demanding openness from the artwork, agility and adaptability from its institutions, and adventurousness from artists, curators and audiences alike.

Notes

1. According to literary critic N. Katherine Hayles (1999, p. 69): 'Virtuality is the cultural perception that material objects are interpenetrated by information patterns.'
2. The full archived version of *Liquid Architectures* forum can be accessed from: http://www.tate.org.uk/forums/category.jspa?categoryID=16.
3. Scholar Richard A. Lanham (1993) recognises such a 'digital rhetoric' in much contemporary intellectual and artistic endeavour. In his discussion of electronic textuality and its rhetorical implications, he asserts:

> Technology isn't leading us in these new directions. The arts, and the theoretical debate that tags along after them, have done the leading, and digitisation has emerged as their condign embodiment. We needn't worry about digital determinism. We must explain, instead, the

extraordinary convergence of twentieth-century thinking with the digital means that now give it expression. It is the computer as fulfilment of social thought that requires explanation. (p. 51)

4. Bernard Cache (1995) theorises the idea of a technologically integrated, quasi-object open to the possibility of unpredictable variation from drawing upon the possibilities offered by parametric modelling for nonstandard production of forms through computer-assisted design and fabrication systems. Cache recognises how these systems enable unique objects to be produced industrially by modifying the parameters of their calculation, distinguishing between objects created from varying the coordinates of their surface ('subjectiles') or volume ('objectiles').

5. An interior can be defined for simplicity as a spatial enclosure that is discrete and self-contained. For the purposes of broadening its relevance to this discussion, Dorothea Olkowski (1999) relates how the concept of interiority translates to philosophy, by illustrating how the philosophical perspective of Merleau-Ponty sought to maintain a relation of continuity between 'interiority' (understood as subjectivity) and the 'exteriority' of the world:

> Only on the human level is life fully able to be called existence. For humans can vary their relations to things, not only by moving their bodies as animals do but also by manipulating objects in the world, thereby giving them multiple relations while recognising that these are simply different properties of the same thing. Precisely this ability to both vary relations and to recognise unity are characterised by Merleau-Ponty as symbolic behaviour. Symbolic behaviour includes the ability to imagine the future or remember the past and its importance to human life cannot be overestimated. This complex behaviour, the ability to vary a point of view, is the basis of human freedom. (p. 3)

Chapter 2

The Art of Exhibition

Synopsis

The integration of digital media within museology has far-reaching implications for the role of the museum and for how the discursive act of exposition functions through the medium of the exhibition. Techniques of visual display reveal how meaning is constructed in the contemporary museum as a result of the fundamental interdependence between art object, gallery space and museological processes.

The museum plays an instrumental role in modelling the contours of artistic practices. Revealed in the light of new technologies, its spatiality and structure are reconceived as a matrix of increasingly interrelated spaces. No longer can the museum be viewed as simply a physical container, its operations consigned to a homogenous display space bounded by four walls. With the relatively recent augmentation of the hidden infrastructure of multimedia technologies that are to be found 'behind the walls', as it were, the architectural issues of organising spaces and manipulating settings for displaying artworks is now more decisive, and as much virtual as physical.

What might the admixture of physical and virtual qualities bring to experiences (aesthetic, communicative, educative) that take place across museological spaces? How can the array of spatial practices associated with modes of artistic and curatorial production, such as the architectural factors of gallery space or the curatorial issues associated with the exhibition form itself be explored? These questions have far-reaching implications for the roles and interactions between artist, curator and designer within what might be described as the *exhibition complex* of contemporary art.[1]

Inspired by the way that the design of mediated spaces are influencing the structure of contemporary art practices, distinctively altering their interactions and resulting experiences, my investigation into the art of exhibition aims – by surveying the adaptation and integration of digital media within museological practice – to speculate upon the exhibition as an event-structure and the influence that virtuality might pose to curatorial design. The expanded field opened up by virtual technologies, as a space composed of a variety of relationships (between subjects, objects and environments) and shifting vectors (involving institutional practices, types of information flow) offers a distinctively new environment for art to function within. While it is the nature of museums to operate across many levels (as tresorium, conservatorium, imprimateur), the form through which it transacts most directly with its audience is through the interface offered by the exhibition.

Institutionally, the museum can be conceived as a belief system in which every act of collecting, preserving or presenting carries implicit political, ideological and aesthetic values.[2] Disentangling the subtext of these diverse (often contradictory) strands, methods and techniques that encompass administration, conservation and display is recognised as the subject matter interrogated by the 'new museology' (Vergo 1989a, Bal 1996b).[3] According to art historian and theorist Peter Vergo:

Whether we like it or not, every acquisition (and indeed disposal), every juxtaposition or arrangement of an object or work of art, together with other objects or works of art, within the context of a temporary exhibition or museum display means placing a certain construction upon history, be it the history of the distant or more recent past, of our own culture or someone else's, of mankind in general or a particular aspect of human endeavour. (1989a, pp. 2–3)

But just how new is this 'new' museology?[4] Set in motion by a process of general social and cultural critique during the 1960s, this self-analytical approach is now a relatively commonplace expectation of curatorial practice (Schubert 2000, p. 66). It can, however, be argued that self-consciousness has been closely associated with the museum's evolution, in particular through the phase of industrialised art culture.[5] It can be contended that the emergence of the mass audience in the mid-nineteenth century was a fundamental step for museums, confirming their status as the most democratic of cultural institutions (p. 75). It is not surprising, therefore, that the operations of the modern museum (particularly in terms of making manifest the acquisitive impulse of collecting and through its techniques of exhibition) would fall under the inquisitive scope of Walter Benjamin's larger historical project, *The Arcades Project*.

For her part, Mieke Bal's investigations of museology have used the exhibition as her primary subject for cultural analysis. Drawing out the interconnected meanings of *exposition, exposé* and *exposure*, she has described their confluence for an interdisciplinary investigation of the art of exhibition:

Something is made public in exposition, and that event involves bringing out into the public domain the deepest held views and beliefs of a subject. Exposition is always also an argument. Therefore, in publicising these views the subject objectifies, exposes himself as much as the object; this makes the exposition an exposure of the self. Such exposure is an act of producing meaning, a performance. (Bal 1996a, p. 2)

According to Bal: 'Discursivity, most notably rhetoric imbricated with narrative, is in effect a crucial aspect of the institution' (1996b, p. 205). While easily borne out in the copious amounts of discursive material produced by museums in the form of didactic panels, information pamphlets and exhibition catalogues, this observation is actually directed at something far more fundamental to the nature of the museum, and operates at the heart of the very idea of exhibition itself.

The various roles assumed by the museum can be combined under one singular, overarching interpretive function. In *Rethinking the Museum*, Stephen E. Weil (1990) extracted three essential, core functions of the museum: to preserve, to study, and to communicate. He noted that these functions are not separate but overlap and intertwine. It is through the medium of the exhibition that the range of interactions and experiences arising from the meeting of ideas and objects, of aesthetic perception mediated through presentation, are communicated most intensely. Reflecting the notion that 'at the center of the idea of a museum lie not things, but people' (de Varine cited in Hauenschild 1998, unpaginated source), it is through the 'medium' of the exhibition that the idea of the museum as a system composed from the interaction of ideas and objects is experienced (Saumarez Smith 1989). According to Charles Saumarez Smith, while most museums might still be structured in accordance with taxonomic and classificatory ideals that were established in the late nineteenth century, 'intellectual ideas have moved away from a belief in a single, overriding theoretical system towards a much more conscious sense of the role of the reader or the spectator in interpretation' (1989, p. 19).

This transformation of the monumentality associated with the museum (the imposing physical presence of its architecture, the historical assurance predicated by its regimes of conservation and display) into a more abstract, communication channel was heralded most obviously by André Malraux through his conception of the 'Museum without Walls':

> A 'Museum without Walls' is coming into being, and (now that the plastic arts have invented their own printing-press) it will carry infinitely farther that revelation of the world of art, limited perforce, which the 'real' museums offer us within their walls. (1974, p. 16)

Increasingly sophisticated strategies around what can broadly be described as the institution's 'public relations' have undoubtedly transformed the contemporary museum. Theorists from Bourdieu to Bourriaud have charted the changes that the museum has undergone: 'from mausoleum to "white cube", department store or theme park; to either a modernist palace of the elite or a purveyor of mass spectacle' (Blazwick & Wilson 2000, p. 30). [*Figure 2*] Techniques of exhibition and aesthetic experience go hand-in-hand:

> Works of art are rarely encountered in isolation. They are experienced in relation to each other and articulated by the architectonics of a building and the unconscious choreography of other people. Museums are activated by wandering groups and individuals who are busy looking at art and each other. Museums can be playful, even libidinous spaces, where images of the human body abound. (p. 31)

It may seem self-evident, but the 'context' established by the exhibition confers upon objects a meaning that is above and beyond any significance they may already possess, whether as cultural artefacts or artworks. The set of objects the museum displays is sustained only by the fiction that they somehow constitute a coherent representational universe. Should the fiction disappear, there is nothing left of the museum but 'bric-a-brac', a heap of meaningless and valueless fragments of objects which are incapable of substituting themselves either metonymically for the original objects or metaphorically for their representations (Donato 1980, p. 223). By being incorporated into an exhibition, they become not merely works of art or tokens of a certain culture or society, but elements of a narrative, forming part of a thread of discourse which is itself one element in a more complex web of meanings (Vergo 1989b, p. 46). Through exhibition, the resulting complex – or 'epistemic matrix'[6] – reveals a

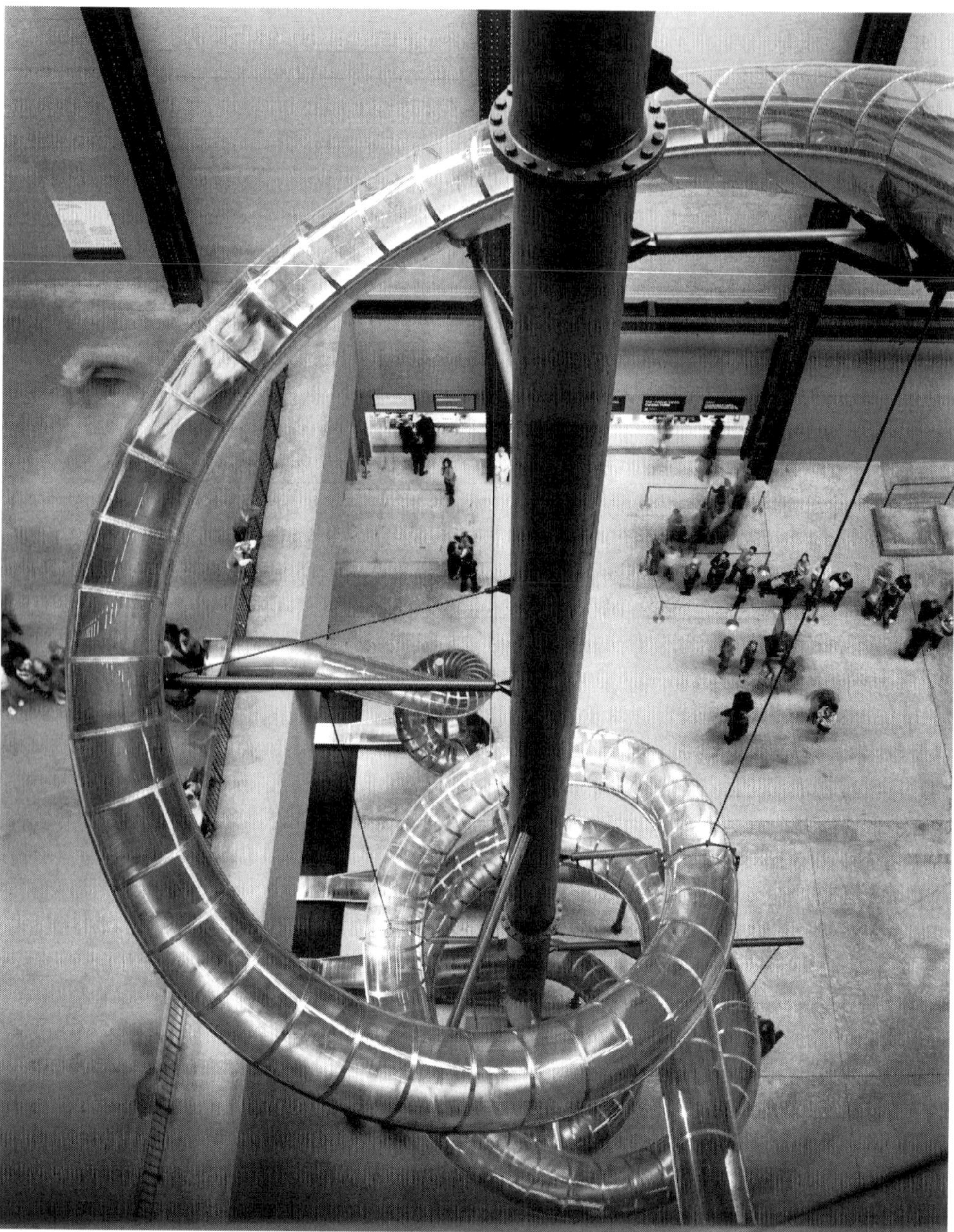

Figure 2: Installation view of Carsten Holler, *Test Site* (2006). Slide Installation (*Unilever Series*, Tate Modern: London, 2006–7). Photo credit: Attilio Maranzano.

hypertextual structure, with intertextual references, passages, allusions and linkages woven together to achieve an overall 'texture'. Henri Lefebvre made use of this term to denote how the interventions of spatial practices are informed by knowledge and ideology:

> It is helpful to think of architectures as 'archi-textures', to treat each monument or building, viewed in its surroundings and context, in the populated area and associated networks in which it is set down, as part of a particular production of space. (Lefebvre 1991, p. 118)

Representatively, curatorial design makes the connection between artworks and space emphatic, supplanting the self-contained artwork through techniques of assemblage, arrangement and spatial composition. From a curatorial standpoint, this spectrum of techniques cycle through exhibitions characterised as 'aesthetic' at one end, through to overtly 'contextual' ones on the other extreme (Vergo 1989b, pp. 48–9). In an aesthetic exhibition, the object is treated as paramount. Understanding is derived from the viewer's experience through a process of 'private communion' with the artefact or artwork. In contrast, contextual exhibitions might be said to place more emphasis on the 'representational' qualities of the object-as-token. Most often used to serve an educative purpose, this type of exhibition presents original objects alongside an array of other kinds of material (informative, comparative, explicative). While most common in historical and scientific museums, this form of display is being found increasingly in art museums.

The focus on visual display is integral to any reconsideration of the epistemological status of artefacts and their reconstitution as outcomes of the overall performance that takes place in and through the museum. Recognizing the spectrum of presentation strategies that operate in museums for the public display of artefacts, Suarez-Smith has observed that:

> It is important that museums acknowledge that these strategies of display are necessarily artificial and that the museum visitor be made to realise that display is only a trick which can itself be independently enjoyed as a system of theatrical artifice. The best museum displays are often those which are most evidently self-conscious, heightening the spectator's awareness of the means of representation, involving the spectator in the process of display. (Suarez-Smith 1989, p. 20)

The revelatory power of display, especially under the conditions of technologised media culture today, should not be underestimated.[7] Considered as different regimes under the one guiding principle of exposition, each of these modes of display aims to reveal something more about the artworks than appearance; however, their rhetoric of display can equally be said to expose truths meant to be concealed (Wollen 1995, p. 10).

The perceived conflict between the institution's power structures and artistic freedom has preoccupied much artistic practice since the 1960s. Characterising an 'Oedipal relationship' between practitioners and institutions, artists – ranging from Marcel Broodthaers, Daniel Buren, Hans Haacke, Mark Dion, Antoni Muntadas to Thomas Struth – have increasingly made the museum the actual subject of their art (Blazwick & Wright 2000, pp. 29–30). In his study of the evolution of the museum concept, Karsten Schubert noted that since the 1960s artists have 'developed a multiplicity of techniques (ranging from mere reference in-passing to total usurpation of the museum concept) that simultaneously acknowledge and undermine the museum' (2000, p. 84). Employing self-reflexive techniques, artists have 'dissected the processes of classification, the formalities of labels, plinths, frames and display cases, the legitimisations of value that characterise museum practice. Their art has revealed the unconsciously surreal poetics of these rationalisations, or exposed the ideological framework which lie behind them, making explicit the economic and political agendas that inform acquisition and exhibition policy, patronage and sponsorship' (Blazwick & Wright 2000, pp. 29–30). Common to their respective practices is the exploration of the reciprocal movement between art object and the museum. These interventions focus upon how meaning is constructed in the postmodern museum and, by extension, critically informs the emergence of the multimedial museum.

For its part, the influence of design in this context has also become increasingly apparent. Strategies employed in recent museum architecture illustrate symbiotic approaches that create a continuum across external architecture, interior architecture and exhibition design. Dramatic methods of display and presentation are characteristic of this new ecology and instil in the viewer preparedness to recognise the artwork as an outcome of a performed process (both in the sense of simulated, read 'staged', and lived, read 'experienced'), rather than as a fixed, consolidated artefact. The added dimensionality of the virtual is exaggerated in examples of artistic and museological practices that enact a rhetorical inversion of the relationship of object and exhibition.

From a curatorial perspective, the exhibition mediates the relations operating between artefact, gallery and museum. To approach this complex relationship from an ecological perspective suggests that there exists a fundamental interdependence in operation between all constituent parts of the process: 'In this sense, ecology does not exist as a thing, but as a fluid structure involving meaning, which we will treat as a kind of discourse or frame' (Altheide 1995, p. 11).

Notes

1. In employing this term to describe the formally constructed interrelationship that exists between art object, exhibition and museological spaces, I am conscious of its close relationship to Tony Bennett's usage of the term, the *exhibitionary complex*. In *The Birth of the Museum*, Bennett draws a parallel history for the emergence of the museum in the period spanning the late eighteenth to mid-nineteenth centuries. In doing so, he contextualizes how the museum's power and knowledge relations operated between those conventionally understood as predicated on confinement with others more closely oriented towards exhibition (exemplified by synthetic image spaces, such as dioramas and panoramas, and popular forms of entertainment including menageries and amusement parks). In contrast to the Foucaultian 'carceral archipelago' of institutions whose principles were modelled

on the prison, the institutions, disciplines and discursive formations that make up the 'exhibitionary complex' employed new technologies of vision to affect the transfer of 'objects and bodies from the enclosed and private domains in which they had previously been displayed (but not restricted to a public) into progressively more open and public arenas where, through the representations to which they were subjected, they formed vehicles for inscribing and broadcasting the messages of power (but of a different type) through society' (Bennett 1995, pp. 60–1).

2. According to the International Council of Museums (ICOM), a museum is defined as 'a non-profit-making permanent institution in the service of society and of its development, open to the public, which acquires, conserves, researches, communicates and exhibits, for purposes of study, education and enjoyment, the tangible and intangible evidence of people and their environment'.

3. The *new museology* describes a widely adopted approach to museological practice that places emphasis upon the values and meanings that operate implicitly within museums. The use of the term is connected with the changing role of museums in education and in society at large. It promotes a perception that current museum practices are obsolete and the professional practice of museum professions (ranging from museum director to curator, through to educator, designer, archivist and conservator) are subjected to critique. The profession, at large, is urged to reflect critically upon its own values and practices itself, most often taking shape in the form of a renewed social commitment to its public. The role of installation techniques and curatorial strategies is viewed as fundamentally important to the interpretation and experience of artworks.

   Peter Vergo has made a significant contribution to the debate about the role of museums in society as editor of the anthology, *The New Museology* (1989) and contributor to *Towards the Museum of the Future* (1994), which addresses developments in museums and exhibitions practice taking place in the context of a rapidly changing world; while Mieke Bal posits the new museology as a self-critical study of the museum and its often-contradictory purposes, motivations and allegiances, which appeal as an object of study across both the humanities and social sciences (Bal 1996b, pp. 201–2).

4. The editors of *Towards the Museum of the Future* distinguish between two contrasting meanings of the term 'new museology' in contemporary European museum studies. One perspective links its use with the French 'ecomuseum' movement of socially inclusive, community museums. The other – which is of direct relevance to my interests – relates to a self-reflective approach towards the making and theoretical study of museums (Miles and Zavala 1994, p. 147).

5. In his contribution to *The New Museology* anthology, Charles Saumarcz Smith (1989) puts forward an historical example of how Moncure Conway's *Travels in South Kensington* stimulated growing intellectual interest towards techniques of museological discourse. This interest was stirred by the general public enthusiasm surrounding the formation of the South Kensington Museum, later to become the Victoria & Albert Museum in 1882. The desire for industrial art culture was made manifest through the museum's capacity to demonstrate aspects of cultural difference through the systematic organisation of artefacts, recognising that 'objects were not viewed purely for their own sake as fragments from a shattered historical universe, but rather as possible indicator, as metonyms, for comparative study' (Saumarez Smith 1989, p. 9).

6. The work of historian Stephen Bann has been influential in focusing scholarly attention toward connections between the history of art and visual culture. Concerned primarily with the historical consciousness particular to the nineteenth century, Bann's conception of 'the poetics of the museum' establishes how approaches to recreation and display structure representations of the past in museum collections. In his contribution to the anthology, *Visual Display*, Bann (1995) discusses how visuality and the actual techniques of display reflect qualities (the holy, the marvellous, the

antique) that are achieved not simply by the objects exhibited but on the rhetorical power of the presentation itself and how this instilled the desired experience of viewers.

7. Theorist Peter Wollen describes visual display as 'the other side of the spectacle: the side of production rather than consumption or reception, the designer rather than the viewer, the agent rather than the patient. It is related to exhibitionism rather than scopophilia' (1995, p. 9).

Chapter 3

Spatial Practice

Synopsis

Through focusing on the relationship between artwork and museum, artistic interventions provide useful insights for exploring the interrelationship between art and the expanded dimensions in which it operates today. The spatial interventions of Marcel Duchamp are particularly inspiring in this respect. Through exploring the types of exchanges that take place between object and site of exhibition, 'site-specific' practices critique the museum as both an institutional set of values and as self-reflective subject. Foregrounding the creative act of mediation, these artistic investigations intervene most broadly with art's encompassing cultural framework.

The construction of meaning in the postmodern museum – and by extension the foundation for the emergence of the multimedial museum – has been informed by artistic interventions that have explored the relationship between artwork and museum. Intriguing precedents such as Kurt Schwitters' *Merzbau*[1] and Piet Mondrian's *Salon de Madame B. à Dresden*[2] historicise the reconceptualisation of the gallery. El Lissitzky's expanded three-dimensional expressions of his architectonic compositions first realised in the *Prounenraum* designed for the Great Berlin Art Exhibition of 1923 would lead to his experimental design of the *Cabinet of Abstraction*. Conceived as a demonstration space suited explicitly to the presentation of avant-garde art, the gallery was designed with moveable panels that simultaneously hid and revealed the collection of works displayed within (which included his own work along with works by Picasso, Léger and Schwitters, amongst others). Commissioned by the Hanover Provincial Museum in 1927, this installation is arguably the first functional interactive exhibition environment.[3]

Exemplified by his infamous, hybrid architecture for Peggy Guggenheim's *Art of This Century* exhibition in New York in 1942, Frederick Kiesler tested the limits of exhibition design. This new method involved incorporating aspects constituting the exhibition – artworks (paintings, sculptures) as well as architectural supports, wall surfaces, gallery seating – in a continuous, potentially 'endless' tension. In his 'Manifesto on Correalism' of 1947, Kiesler stated:

If by painting we mean painting in frames or frescoes, we are trapped in a dead end.

If we speak only of sculptures on pedestals, in niches, and of *bas-reliefs*, we are bound to the tradition of our grandparents.

If we speak only of an architecture that is 'monumental', we are hiding behind religion and politics. (Kiesler 2001, p. 96).

Likening these environments to 'galaxies', his system aimed to achieve a 'triangular correlation' between space, art object and viewing subject in an attempt to dissolve the 'artificial duality of vision and reality or image and environment'. Kiesler's ideas were inspired by a sense that the universe is a continuum. Since space is endless, the differentiation of 'inner space' from 'outer space' is rendered meaningless. And so art, he believed, should operate in the same way (painting and sculpture should not be treated as isolated objects but as parts of a living space). In this context, I am particularly drawn to Kiesler's use of the term 'galaxies' to describe the exhibition environment and the way it can be juxtaposed alongside other keywords that have been used to describe the relationships operating within art and visual culture, such as 'constellations' (Benjamin), 'force-fields' (Adorno) or 'fields' (Bourdieu).

Regardless of whether the impact of any of these designs have proven to be too esoteric and exaggerated or, alternatively, represent particularly insightful and visionary approaches that can be repurposed as useful models today, the recognition of these examples in this context is a useful way to focus the interrelationship between art and an expanded sense of the dimensions (curatorial, exhibitionary, museological, architectural and multimedial) in which it operates today.

It would be remiss to not directly recognise the important legacy of Marcel Duchamp and his range of spatial interventions, most notably his legendary *A Mile of String* installation from the *First Papers of Surrealism* exhibition.[4] [*Figure 3*] Visualise a gallery, lined with hung canvases. Consider these internal walls, temporary flats and paintings as the 'positive space' that makes up this conventional spatial enclosure. Then, notice a strange, cobweb-like weave of string that courses across and 'in-between' these features of the room, connecting up these

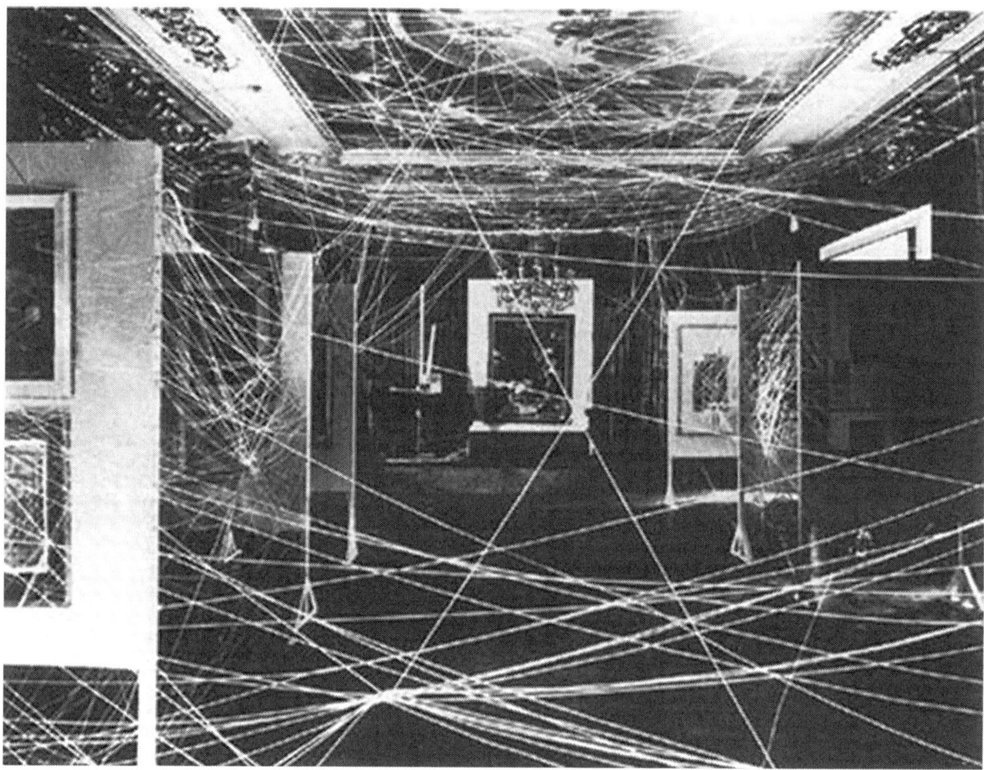

Figure 3: Installation documentation of Marcel Duchamp, *A Mile of String* (1942). String installation (*First Papers of Surrealism*: New York, 1942). © Marcel Duchamp/ADAGP. Licensed by Viscopy, 2011.

separate surfaces. Any conventional viewing of the exhibited artworks is frustrated because of this obstruction; accessibility is paralysed by the looping of a continuous, indeterminable length of string across and through the entire gallery space. This intervention of line, strung at exaggerated tangents and knotted in densely interwoven clusters throughout the 'negative space' of the gallery somehow even seems to actualise the virtual space represented in many of the pictures on display, transforming the experience of their representational spaces into something palpable.

This creative gesture, along with his earlier site-specific intervention of lining the ceiling of the Galerie Beaux-Arts with *1200 Bags of Coal* for the *International Exhibition of Surrealism* in 1938, reveals a central trope of Duchamp's practice: the production of rhetorical effects that combine the creative agendas of artist and curator inextricably, and entangle the artwork with its site of exposition. These interrelationships are synthesised at the level of the exhibition form itself. It is the exhibition, with its own creative value superseding the aesthetic primacy conventionally attributed to the artefact, that emerges in sharper relief as a result of the conceptual shift that Duchamp enacts. As Brian O'Doherty discussed in his highly influential text *Inside the White Cube: the ideology of the gallery space*: 'dissolving the frame transferred that function to the gallery space. Boxing up the space (or spacing up the box) is part of the central theme of Duchamp's art: containment/inside/outside' (1999, p. 73).[5]

In both cases, Duchamp assumed the role of *Generator-Arbitrator* of the exhibition.[6] This role – which intimates the innovative combining of the practices of artist and curator, also draws illustratively upon design method and process. In the *First Papers of Surrealism*, this approach assumed an exaggerated performative character when Duchamp amplified the effect of the interruption he created by running string throughout the space by arranging for a pair of children to play ball games in the gallery amongst the guests assembled as part of the exhibition's opening night.[7] Coming back to the *International Exhibition of Surrealism* exhibition: Duchamp effectively coordinated the visitor's experience of the entire exhibition. He did so, on one hand, by having revolving doors installed at the entrance and exit of the gallery. Through accounting for the access and egress to the exhibition, this intervention was intended to further reinforce the confusion of inside and outside, as well as complement the inversion of the gallery space he achieved by literally turning the gallery upside down by installing a ceiling full of coal bags suspended above an open, lit brazier. In discussing this spatial intervention, O'Doherty articulates a devious interpretation of Duchamp's curatorial motivations:

If he were accused of dominating the show, he could say that he took only what no one wanted – the ceiling and a little spot on the floor; the accusation would underline his (gigantic) modesty, his (excessive) humility. No one looks at the ceiling; it isn't choice territory – indeed, it wasn't (until then) territory at all. Hanging over your head, the largest piece in the show was unobtrusively physical but totally obtrusive psychologically. (1999, p. 69)

As creative practice, curatorial design develops upon site-specificity, which – as illustrated by the preceding exemplars – has its roots firmly set in the tangible relations that exist between object and its site of exhibition.

Broadly defined, the term *site-specificity* encompasses a wide range of artistic approaches that 'articulate exchanges between the work of art and the places in which its meanings are defined' (Kaye 2000, p. 1). Initially characterised by a self-critical negotiation of spatially 'grounding' the work *in situ*, site-specific practices were commonly preoccupied with the 'presence' of the artwork. In this paradigm, the relationship of artwork to site was inseparable – an artwork could not be transposed or transported to any other site without its integrity as a work being compromised. An integral relationship is implied between the artwork's site of production and space of exhibition. This understanding gave rise to a host of artistic interventions that explored alternative environments for art, while also bringing added critical exploration of the role of the gallery itself. As Nick Kaye has observed, 'site-specificity presents a challenge to notions of "original" or "fixed" location, problematising the relationship between work and site' (2000, p. 2). A crucial elaboration upon the understanding of site-specificity is that its 'practice' also comes to address a broader institutional 'dimension' (that entails critique of the modus operandi and material conditions operating that sustain the art system). While intimately associated with Minimalist sculpture of the 1960s (premised as it was upon establishing an unequivocal relationship between the material presence of the artwork and its physical site), the emergence of this mode of artistic practice can also be contextualised as part of a widespread preoccupation with the machinations of the 'art system' during the period. As Boris Groys has noted:

> Accordingly, the advanced art of this time understood the individual act of art production as being originally regulated by a 'system,' as following a certain general rule from the beginning, and as being inscribed into a certain social practice even before its product was submitted to a definite social use. (2005, p. 52)

A number of distinctive responses to the museum as system emerged in the advanced art of the 1960s. In retrospect, installation art and forms of institutional critique have become extremely influential to the art of recent decades, including new media practices. Taking the form of sculptural obstructions, 'anti-forms' – exemplified by the sculptural practice of Robert Morris – abolished the integrity of the physical object in favour of exploring the interrelationship between form, space and viewer. Morris' *Untitled, Mirrored Cubes* (1965) offers a representative example. Encapsulating this idea in his theoretical writing, he describes how:

> In the simpler regular polyhedrons such as cubes and pyramids, one need not move around the object for the sense of the whole, the gestalt, to occur. One sees and immediately 'believes' that the pattern within one's mind corresponds to the existential fact of the object. Belief in this sense is both a kind of faith in spatial extension and a visualisation

of that extension. In other words, of those aspects of apprehension that are not coexistent with the visual field but rather the result of the experience of the visual field. (R. Morris 1993, p. 6)

Installations, environments and tableaux assume forms and scales that range from grand spatial epics (taken to its ultimate extreme when the Museum of Contemporary Art in Chicago was wrapped by Christo and Jeanne-Claude in 1969) through to subtle, almost imperceptible 'gestures'.[8] Diverse examples ranging from William Anastasi's *Six Sites* (1966), Mel Bochner's *Measurement Room* (1969)[9] through to Nam June Paik's *TV Garden* (1974)[10] reflect the myriad approaches taken by artists to gallery-based interventions during this period. Museum 'fictions' directly blended art production and spatial practice with a curatorial approach. The interpretation of forms of museum display and reliance upon exhibition documentation play a crucial role in sustaining this practice. While Marcel Broodthaers is acknowledged as the pre-eminent exponent of this approach, other relevant examples include the *Museum of Contemporary Ideas* by Australian artist Peter Hill[11] and Michelangelo Pistoletto's *Le Stanze (The Rooms)*. The latter of these extended projects was staged as an intertextual programme of consecutive installations at the Christian Stein Gallery in Turin between October 1975 and September 1976. According to Kaye, this project exposes:

> The conditions in and under which the work is always in the process of being anticipated, produced and remembered, where 'real space' is subject to being 'written over' by experience and imagination. Pistoletto traces out a series of complex relationships between the real and virtual spaces of the rooms and their various reflections. (2000, p. 31)

Reflecting how terms like 'system', 'structure' and 'process' held a distinct currency in the art culture of the period, the gallery acts as the catalyst for the redefinition of the work of art and modes of representation during the late 1960s and early 1970s, 'taking place against a backdrop of technological and communications innovations that we now see as the foundations of today's global society' (De Salvo 2005, p. 11). Collectively, these practices can be characterised by the dialectical nature of the aesthetic experience they establish between real encounters with artworks in gallery space overlayed with more open, potentialities associated with virtual space: 'real and virtual space are defined only *in* each other' (Kaye 2000, p. 32).

During the 1980s, art that approached the museum as subject matter was markedly influenced by critical theories surrounding contemporary visual culture. Postmodernist critique of the museum institution and its function of preserving 'the auratic status of art that was Benjamin's main target' (Crimp 1993a, p. 248) operated within a more general culture of quotation and homage in popular, mass media. Most directly, photographic investigations by Louise Lawler address the museum as a self-referential subject. More recently, Thomas Struth's project devoted to museums operates as a contemporary version of eighteenth-century art pilgrimage, or 'Grand Tour'. Since the mid-1980s, Struth has focused on art's social arena and the nature of aesthetic experience under contemporary conditions; not directly on the art or architecture, but the fleeting experience of these virtualised spaces. Struth's exhibition from early 2007 celebrating the new extension of the Prado Museum in Madrid mirrors photographic works with the site of their origination, presenting arguably the most advanced realisation of his project to date. This exhibition was translated through a double installation. In the first instance, Struth's photographs of art spaces (from the founding series in 1987 through to work produced in the Prado itself) were inserted throughout a range of the institution's spaces. Juxtaposed alongside emblematic works from the collection, a direct dialog between real (immediate, present, here) and virtual (representational, absent, there) was established. The museum's new expansion into the Cloister of Los Jeronimos provided the setting for an accompanying presentation of recent work. This installation drew together works executed contemporaneously at two of the great European museums (involving Leonardo's *Madonna Benois* at the Hermitage, St. Petersburg, and the Michelangelo's *David* at the Accademia in Florence). Adding a further vertiginous layer to this, a series of works produced in the Prado Museum itself (concentrating on Velasquez's *Las Meinenas*) were also installed. The relationship of the artist to the workings of the institution and the wider art system has been explored by the likes of Hans Haacke, Fred Wilson and Robert Gober[12], whose museological interventions inevitably provoke the central issue of how the position of the artist relates to critique or complicity.

Throughout this period, the artistic projects of Antoni Muntadas have deconstructed the nature of culture under conditions of networked society. As described by Mary Anne Staniszewski: 'These projects have been constructed to make visible social conventions and frameworks within which meaning and value are created' (2003, p. 25). Muntadas' projects have taken as their subject the models of exposition involved in the production of culture. In *Between the Frames*, hours of video recordings of international art-world figures are divided into thematic 'chapters' ('The Dealers', 'The Collectors', etc.). In its presentation at Bordeaux's Musée d'Art Contemporain in 1994, Muntadas drew attention to the discursive qualities of the environment itself by distributing these episodes across selected locations throughout the museum ('The Critics' section was shown in the library, 'The Docents' screened in the education department). In *Exhibition* (1985–87), 'the centrepiece is missing' (Staniszewski, p. 28); instead, nine installations adopting the standard display conventions associated with different types of work ('The Print Series', 'The Triptych', 'The Slide Projection', 'The Light Box Display', etc.) were put on centre stage. In the case of 'The Video Installation', a single video monitor was displayed with a blank screen. As discussed by Celine Condorelli (in Dipple 2005):

By accentuating light – traditionally associated with idealist and metaphorical aspects of fine art – Muntadas paradoxically rendered the historical and material conditions of the modern art gallery. Illuminated in this installation was what the viewer does not normally see: the social conventions that shape aesthetic worth, the political unconscious of an art exhibition.

Intriguingly, some of the most exaggerated expressions of such self-reflection have been initiated by the museum itself. The Tate Gallery in London has undergone significant redevelopment since 1988 leading up to Tate Modern expansion. Operating for the most part within the pre-existing shell and exterior of the decommissioned Bankside Power Station in Southwark, Herzog & de Meuron's architectural solution provided the impetus for a reorientation of spatial practice and an opportunity for developing alternative curatorial principles and accompanying methods of display responsive to art's changing conditions. Capitalising on the vast cavernous space which originally housed immense turbines and boilers, the Turbine Hall has become the site of a series of specially commissioned artistic works over the past decade (under the auspices of the Unilever Series), resulting in projects that have proven inspiring and contentious in equal measure; arguably, the most celebrated to date being Olafur Eliasson's *The Weather Project* in 2003, which filled the interior of the museum with an ethereal blending of atmosphere and light. Using humidifiers to create a fine mist that permeated the air, Eliasson transformed the entrance space using a semi-circular disc made up of hundreds of lamps emitting a pure yellow light. In addition, the imposing vault of the Turbine Hall was lined with a huge mirror, which induced visitors to look upwards to watch themselves represented as tiny shadows bathed in a field of orange light. This sensory intervention, along with numerous other works by the artist which have explored the relationship of artwork to space, acknowledge the role of perceptual behaviour to viewing experience in museums.[13] The dialectical qualities afforded by preconceptions, perceptions and apperceptions – not only of sensory impressions, but also of the conventions and expected routines for viewing art – offer subtle modulations than outline the exhibition event. Acknowledging that this interaction takes place under the conditions of exhibition space, Eliasson's work is celebrated for creating effects that are facilitated by the qualities of space along with its 'temporal dimension'.[14]

Implicated in such practices, is it possible to differentiate between when social, technological and physical architectures function as the work of art itself or act as the site of the work? In her revision of site-specificity, Miwon Kwon has recognised that the artistic investigation of site never operates along physical or spatial lines exclusively but rather operates embedded within an encompassing 'cultural framework' defined by art's supporting institutional complex (1997, p. 88). Formulating site as more than place is crucial to making the conceptual leap of redefining the role of art under present-day socio-cultural conditions:

> A provisional conclusion might be that in advanced art practices of the past thirty years the operative definition of site has been transformed from a physical location – grounded, fixed, actual – to a discursive vector – ungrounded, fluid, virtual. (Kwon 1997, p. 95)

Collectively, the examples of spatial practice outlined above foreground the act of mediation as a form of creative production. Through the development of institutional critique as a form of self-critical artistic practice, the role of the contemporary curator has been affected dramatically. Determining how a viewer encounters artworks through the spatio-temporal frame of the exhibition is defined as a priority for curatorial design.

Notes

1. Kurt Schwitters was a quintessential avant-garde artist who worked in several genres (Dadaism, Constructivism, Surrealism) and media (including poetry, sound, painting, sculpture and design). His *Merz* works — art constructions built up of assorted objects – pioneered installation art. Schwitters' *Merzbau* was created as a private room within his former studio between the years of 1923 and 1936. This imaginative architecture transformed rooms in Schwitters' house in Hannover, including the ground floor, attic and basement. The original *Merzbau* was destroyed in an air raid during World War II. The Sprengel Museum in Hanover reconstructed it from photographic evidence in 1983. The work forms an important part of their Kurt Schwitters Archive, which contains the most comprehensive documentation about the artist.
2. Based on Mondrian's original concept drawing from 1926, this space would only be realised as an actual environment in 1970 at the Pace Gallery, New York.
3. The original cabinet was destroyed in 1937. It was reconstructed in 1969 from the original plans and is now an exhibit at the Sprengel Museum in Hannover. Henk Puts provides extensive detail about El Lissitzky's designs for exhibition spaces in the catalogue for the exhibition *El Lissitzky (1890–1941) architect painter photographer typographer*, organised by the Municipal Van Abbemuseum, Eindhoven (Puts 1991, pp. 19–24).
4. The *First Papers of Surrealism* exhibition was staged at the headquarters of the Coordinating Council of French Relief Societies, the Whitelaw Reid Mansion, New York, during October-November 1942. The exhibition's title makes reference to the immigration papers of recent arrivals to America seeking refuge from war-torn Europe.

   In his documentation of this exhibition compiled in *The Avant-garde in Exhibition: new art in the 20th century*, Bruce Altshuler (1994) relates a number of illuminating aspects behind Duchamp's string intervention. Interpretations of Duchamp's artistic 'action' were far-ranging and varied: the cobweb effect created by the skeins of string alluded to decay and reminded of old wine cellars, as a representation of obfuscation and the difficulty in understanding the advanced art of the time, or as a statement about the exhaustion of European Surrealism (p. 152). While intimating that 'sixteen' miles of string were involved, the work was actually completed with Duchamp only needing to use a single mile's worth of string. In addition, the work had to be fully reinstalled after the string mysteriously was damaged by fire.

5. Brian O'Doherty's series of essays appeared originally in three separate issues of *Artforum* in 1976.
6. As ascribed by O'Doherty (1999, p. 67). Further to this: André Breton is credited with assembling the exhibition, with assistance from Max Ernst and Marcel Duchamp. While Breton is credited with the actual hanging, Duchamp is directly cited in the catalogue for his string intervention, which exerted an overwhelming influence over the exhibition as a whole. In addition, Duchamp contributed the cover design of the publication, which showed a picture of a bullet-ridden wall complete with actual holes on the front cover, with a close-up image of Gruyere cheese on the back.
7. On the evening, six children played in pairs in each of the three rooms that comprised the show. Duchamp's instructions directed the children to play ball without speaking to anyone; should they be approached and told to stop playing they were to reply that Marcel Duchamp told them to play there. Intriguingly, Duchamp himself was absent at the opening (Altshuler 1994, p. 154).
8. Singling out Gene Davis' *Micro-Pictures* of 1968, O'Doherty writes: 'Now a participant in, rather than a passive support for art, the wall became the locus of contended ideologies' (1986, p. 29).

9. This work is discussed extensively in Mark Godfrey's contribution to the publication accompanying the exhibition *Open Systems – Rethinking Art c.1970* at Tate Modern (Godfrey 2005, pp. 32–5).

10. John G. Hanhardt (2003) discusses the issues related to preservation and determining the effective reconstruction of this seminal work as a representative case study of the Variable Media Approach.

11. Inaugurated in 1989, Peter Hill's *Museum of Contemporary Ideas* (MOCI) involves creating what he terms 'Superfictions', whose motivation he describes as 'an umbrella under which to work. I could create fictional artists, curators, editors, collectors, and auctioneers and through them create an alternative art world' (Hill 2006, unpaginated source). Since 1992, the Internet has become a major channel for the project's promotion and distribution.

12. *The Meat Wagon* (28 October 2005 to 22 January 2006) was conceived as a critical examination of the museum as an exhibition space. Combining works by the artist with items drawn from the Menil Collection in Houston, Gober's exhibition was promoted as an American embodiment of Malraux's imaginary museum. The installation was developed as a response to the artist's relationship to museum curators, and the relationship of works of art to the culturally determined context of the art museum.

13. Olafur Eliasson's art exhibits a general tendency towards 'engag(ing) the viewer in a creative reconstruction of his perception of the environment' (Arnason 2004, p. 13). Works involving structurally altered or reconstructed architectural features (*Your Activity Horizon*, 2004) and built self-contained environments (*La Situazione Antispettiva*, for the Venice Biennale in 2003) are illustrative cases in point.

14. As Gunnar Arnason expands:

> Once time enters the equation the whole nature of aesthetic qualities changes. We are used to thinking about art in terms of static concepts of visual aesthetic qualities, inherited from the classical notion of beauty, and formalist notions of the aesthetic qualities inherent in images. But if we introduce the temporal element into the equation a whole new array of qualities come into play, like symmetry and equilibrium, cyclical change and periodicity, transition from chaos to order, reflection and refraction. (2004, p. 15)

Chapter 4

Digital Mediation

Synopsis

The increasingly digitally mediated context of the contemporary art museum provides the impetus to consider the virtual as an expanding space for museological practice. The virtual interface initiates a new arena for exhibition practices and precipitates cultural discourse about the nature, value and function of art. The adoption of digital mediation by museums exemplified by forms such as Net Art reflects their new multimedial condition as multi-platform and distributed. In response, curatorial practice orients itself towards the presentation of perspectives and context that facilitate dialogical transactions between artefact and mode of display through exploring new possibilities for viewer and spatial experience.

The digitally mediated context of the contemporary art museum presents a challenge to rethink the institution's material interface in response to its increasingly 'virtualised' situation. Embedded in the missions of institutions across a broad range of departments or services, information communication technologies have found themselves playing a central role across an ever-widening range of organisational functions and cultural activities, to the point that it can be generalised that human-computer interaction is on the verge of becoming the primary interface for many museums to engage with their public. The rapid development of the new media field has also provided the impetus to consider the virtual as an expanding space for museological practice. Prominent new media curator Steve Dietz (1998) forecast more than a decade ago that as museum audiences become ever more fluent in processing 'information' in digital forms and through the Internet, 'we may need to refine our notions of what the best roles of museums and curators are'.

Distributable media are making a significant impact on contemporary aesthetic practices. While redefining how an artwork might actually take shape, these forms also challenge how artworks might conventionally be exhibited. A reliance upon participatory modes of engagement is a feature of many forms of digital communication, whether found in popular media or artistic contexts. According to media theorist Darren Tofts (2005), these forms 'have modified the spatial and temporal dimensions of what constitutes an art event and an experience of it'. That being said, the field is particularly fluid and responses can prove contradictory. Over the past 20 years, notions of the 'virtual museum' have significantly altered. From early graphical forays that explored the screen spaces native to the computer to establishing alter egos in the realm of *Second Life*,[1] ideas about what kind of virtual presence best serves the ambitions and audiences of individual museums has evolved dramatically. Even within this relatively short time-frame, we have witnessed new digital technologies that have heralded the advent of the participatory web, social computing and mobile media. The ubiquity of the mobile phone and *iPod*[2] – arguably the single most significant influence on the consumption of media content of recent times – and their subsequent application towards augmenting and extending the viewer experience of art could barely have been contemplated even just a single generation ago.

The nature of new media art also poses fundamental questions about the traditional role and purview of the museum reflected in its mission to collect, preserve and interpret works of art. Addressing the relationship that connects the artwork, museology and digital technology has become a key dialog within cultural practice and policy. This assertion is supported by a number of significant studies conducted by leading government bodies and cultural organisations around the turn of the millennium during a particularly formative era of deliberation and debate over new media's place in the museum. Viewed in retrospect, their respective observations provide an overview of contentions that continue to influence the application of digital mediation today.

Arguably, the most highly profiled of these was a research report on museums and new media art commissioned by the Rockefeller Foundation (S. Morris 2001). The report identified a set of options for art museums to define their role in relation to new media art. The alternatives outlined in the report fell under the categories of commissioner, portal or collector. The direct commissioning of new media art was put forward as a continuation of a distinctive trend since the 1970s taken by a number of museums with regards to contemporary art more generally. The report cites the Guggenheim's patronage of Shu Lea Cheang's *Brandon: A One-Year Narrative Project in Installments* (1998) as the first commission of an online artwork by a museum, although MoMA's first web-specific project dates back to Peter Halley's *Exploding the Cell* interactive.[3] In contrast, museums may instead choose to act as information 'hubs', providing links to alternative platforms and dedicated new media art sites or operate open-access forums for promoting interactive public dialogue. The role of the museum as a 'filter' can be thought to run counter to a more conventional, institutional stance that is based on maintaining its 'neutrality'.[4] The notion that the museum acts as an information 'hub', it can be argued, may be more attuned to where the institution may sit within today's media ecology or 'infosphere' (Appadurai 1996). The framework for the cultural study of globalisation proposed by Arjun Appadurai is characterised by the combined forces of mass migration and electronic mediation. In *Modernity at Large: cultural dimensions of globalization*, he investigated how images are circulated through globalised mass media, appropriated and reinvented by their local recipients.

In terms of collecting policy, the report acknowledged some of the contentions that exist over classifying new media artworks in relation to established, pre-existing categories of 'original, unique work of art', an 'edition' or a 'performance'. The performance model is given the most credence of these options. As noted in the report:

> It is ephemeral, exists as an experience in time, which vanishes after completion, unless recorded for posterity. Whitney curator Christiane Paul says new media art is like performance because 'the artwork has been transformed into a structure that relies on a constant flux of information and engages the viewer/collaborator the way a performance might'. (S. Morris 2002, p. 9)

I would extend this observation by positing that this 'real-time' quality is activated in any exhibition that features species of new media art or mediated forms. While other traits commonly associated with digital media – such as intangibility, variability, interactivity and reproducibility – may in fact set out an irreconcilable contradiction between the respective cultures of future-oriented new media and that of the traditional museum, with its view to preserving historical legacy.[5]

Offering a pre-millennial perspective, Dietz (1998) associated the virtual museum with a 'potential museum' that is not predicated on ' a collection, education, connoisseurship or any other aspect of our current institutions but on what the muses (the daughters of memory) promise – potentiality'. Warning that 'museums ignore the reality of the virtual at their peril', he professed that such a shift brings with it the inevitable consequence of questioning the curator's central role in the museum. On a social level, as the museum's audience becomes increasingly fluent in processing 'information', prevailing notions of the role of museum curator would be tested. For example, developing upon the notion of 'auto-curation', in pointing out how databases have enabled increasingly sophisticated methods of exploring and interrogating a museum's resources, Dietz muses that 'the value of the curatorial role will lie not so much in what is known as in how well the stories can be told'. Curation, through its professional position within the museum, negotiates the intersection of the artwork and institution, artists and audience. Supported by the observations of Steven Johnson – a futurist who draws upon a wide array of cultural and historical examples that trace a lineage from computer and information graphics back to the Victorian novel, early cinema and beyond to address how technological innovations have transformed society – Dietz pointed out that: 'the most profound change ushered in by the digital revolution [...] will lie with our generic expectations about the interface itself. We will come to think of interface design as a kind of art form'. Examples ranging from online guides to mixed-reality environments continue to provide us with examples that indicate ways in which the museum can use digital technologies to respond to this interface.[6]

Switching focus to the Australian context, the Myer Report (DCITA 2002) set out a case for national arts organisations to become more fully engaged with this virtual interface. In it, the impact of new technology upon the operations of these institutions was surveyed and a number of consequential factors highlighted. In the report, the following restrictions and impediments to fuller scale adoption were identified:

The use of new technologies in digital and other arts has added an extra cost factor for artists and organisations, both those producing and those presenting such works. Due to the rapid evolution of technology, levels of obsolescence are high. A lack of access for artists will increase the digital divide forming between those who do have easy access to technology and those who do not. Australian artists have achieved international standing, but may lose representation in international exhibitions if they are unable to contribute in the fields of new technology-based and digital art. If galleries and other art spaces do not have adequate access to new technology, works based on new technology will be unable to be shown and collections will be reluctant to acquire them.

While cautionary in cases, the report did recognise that the up-take of digital technologies by artists and museums 'initiates a new virtual arena for artistic expression and exhibition', leading to new cultural discourses about the nature, value and function of art itself in an era of human-computer interaction and networked participation.

Back on the international stage, the Tate provides an illustrative example of how a gallery can be transformed through its encounter with new programmes and architectures that characterise the multimedial museum. At an institutional level, the Tate has responded innovatively to a number of issues facing the postmodern museum. No longer embodied in a single building, let alone geographic location, the Tate 'brand' has become increasingly dispersed across a number of 'campuses'. This physical dispersal across four 'real' locations (Tate Britain and Tate Modern in London, Tate Liverpool and Tate St. Ives) was further exaggerated by the establishment of its online presence, Tate Online, in 1998. Based on conversations with Jemima Rellie, Head of Digital Programmes at the Tate in London, during late 2002, statistics drawn from annual visitor numbers anecdotally supported the recognition of Tate Online as the organisation's second most visited campus (second only, at that time, to the then recently opened Tate Modern). Complementing their overarching policy for expanding access and audiences, the Tate continues to be a representative example of a cultural organisation that has come to embrace increased virtualisation as a fundamental part of its institutional mandate.

The gallery introduced its curatorial focus on Net Art commissions in 1999. Charged with the brief to initiate the commissioning of art projects for their website, Matthew Gansallo described Tate Online's programme as 'a platform for more research, experiments and dialogue in museum curating and presenting new media' (Gansallo quoted in S. Morris 2002, p. 72). Initiated through Tate National Programmes (Fall 1999), the curating and commissioning of art coincided with the opening of Tate Modern in Spring 2000. The Tate's first online project went 'live' on 26 June 2000. Titled *Uncomfortable Proximity* (or 'Tate-Mongrel', as it more popularly became known), this work by the media art group Mongrel gave the impression of the Tate website being 'hacked' and its history rewritten. Initially, it was proposed that this alternative version of the site would subversively activate on every fifth visit or 'hit' to the official website. This work was followed closely by a work devised by artist Simon Patterson. *La Match de Couleur* (launched 12 July 2000) explored coding and information systems associated with the Internet on a more aesthetic level by matching the hexadecimal values of a colour table shared with teams from the French football league. While a focus on the innate qualities of the art form itself naturally drove this initiative, a number of related curatorial concerns also spiral out from their commissioning. For instance, how the gallery-going audience relates to the work's exhibition places particular emphasis on determining the most suitable method of presentation, leading to the investigation of how the virtual dimension associated with the computer and Internet could be presented within the physical spaces of the museums. On this point, Gansallo makes note of the initial difficulty he encountered with regards to the predisposition from within the institution to simply resort to providing a computer in a 'stuffy room within a gallery'. The shape this decision takes goes some way to revealing the institution's own predisposition to such a programme: 'How these commissions would be perceived as art in the way that contemporary art museums like the Tate, define and present art' (Gansallo quoted in S. Morris 2002, p. 62).

This vexed relationship precipitated one of its most intriguing commissions: *Tate in Space* by artist Susan Collins. [*Figure 4*] Launched in 2002 following in the wake of the highly publicised opening of Tate Modern, *Tate in Space* heralded the next stage of the organisation's expansion ('continuing the Tate tradition of innovation and exploration') that would see it conquer the 'final frontier' of outer space. The work operated insidiously by blending seamlessly into the Tate's institutional website. Branded and designed in accordance with the style guide adopted across the site and drawing upon corporate language (with its rhetoric of extending audience access and expanding the mission of the organisation), *Tate in Space* presented itself as an almost-plausible programme. The artwork functioned as a conventional website designed around sections dedicated to 'Space Art' and 'Space Architecture', plus 'Public Programmes' and 'Visiting Information' pages. An obligatory director's introduction announced the aspirations of the mock-programme, while a webcam relay from the fictitious orbiting gallery module added a level of pseudo-realism. As Paul Boneventura (2002) observed in the accompanying critical essay: 'Arguably, no artwork encapsulates the reality neutral position of the web quite so succinctly as *Tate in Space*'.

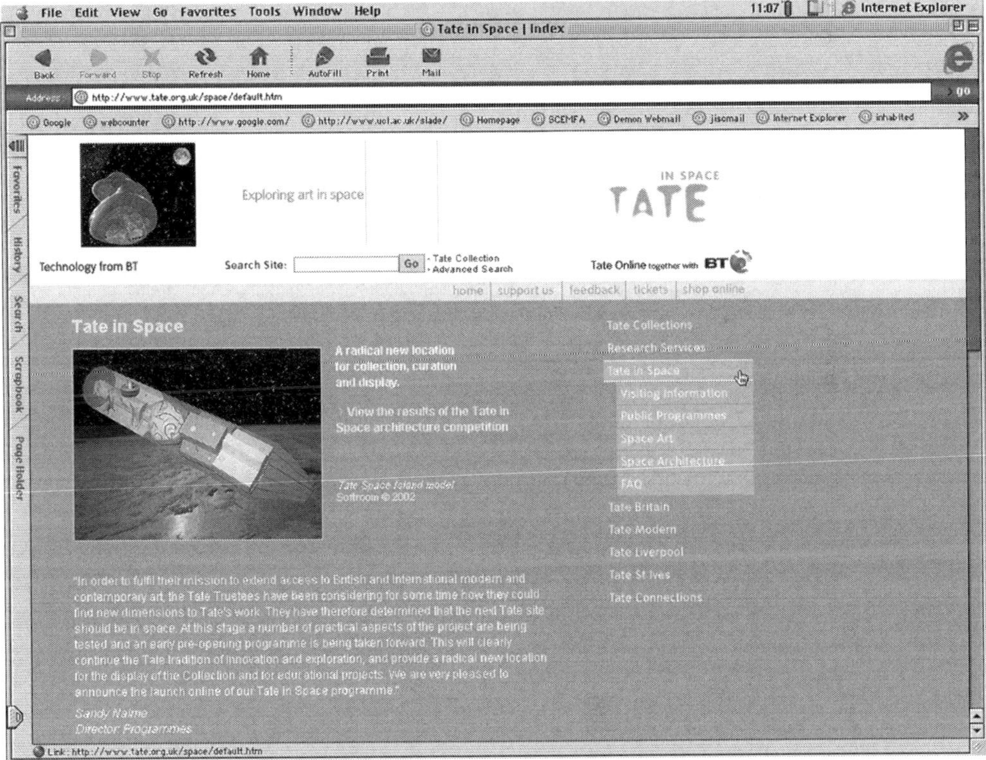

Figure 4: Screen documentation of Susan Collins, *Tate in Space* (2002). Website (Tate Online: London, 2002).

Deliberately causing a suspension-of-disbelief in the mind of the visitor, the resulting disorientation drew attention to the tenuous separation of the artwork – its perceived aesthetic autonomy – from the actual public operability and functioning of Tate Online as interface for the institution's 'public relations'.[7]

As these points illustrate:

> Collins' project is less to do with real or imagined artefacts in space or opportunities for artists outside the earth's gravitational pull and more about examining the contexts in which art institutions, artists and viewers play out their interconnecting roles. (Boneventura 2002)

Exemplified by this example, the Tate's general response to digital mediation over the past decade has reflected how the new ecological condition of the contemporary museum is multi-platform and distributed along the lines of physical/virtual as well as onsite/online.

Along with conservation and provenance, the role played by museums in displaying new media art raises a particularly contentious issue.[8] Extending the exhibition of an artwork into the digital domain is not only about re-presenting it. In weighing up alternatives offered by physical gallery environs versus an exclusively online presence for showing works, the Rockefeller Foundation report indicated that most museums have adopted 'object-based' display techniques reliant largely upon existing museum exhibition models (S. Morris 2001, p. 12). The case related to Tony Oursler's *TimeStream* was singled out to illustrate this assertion. Originally conceived as the first in a series of projects by online artists and commissioned by MoMA, the work was transformed into a special installation because of the perceived 'inaccessibility' or 'dullness' that either an online-only or kiosk-based presentation would offer museum visitors.

Further opportunities exist in re-formatting notions about what constitutes the work itself. However, in order to optimise the potential of digital mediation, Dietz (1998) has duly cautioned: 'It's a fine line between presenting the work in an exhibition and extending it appropriately – appropriate to both the work and the medium.' Curatorially, this digital interface carries with it a reassessment of established values – reorienting the curatorial 'compass' in favour of presenting perspectives, establishing contexts and providing platforms over more conventional institutional concerns with preservation, reproducibility and issues of ownership. Just as categorising new media art presents difficulties, so too does accommodating the multidisciplinary nature of the role of new media curator within pre-existing professionalized structures. The Rockefeller Foundation report recommended that the founding of departments dedicated to 'New Media' – as distinct from pre-existing departments working under labels such as 'Media', 'Contemporary Art' or 'Photography' – would need to be structured differently from other departments that are defined by media affiliations, because of new media's distinctive interdisciplinary nature (S. Morris 2001, p. 15). On this point, the report made an important observation that is central to the practice-base of the curatorial design enterprise:

Just as museums have expanded their roles in the twentieth century, so too have curators. The enlargement of the original role of 'keeper' of objects has enabled the curator to be an active participant in the commissioning and creation of new artwork. This development coincided with the rise of site-specific installation art, and has continued with new media art. (S. Morris 2001, p. 14)

Adapting contemporary curatorial practice to the cultural discourses and conditions of the new virtual arena is a main objective of this book. The question of curatorial process is delicately poised on the issue of artistic autonomy versus curatorial 'co-creation', as it involves collaboration and dialogue with artists on the realisation of projects. Further, inspired by the language and techniques associated with interactive multimedia, processes of annotation, mapping and navigation can be posited as distinctive new curatorial functions. Because of the interdisciplinary nature of the role, the curator in the future ultimately needs to be capable of operating as a 'producer', act as a 'mediator' between the artists and institution, and be skilled in 'negotiating' across disciplinary borders and conventional organisational structures of the museum.

Today, virtuality characterises the quality of aesthetic experience under contemporary conditions. These conditions are influenced, to a significant degree, by the range of practices encompassed by digital mediation and how they facilitate transactions between artefact and mode of display, viewer and spatial experience. These dialogical exchanges are not limited to a single scale, dimension or channel, but remain open, continuously cycling between response and anticipation, influence and reinterpretation. 'Browsing' – commonly applied to the experience of traversing and sifting through information on the Internet – may well prove to be a most apt description of the form of engagement that is becoming increasingly applicable to museum-based experiences. While used derisively to describe a state of indiscriminate, distracted interaction, 'browsing' draws attention to the way that 'searching' might be shown to supersede authored narrative within interactive media. In a digital milieu, proximity (a spatial property) and connectivity (a relational one) stitch together an experiential fabric that contrasts with time-honoured tropes like linearity and narrative. These properties exhibit a recognisable affinity with the discursive requirements placed upon curation and the formatting of exhibition space.

Digital mediation adds to the ways in which exposition can take place, extending the possibility for interactions, interpretations and viewing scenarios to occur across real and virtual spaces. Curator Nicolas Bourriaud has spoken of: 'the space where works are displayed is altogether the space of interaction. The space of openness that ushers in all dialogue' (Bourriaud 2002, p. 44). Digitally informed artistic and curatorial design practices are ideally situated at this time to explore the relationship between spatial practice and digital mediation dialectically, and there is arguably no better place to play this out than in the multimedial museum.

Notes

1. *Second Life* is a virtual world developed by Linden Labs and launched on the Internet in 2003 [http://www.secondlife-art.com/]. There are believed to be well over 2000 'museums' in *Second Life*. Members of the virtual community can use *Second Life* as a platform to express themselves and create virtual art. Using the software's modeling tools enables artists to create new forms of art that otherwise would not physically be possible.

2. The *iPod* was launched by Apple on 23 October 2001. On 9 April 2007, it was announced that Apple had sold its one hundred millionth *iPod*, making it the biggest-selling digital music player of all time. In addition to dominating the portable media player market, the *iPod* has been adopted by major institutions, including universities and museums, as a delivery mechanism for communication, education and public access through 'podcasting'.

3. Documentation related to virtual projects commissioned by the Guggenheim are available online [http://www.guggenheim.org/exhibitions/virtual/].

4. This approach is informed a number of initiatives, including *CyberMuse* (National Gallery of Canada and Canadian Museum of Contemporary Photography, Ottawa [http://cybermuse.gallery.ca/cybermuse/home_e.jsp]) and *Design Hub* (a project initiated through the Powerhouse Museum, Sydney [http://www.dhub.org/]).

5. In March 2001, the Guggenheim convened a symposium titled 'Preserving the Immaterial: A Conference on Variable Media'. This event focused directly on conservation-related issues to the preservation of new media art. Subsequently, further study based on the Variable Media model for preserving non-traditional media was supported by the Daniel Langlois Foundation based on a proposal from Jon Ippolito, Associate Curator of Media Arts at the Guggenheim.

6. At the time, Steve Dietz (1998) singled out the Institute for Contemporary Art (ICA), London's approach to their 'curatours' programme which provided a means to support 'explor[ing] ideas and themes across web sites. Each curatour explores a different theme and is curated by a specialist within the field'. The Guggenheim's 'Cyber-Atlas' was also highlighted for its mapping of Web sites related to visual art and culture.

7. The Tate's Net Art commissions are exhibited within the context of the institution's Web presence. More recently re-branded as Tate Media, the present mandate encompasses an evolving range of activities. Through its 'digital channel', a continuously expanding resource of artist talks, performances and cultural debate is made available to the Tate's audience in a variety of formats.

    Included amongst these has been a programme of online event forums. Generally, these forums have operated in conjunction with an umbrella, cross-platform programme. For example, the 'Code of Practice' online discussion was linked to the *Open Systems* exhibition at Tate Modern in 2005. In addition, two associated symposia were webcast and archived. But unlike a conference, they provide the opportunity for a discussion to be explored over time and at length. Convened as 'asynchronous' discussions, these online forums were conducted over three to six weeks. By being hosted online, external links to papers, related projects and other reference points were easy to accumulate and make available to their audiences. According to convenor Kelli Dipple, success with engaging audiences in dialogue through these events has proven variable. The most successful public discussion was linked to the Common Ground forum, which discussed Open Source methodologies. While statistics charting online activity in the form of 'postings' revealed that not many people participate actively in this way, it was determined that around 2000 visitors accessed the discussion during its 'live' period.

8. The 2000 Whitney Biennial has been identified as the watershed for digital art's acceptance into the museum. While it was noted that Web pieces by Fred Wilson and Allan McCollum were

commissioned by MoMA for *Museum as Muse*, curated by Kynaston McShine in 1995 [http://www.moma.org/exhibitions/1999/muse/index.html], the inclusion of new media works curated jointly by Christiane Paul and Larry Rinder for the 2000 Whitney Biennial has been given particular credence.

Along with the Whitney Museum of American Art, the Guggenheim Report singled out other major American museums for their early commitment and patronage of new media art. These included the Dia Center for Art, the Solomon R. Guggenheim Museum, The Museum of Modern Art (MoMA), the San Francisco Museum of Modern Art (SFMOMA) and the Walker Art Center.

For the most part, electronic art has found itself historicised in the lineage of installation art practices and digital technologies viewed as providing the means to expand upon that art form's possibilities. However, the exhibition *Net_Condition* shown at ZKM/Karlsruhe in 1999 is notable for the influential role it played in gaining Net Art a wider audience [http://on1.zkm.de/netcondition/]. Hans Peter Schwarz (1999) has provided a review of the exhibition and, in particular, its approach to the exhibition of screen-based artworks in a gallery setting.

Chapter 5

The Multimedial Museum

Synopsis

Describing the museum as multimedial signals a pervasive revisioning of the museum apparatus in response to changing social, cultural and technological conditions. Proving an innately adaptable cultural construct in the face of new technologies, the idea of the museum has itself been transformed through conceptualisations such as André Malraux's *musée imaginaire* or 'museum without walls'. The National Gallery of Victoria provides a case study for a major cultural institution's transformation into a multimedial museum through its embrace of digital mediation in the form of networked communications and display-based applications as part of its redevelopment. Entailing a more dialectical approach, the museum's role begins to shift from presentation to providing an infrastructure for aesthetic experience and, as a result, the conceptualisation of how exhibition space operates in this configuration is altered.

The preceding chapters, which have centred around virtuality and the art of exhibition, are underlined by the observation that adapting to changing social, cultural and technological conditions has become a primary concern for all museums. (Schubert 2000, p. 133) Most apparent in contemporary art museums, the transition from a more static and monolithic *modus operandi* to curatorial approaches and artistic practices that instead embrace the dynamic, temporal and contingent nature of exhibitions has transformed how museums approach the act of exposition over the last quarter of a century. Poised at the fulcrum of the new millennium, the development of a more, 'open' museum can be seen as indicative of a pervasive revisioning of the museum apparatus:

> As the gap between material and interpretation widened during this century, the limitations of the historical models of museum organisation became painfully clear. As a result, displays have shifted from the static towards the dynamic. The transition arguably marked the greatest revolution the museum concept has undergone in its entire history. (Schubert, p. 134)

A museum can be explored as a formation of surfaces and statements. In the postmodern era, the museum's role shifted away from creating an arena for the contemplation of the unique artwork and its aesthetic immediacy to staging virtual experiences (Krauss 1990). Extending this observation by using the term 'multimedial' to describe this situation today locates the crux of the issue in negotiating how the wide array of aesthetic transactions on offer as part of virtually any museum experience might elaborate upon relationships that might exist between material/immaterial, experience/information, fixed/variable. According to cultural analyst Mieke Bal, developing this 'multimedial' aspect of the museum raises far-reaching implications about 'what could happen if the mixed media nature of museums were to become a paradigm of cultural practice, in general' (Bal 1996a, p. 3). Positioned in a consumer society of mass markets in which subjectivity is fragmented and dispersed by information and media, the contemporary museum is compelled to address the importance of multimedia, defined both as content delivery and technology infrastructure, towards its expository techniques. Considering exposition – the public presentation or demonstration of arguments, through events that bring values, beliefs and their points of view into the public domain – as the primary function of the museum extends the analysis of it as a material object and directs critique towards the idea of the museum and its discursive behaviour.

The museum has proven to be an innately adaptable cultural construct. During the twentieth century, the foundations of the eighteenth-century ideal of the museum were put under incessant pressure by technological advancements. Technologies such as photography, film, television and video have each in their own respective ways altered the relationship that exists between the objects they display and their audience dramatically. As a consequence of technological mediation, the hierarchical 'order of things' in museums has been irreversibly affected, if not fully undermined. Walter Benjamin's insights in relation to the transformation of the work of art by forms of mechanical reproduction – including how mediated images might overlay a different pattern of visual realities over what might be thought of as 'objective' reality – cannot be understated in this regard. Advancing Benjamin's theorising of the impact of photographic reproduction on the social and cultural significance of art in the modern era, André Malraux formulated the concept of the *musée imaginaire*.[1] Malraux's 'museum without walls' provides an expression of the potentially endless discursive possibilities of the museum. According to Malraux, while the primary value of artworks may no longer reside in them as physical objects, they are remunerated through the process of reproduction: 'We might almost call them not "works" but "moments" of art' (1974, p. 55).

Conceived as an 'open field into which the viewer's own imaginative, projective, play was welcomed' (Krauss 1996, p. 346), this concept was particularly resonant during Postmodernism's formative period in the early 1980s. Pre-eminent art historians Douglas Crimp and Rosalind Krauss have provided critical examinations of Malraux's museum construct. Krauss explains her attraction to the *musée imaginaire* for the way it 'anticipated Postmodernism's levelling of formal value, its interest in constant play of exchange and its practice based on the interchangeability of style and form' (1996, p. 348). Instead of seeing his imaginary museum as a place where notions 'essential to the ordered discourse of the museum' such as originality, authenticity and presence are challenged or undermined, Malraux was enamoured by the prospect of 'establishing ever new stylistic series simply by reshuffling the photographs' (Crimp 1993b, p. 58). Through style, the collective corpus of art is simultaneously differentiated and unified. It is on the point of photography that Crimp's critique turns. In his essay 'On the Museum's Ruins', he stated:

> The set of objects the museum displays is sustained only by the fiction that they somehow constitute a coherent representational universe [...] Such a fiction is a result of an uncritical belief in the notion that ordering and classifying, that is to say, the spatial juxtaposition of fragments, can produce a representational understanding of the world. Should the fiction disappear, there is nothing left of the museum but 'bric-a-brac', a heap of meaningless and valueless fragments of objects' (Crimp 1993b, p. 53).

Neutrality has been instated as a precondition of the modern museum, enabling it to operate as a coherent field (Krauss 1996, p. 342). Krauss has formulated how the interpretive work of the museum curator or art historian proceeds from this form of museological organisation, 'establish[ing] meaning as a function of comparison' (p. 343). In its earliest form, the museum drew upon the spatial characteristics of the Renaissance palace. Through this building type, with its architectural arrangement of *en filade* series of rooms, the chronology of art history is reinforced as the spectator's movement is guided sequentially through these spaces. More contemporaneously, Brian O'Doherty has recognised the self-sustaining ideology of the Modernist museum reflected in its spatial dogma, the 'white cube':

> The ideal gallery subtracts from the artwork all cues that interfere with the fact that it is 'art'. The work is isolated from everything that would detract from its evaluation of itself. This gives the space a presence possessed by other spaces where conventions are preserved through the repetition of a closed system of values. Some of the sanctity of the church, the formality of the courtroom, the mystique of the experimental laboratory joins with chic design to produce a unique chamber of esthetics. So powerful are the perceptual fields of force within this chamber that, once outside it, art can lapse into secular status. (1986, p. 14)

Douglas Crimp has drawn attention to the issue raised by photography's own accommodation into the museum without walls and how this undermines the museum's ambition to preserve its universality. Whereas Benjamin recognised in photography and reproductive technologies the propensity to undo art's aura, Crimp interprets Malraux's formulation as serving to perpetuate this specious unity in the comforting knowledge that sees art sustained by its Humanist project with artworks providing evidence of the human 'spirit'. While photography is simply used at the service of this project – as the 'vehicle by which art objects entered the imaginary museum' – the coherence of Malraux's museum is otherwise maintained. However, once photography itself is granted admission to this pantheon, the museum's homogeneity is disrupted: 'once photography itself enters, as an object amongst other, heterogeneity is re-established at the heart of the museum; its pretensions to knowledge are doomed' (Crimp 1993b, p. 56). If we turn our attention today from reproducibility to the issue of digitisation, does a similar deconstruction await in prospect? As the modern museum is in the process of transforming itself into a multimedial museum, what consequences can be drawn from the postmodern critique of Malraux's museum, given the prospects of increased digital mediation? While multimedia is used at the service of the museum, its difference is neutralised. However, do network-based applications of multimedia – as illustrated by the examples presented earlier when discussing the Tate's Net Art commissions – along with other media practices such as projectual media raise a disruption to the overall scheme of things, similar to that of photography when it was first allowed to enter into the museum as an artform in its own right?

Rosalind Krauss makes much of the linguistic turn from *musée imaginaire* to 'museum without walls', thereby raising the issue of the translation – the spatial visualisation – of Malraux's concept. According to Krauss' reading, Malraux's conception of his museum was not so much architectural as museological. Taking particular note of the act of translation that turns Malraux's original *musée imaginaire* into 'museum without walls', Krauss (1996) has interpreted this as a shift in emphasis of the original orientation of his argument towards subsequent interpretations that have proceeded along more spatially analogous lines. Drawing attention to his original text, she points out that museum architecture was not addressed directly, but implicitly through two images included as illustration in its publication. According to Krauss, 'each is intended to function more as the paradigm of a way that art had historically been conceived, or valued, or systematised, a specific way, in short, in which it was previously imagined' (1996, p. 342). The first of these, *The Gallery of the Archduke Leopold at Brussels* by Teniers, offers a representation of the classical standards on which the nineteenth-century museum was founded, while the photograph of an installation of El Greco paintings at the Washington National Gallery illustrates the twentieth-century museum's reorganisation of those values. In this image – with its rational proportions, uniform lighting and imposed ordering (semiotically signified by the guard rope, which enforces the respective spaces of artwork and its beholder). More relevantly to subsequent transformations of the museum, she raises two contemporaneous models that she identified as influencing Malraux's conception of the *musée imaginaire*: the 'universal space' of Mies van der Rohe and the spiral ramps of Le Corbusier and Frank Lloyd Wright, which render the 'endless imaginative production' of the museum's user. 'Being an immense enclosure which nonetheless defines a space', the spatial plan or 'idea' of Mies' Neue Nationalgalerie in Berlin is that of a 'value-free network within which to set individual objects in (changing) relation' (Krauss 1996, p. 344). In Wright's Guggenheim Museum, its spiral ramp is interpreted as exemplifying the increased effect of democratisation and act of imaginative projection ('fiction') privileged by the individualistic experience of art.

Applicably today, the virtual museum raises the question of what shape or space it might take. How does it interface with architecture? To what purposes might the integration of digital technologies through augmentation strategies involved in exhibition design serve, particularly as this relates to art museums? While widespread in non-art museums, Karsten Schubert has noted that the deployment of information technologies into museum displays has been relatively limited in comparison, pointing out that interactive displays appear to hardly ever be deployed in gallery settings. More conventionally, this form of kiosk has tended to be seconded away in specially designated areas, clearly separated away from the display of artworks (2000, p. 151). As Matthew Gansallo has summarised:

Contemporary art museums of the future will exhibit the virtual and the real alongside one another, crossing and overlapping each one's boundaries, creating an amazing visual and interactive experience within and without walls. It is therefore inevitable that museum architecture will have to change to accommodate the ever-growing advance and innovation in technology. I believe this will enhance the way we use, view and live with new media as part of our cultural consumption. (quoted in S. Morris 2001, p. 72)

While predictions that the Internet would make museums obsolete overstate the point, what values are promoted as museums move towards closer integration of physical and virtual spheres of engagement, becoming more fully multimedial as a result?

Serving as an illustrative case study, the National Gallery of Victoria (NGV) in Melbourne offers a prime example of a major art gallery's transformation into a 'multimedial' museum.[2] The cultural landscape of Melbourne has been significantly transformed since the 1990s. While its own local features, influences and vernaculars distinctively shape this geography, this terrain can be viewed as representative of the status and role of the museum at this particular historical moment. Collectively, Melbourne's spate of new art galleries offers a case study of the 'cultural logic' of the contemporary museum (Krauss 1990). The redevelopment of NGV into a twin-campus institution that has taken place over the past decade has seen the strategic integration of information technologies and multimedia systems across the full range of its institutional functions (encompassing curatorial, educational, retail and operational activities). Through acknowledging the pressing need to address digital mediation, the NGV set out to reposition itself in order to respond to 'the challenges of how to present, interpret, preserve and store its precious holdings in keeping with standards and expectations in the twenty-first century' (Webster 2000, p. 5). In its particular case, the 'core business' of the institution has been supported by its development of a comprehensive technology infrastructure. The incorporation of 'state-of-the art' multimedia facilities, meeting the aspirations of a major cultural institution, were signalled as a strategic imperative of the original architectural briefs for its two overlapping building projects. This process involved the renovation of the gallery's main building along with the creation of the new building forming an integral part of the major urban development of Federation Square. Designed by Lab Architecture Studios, the Ian Potter Centre: National Gallery of Victoria Australia (NGVA) is now dedicated exclusively to displaying the museum's Australian Art collections. Reopened in 2003 as the National Gallery of Victoria International (NGVI), the original building (designed by leading Australian modernist architect Roy Grounds) now acts as the primary venue for showcasing the gallery's vast international collection and hosting touring 'blockbuster' exhibitions. With its programme dispersed across two physical campuses, multimedia has been deployed extensively across the full range of the organisation's operations, including collections, education, marketing and communications.

Two distinct approaches have illustrated how digital mediation has been applied at the NGV. These examples involve networked communication on one hand and spatial considerations associated with exhibition practice on the other.

Network-based applications relate to media production, website, public screens and kiosks. From the outset of its redevelopment, the NGV's web presence was recognised as key strategy for enhancing the institution's international reputation and engagement with the general public. During the period of closure for renovation (between June 1999 and December 2003) a major archiving project was undertaken involving the digitisation of a significant portion of the overall collection (some 20,000 images). Since then, the NGV's multimedia unit has produced a wealth of rich media content, including materials developed directly to complement exhibitions. These productions are not applied exclusively to screen-based presentation, but also have been translated through hand-held exhibition guides and thoroughly incorporated into the design of installations.

A range of screen technologies can be found embedded into the interior architecture of both recent buildings. These screens have introduced a dynamic means of providing graphic communications for public address purposes (as promotion, signage and way-finding). While Lab Architecture Studio's design of the Ian Potter Centre accommodates a far more radical approach, with screen 'shards' dramatically piercing the architectural façade, the redevelopment of the Sir Roy Grounds Building by Mario Bellini demonstrates a much more understated intervention. In addition, a variety of touch-screen kiosks are distributed throughout to assist with visitor orientation as well as offering informative content intended to extend and enrich the visitor's gallery experience. As part of the architectural strategy originally implemented at the NGVI, the main concentration of these were to be found in a custom-designed 'Cyber Café'.[3]

Design plays an increasingly influential role in the field of cultural production (as evidenced by recent architectural design of museums and production values involved in the design of exhibitions). Concentration upon encounters with digital mediation through display-based applications in the physical environment of the gallery explores the shift away from 'hard' design towards anticipating the 'soft' design of events and experiences, modes of interaction and interfaces of museological spaces. It is therefore not surprising that more exhibitions are incorporating digital mediation as part of their exhibition design through employing a strategy of augmentation. The movement towards augmented strategies has resulted in the more recent introduction of podcasting, as only one part of what is being described currently as 'Web 2.0' services that emphasise networked modes of audience interaction and access.[4]

In the intervening years since the NGV's redevelopment there have been strong indications of the gallery's transition away from the 'white cube' and increasingly towards the 'black box'. While the polarisation intimated by this description is too exaggerated, regardless, the gallery's ability to exhibit a plethora of projectual media work continues to be challenged, technically as well as curatorially. The writing was quite literally 'on the wall' when the main temporary exhibition spaces of the NGVI were reopened by a fully projection-based presentation of work by Mario Bellini and the exhibition *World Rush*, whose installation featured customised projection environments for multiple-screen artworks by Doug Aitken and Eija-Liisa Ahtila. A further illustrative example of digital augmentation in exhibition design can be found in the major Edvard Munch exhibition, *The Frieze of Life*, held at the NGVI in 2004–5, which integrated a double-sided projection screen showing archival footage into the exhibition's layout. This intervention had a strong physical impact on the organisation of the exhibition space, with the inserted screen acting as a 'hinge' between the exhibition's larger and smaller galleries that could be interpreted as both opening and closing off the other space. Contrasting with the salon qualities of the larger, expansive room, the smaller gallery offered a more intimate viewing with its hanging of less formal studies and works on paper. This experience was supported by presenting Munch's less familiar photographic works, which were projected onto the screen as well as being provided on a single kiosk set quietly into the room. In this case, digital mediation complemented the exhibition's curation by offering an enhanced sense of quiet introversion.

While the Australian Centre for the Moving Image (ACMI) – which will be discussed more directly in the next chapter – was ostensibly set up as the dedicated venue for the screening of media-based artworks, the NGV has faced a significant broadening of its purview in the past decade in response to the proliferating variety of contemporary art practices. Digital media was largely conspicuous by its non-inclusion in its opening exhibition, *Fieldwork*, a major survey of post-1968 Australian contemporary art. More recently though, co-share exhibitions have been developed between the NGV and ACMI that have seen projectual media artworks distributed evenly between the two venues allowing curatorial decisions to hold sway over any perceived technical or media-specific delineation. Exhibition projects like *2006 Contemporary Commonwealth* and its forerunner *2004 – Australian Art Now* provide indications that the digital divide initially viewed as a means of differentiating the respective programs of the two institutions has significantly blurred. While ACMI presented an interactive installation of Shilpa Gupta and three-channel projection by Isaac Julien as part of *2006 Contemporary Commonwealth*, the NGVA hosted a mixed media/video installation by Yinka Shonibare. Subsequently acquired by the NGV, Shonibare's works were re-installed in early 2008 within the context of European painting galleries of the seventeenth and eighteenth centuries. [*Figure 5*] The installation of *A Masked Ball* (2004) – along with the accompanying tableaux *Reverend on Ice* (2005) – activated sightlines that interconnect the sequence of *en filade* rooms. Presented as a full wall-sized projection, the video work's presence matches the extravagance and pageantry of Tiepolo's *The Banquet of Cleopatra* hung on the opposite side of the room. *A Masked Ball* animates the dramatic potentials inherent in the works on display as well as the gallery space itself, by overlaying the theatricality of these scenes with the actions and movement of the work's observers.

Recognising the museum as a 'constructed space' encompasses it within a history of ideas expressed in tangible forms as well as that of otherwise intangible social practices. Importantly, by studying the museum as an embodiment of ideas and discourses:

> We can consider constructed objects as components of a discursive formation, and relate the practice of construction, inclusion and exclusion of objects to the rules and patterns of such formations. (Hirst 2003, p. 384)

Creative curatorial strategies, such as refreshing the presentation of time-honoured collections by recombining objects to create unexpected permutations to induce new readings, are just one indication of a pervasive revisioning of the museum apparatus. At this juncture in history, museums are presented with an opportunity to capitalise on the potential for a dialectical interplay between intention and interpretation. Recognising how the interrelationship between digital mediation and spatial practice is coming to shape the character of aesthetic experience under contemporary conditions of the multimedial

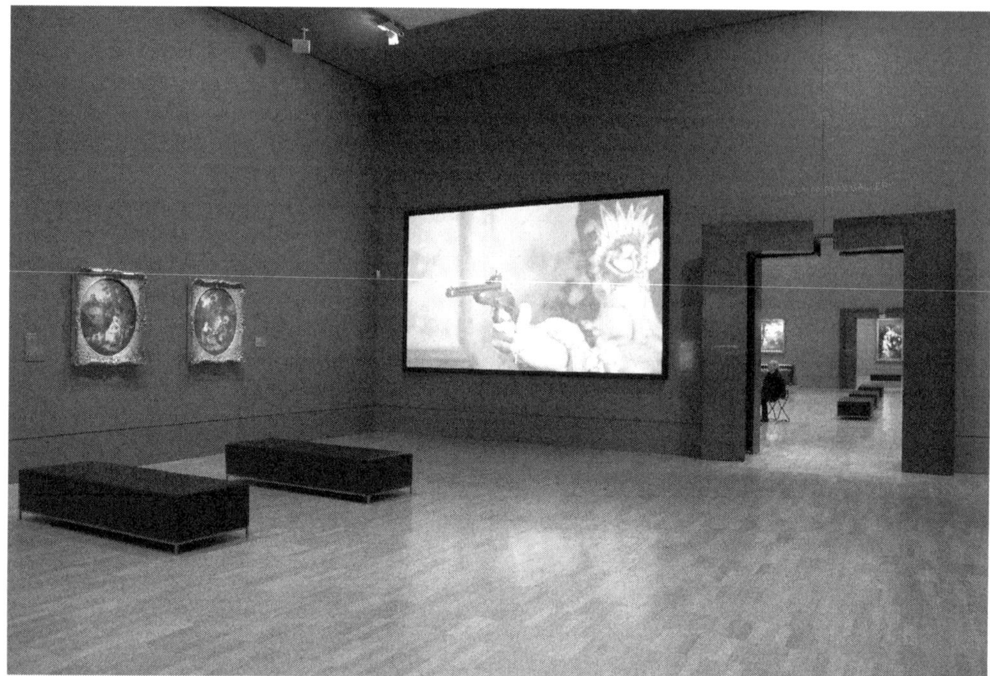

Figure 5: Installation view of Yinka Shonibare, *Un Ballo in Maschera / A Masked Ball* (2004). Video presented in the context of European painting galleries of the 17th and 18th centuries (NGVI: Melbourne, 2008). Photo credit: Vince Dziekan.

museum, the term 'dialectical' draws upon cinematographic associations with the technique of montage. The poetics of montage depends on the reader having expectations that can be overturned. As a technique of exposition, this formation exposes the dynamic relations that exist between author and user-centred orientations; balancing between anticipated, shared reading of conventional situations or norms and their unexpected re-combination or unforeseen juxtaposition – moving from a known towards the revelation of the unknown.

This dialectical approach heralds a movement away from what might be termed as a broadcast model of distribution (entailing a one-way communication approach) by introducing degrees of openness (access, participation) and feedback (exchanges, transactions). Importantly, the realisation of this aesthetic is not achievable only through multimedia – although multimedia does offer a distinctive way of exploring this mode of exposition. This shift entails ideological choices that challenge the museum's ability to respond to a changing mandate, from one founded on its presentation role to that of providing an infrastructure for aesthetic experience. Developing critically and creatively upon the dialectical relationship between virtuality and the art of exhibition could significantly alter the configuration and conceptualisation of how exhibition space operates in this configuration.

Notes

1. This 'museum without walls' builds upon a reliance on the medium of photography combined with the art historical issue of *style*. Malraux viewed style as the great unifying concept of art history, while photography offered the technological means to universalise by providing a basis for comparative analysis and discrimination by rendering everything similar or equivalent (as achieved particularly through the medium of black and white photography). As Malraux writes, 'Nothing conveys more vividly and compellingly the notion of destiny shaping human ends than do the great styles, whose evolutions and transformations seem like long scars that Fate has left, in passing, on the face of the earth' (1974, p. 46).

2. The transformation of the National Gallery of Victoria results from a \$300M (AUD) funding program, which commenced in 1996 with the appointment of Mario Bellini as lead architect on the redevelopment of the Sir Roy Grounds Building, which since 1968 has been the main site of the NGV. In that period the gallery's collection had doubled in size to some 60,000 works of art and the NGV's operations had significantly outgrown the existing building (Goad 2003, p. 41). Undertaking as an extensive re-arrangement of the building's interior (which has effectively doubled the exhibition space available to each category of the Gallery's collection), the architectural project also had to negotiate the building's significant heritage values (involving re-inventing or negotiating such features as Federation Court, the Great Hall, with its iconic stained glass ceiling, and its publicly much-loved 'water wall'). Having radically proposed serious modifications – even eradication – of these features, the pressures upon the refurbishment were significantly offset in 1997 when the opportunity presented itself for the Gallery to consider a purpose-built gallery dedicated exclusively to profiling Australian art as part of the newly-proposed Federation Square site situated just a short distance away. Following an international design competition, Lab Architecture Studio was awarded the Federation Square commission, which would see the new Ian Potter Centre: NGV Australia campus developed alongside a dedicated cinemedia centre, the Australian Centre for the Moving Image.

3. This implementation strategy, which by resorting to a hierarchical approach undermined the dialectical potential of multimedia, proved ineffectual. As a result, this area of the building was redeveloped and refitted back to a more conventional café in 2007.

4. The convenors of the 2008 version of the *Museums and the Web* conference point out how the predilection towards social computing (enabling audiences to make use of the Internet for creating user-generated content, collaboration and virtual communities) dominated this annual conference for the first time. David Bearman and Jennifer Trant noted the following consequence:

   With the pervasive adoption of Web technologies as mechanisms for audience engagement – and the re-situation of the museum on the Web in social application spaces controlled by others, rather than exclusively within the private preserves of museum Web sites – museums are encountering new issues and challenges. (2008, pp. 3–4)

   To illustrate, the 2008 conference hosted in Montreal included a paper by Brian Dawson, et al. that examined how social networking sites, such as Facebook, Flickr and YouTube, offer strategic 'points of presence' for museums, while Peter Samis provided a case study of how SFMOMA encouraged viewer interpretation through maintaining a 'blog' as part of its staging of a retrospective of Olafur Eliasson in keeping with the artist's aesthetic approach to viewer experience and engagement.

Chapter 6

Curatorial Design

Synopsis

Synthetic image spaces (in the lineage of nineteenth-century *phantasmagoria*) promote a dialectical way of thinking about the relationship between art, viewing experience and exhibition space. Drawing upon encounters with interactive environments by leading new media proponents, an alternative reading to immersion is proposed through critically investigating the relationship between virtual images under exhibition conditions, thereby revealing the technoaesthetic of such mediated spaces. Selected installation strategies employed at the Australian Centre for the Moving Image (ACMI) provide further cases that illustrate a reconsideration of the exhibition's design interface and how an integrative approach to digital mediation and spatial practice underpins the conceptual framework for curatorial design.

Digital media has had a significant impact on contemporary aesthetic practices. Critical responses attempt to explain how different modes of perception and engagement develop in relation to new social, cultural and technological conditions. For its part, distributed aesthetics addresses the implications that new technologies such as interactive and networked media are exerting on both the aesthetic and social aspects of contemporary culture. Proposing a revised formulation of the relationship between form and media, Darren Tofts (2005) has written: 'the aesthetics of distribution are indicative of our changing habit of consumption as much as our changing conception of what art is and potentially can be in a networked world'.

Offering the possibility of thinking differently about participation and how relationships between artwork and audience might be reconceived and reconfigured, what characterises these networked conditions and how might they be understood in aesthetic terms? Practices ranging from Net Art through to interactive, networked environments can exhibit highly individualised and introverted forms of engagement or alternatively, draw upon the connectedness and sociability associated with virtual communities. They also redefine how the artwork might actually take shape. Increasingly ephemeral in nature, these forms demonstrate different ways that artworks might be conceived, configured, distributed and exhibited.

Viewing conditions establish new meanings and uses of virtual images, as well as offer alternative constructions of the social space of their exposition. This situation becomes increasingly complex in new media installations. The predominant way of exhibiting digital media artworks has promoted an aesthetic equated with the highly sensory perceptual experience of 'immersion'. Media art historian Oliver Grau has argued that aesthetic distance is antithetical to the illusionistic ambitions and immersive nature of 'virtual art'. In espousing the qualities of this form of artwork, he asserts: 'Virtual installations diminish the faculty or learned ability to objectify or perceive illusory work as an autonomous aesthetic object' (2003, p. 202). In this context, the artwork's installation plays a significant part in establishing an appropriate form of engagement supporting the aesthetic intentions of the artist. Conditions supporting the aesthetic encounter may be established by rendering the spatial considerations of exhibition as unobtrusive as possible (as a remediation of the neutrality of the 'white cube' aesthetic), or through revealing the technologised apparatus of exposition as an incorporated part of the artwork (as illustrated by works by Char Davies, Luc Courchesne and Jeffrey Shaw – three seminal artists who have had a significant influence on shaping the aesthetics and critical formulation of immersion as it relates to the discourse around new media art).

By way of broaching the subject of curatorial design, this chapter will use the term *phantasmagoria* to describe *synthetic exhibition spaces* that first proliferated in the nineteenth century and continue to exert an influence over the projectual and digital media arts of the present day. Phantasmagoria is a term that came into popular usage at the dawn of the nineteenth century as a name for optical illusions produced with magic lanterns. Such illusory 'image spaces' – counting amongst their number the *panorama* and *diorama* plus a diverse and strangely eclectic collection of much more exotic species – are all related because of how they created the appearance of reality by tricking the senses through a mix of technical manipulations. Their proliferation continues to the present day, supported by advancements in digital imaging and multimedia communications.

The phantasmagoria incorporates illusionistic imagery along with the apparatus that is intimately involved in its very production. Implicated in this construction are the relationships between virtual images and the spatial conditions of the private and public spaces in which they are encountered. By drawing upon first-hand encounters with installations at the Australian Centre for the Moving Image (ACMI), I hope to illustrate the way that exhibition space determines the viewer's experience of new media art. An integral feature of Federation Square, Melbourne's major civic project marking the centenary of Australian federation, was the establishment of a cinemedia centre dedicated to the exhibition of new media and interactive and moving image art. ACMI, which was established in 2001, was publicised from the outset as offering 'spatial journeys' realised through the media of light, video and the range of digital media. The founding of this centre dedicated to promoting the exhibition of projectual media artworks provides an opportunity to investigate the particular adaptation of curatorial design to the demands of viewing and interaction with mixed-reality interfaces that characterise new media exhibitions.

Developing from these examples, it is contended that the phantasmagoria actually precipitates a dialectic of relational thinking that points to the inherent tension that exists in the very structure of their exhibition. As the relationship between art and its spaces of exhibition become increasingly mixed, uncertain and conflicting, this analysis of the art of exhibition moves beyond the architectural towards an engagement with the cultural positioning (the institutional, embedded, habitual properties) of the virtual artwork's exhibition space (as enclosed, contained and insulated, or open, distributed and situated in social space). In developing this interpretation, the dialectical implications of such exhibition systems and the contiguous nature of their virtual and physical spaces will be teased out by concluding with an observation of how the spatial practice involved in the presentation of works by Christian Marclay at ACMI exemplify the spatial calibration of an audio-visual experience with its site of exhibition.

The phantasmagoria characterised the cultural values of the modern age. In his ambitious *Arcades Project*, Walter Benjamin undertook to compile a comprehensive inventory of the technologies that serviced the image-making imagination that he sensed was at work in the collective unconscious of the age.[1] Benjamin viewed the phantasmagoria as embodying the field of tensions involving the interpenetration of concrete manifestations of the modern world and the collective dreams of its public. Understood as a deceptive image designed to dazzle, the phantasmagoria expressed 'the ambiguity peculiar to the social relations and products of this epoch' (Tidemann 1999, p. 938). In such a way, an architectural construction such as the Parisian shopping arcades would come to be used by Benjamin as an emblem of the relation between technology and aesthetics in modernity. Through the *technoaesthetic* of mediated spaces dedicated to image consumption and viewing experiences – as evidenced not only by media technologies associated with the pre-history of cinema, but also by spectacles such as world fairs and exhibitions that 'engulf the viewer in a simulated total environment in miniature' (Benjamin 1999, p. 406) – the relation of the subject to their sensory environment was transfigured. The use of the term *technoaesthetic* enables us to recognise how technological developments in the industrial and post-industrial era have transformed aesthetic practices and artistic modes of production from the avant-garde (Futurism, Constructivism and the Bauhaus) through to the contemporary media arts.

The phantasmagoria incorporates illusionistic imagery along with the apparatus that is intimately involved in its very production. This aggregative formation of sight and sound, combining simulated image content, *mise-en-scène* environments and atmospherics, directs a polysensory experience at a receptive subject. Illusionistic success is achieved by overwhelming the viewer's senses with stimuli, effectively drowning the subject's perceptions in a wash of special effects. Submersible and submissive in equal measures, the viewer is subjected to the 'manipulation of [their] synaesthetic system by control of environmental stimuli' that envelops their sensorium leading to the resulting sense of immersion (Buck-Morss 1997, p. 394). Susan Buck-Morss has developed an interpretive reading of the phantasmagoria's immersive effect as part of its technoaesthetics and speaks of the anaesthetic, double-function of technology in her reading of Benjamin's 'The Work of Art in the Age of Mechanical Reproduction'. In the first instance, media extend the human sensorium, opening it up to the world through 'penetration' by the medium's apparatus. This extension however leaves the senses themselves prone to over-exposure in return. Such intense sensory stimulation, or bombardment, 'has the effect of anaesthethetising the organism, not through numbing, but through flooding the senses' (Buck-Morss 1997, p. 394).

The resulting sense of distraction and estrangement associated with such simulated sensoria alter the modern subject's consciousness to waking reality. The loss of perspective distance is a theme that runs through Benjamin's formulation of the viewing subject's modern condition, which he described as 'estranged'. Most significantly, these intoxicating effects don't end at the threshold of the individualised observer but are also experienced at a collective level: 'Everyone sees the same altered world, experiences the same total environment' (Benjamin 1999, p. 395). Implicated in this configuration are the relationships between virtual images and the spatial conditions of the private and public spaces in which they are encountered. In her outline of video installation and virtual environments, Margaret Morse addresses the conditions of existence that support these practices. In *Virtualities: television, media art, and cyberculture, she* recognises presentation-based art's dependence on the validation provided by the museum by noting: 'Installation implies a kind of art that is ephemeral and never to be utterly severed from the subject, time and place of its enunciation' (1998, p. 157).

Of particular relevance to the following discussion of spatial practice is this comment by Morse:

The frame of an installation is then only apparently the actual room in which it is placed. This room is rather the ground over which a conceptual, figural, embodied and temporalised space that is the installation breaks. Then, the material objects placed in space and the images on monitor(s) are meaningful within the whole pattern of orientations and constraints on passage of either the body of the visitor or of conceptual figures through various modes of manifestation – pictorial, sculptural, kinaesthetic, aural and linguistic. (p. 157)

Projecting the phantasmagoria forward to the projectual and digital media art of recent decades, the situation becomes increasingly complex in new media installations given the interpenetration and meshing of perceptual experience, increasingly complex forms of visuality and imaging technology. When Benjamin writes: 'The arcades are passages having no outside – like the dream' (1999, p. 406), how might distributable media's qualities translate given the predisposition towards 'interiority' that is evidenced through a typology of impacted, dark spaces that have become a preferred format of presentation closely associated with new media artworks? The exhibition demands involved with installations such as the three examples to follow has had a significant influence on the resulting praxis of new media curating.

Char Davies' *Osmose* is an interactive environment designed to absorb its 'immersant' in synthetic space.[2] Taking its name from the biological process of osmosis, which involves the passage from one side of a semi-permeable cellular membrane to another, the work synthesises its viewing subject with virtual imagery through a user interface designed to enable the participant's breathing and physical, bodily balance to provide the means by which the work can be navigated. *Osmose* aspires to produce a contemplative, meditative experience. Comprised of stand-alone computer system and a head-mounted VR display, the viewer is provided with the opportunity to explore three distinct realms that represent the physical world through real-time interaction with generative 3D computer graphics and interactive sound. The first journey telescopes from an encounter with forest and trees, through branches and leaves, and onwards ('in'-wards) into subterranean depths of soil and root structures. A second starts on the surface of a pond and descends into an underwater abyss; the third ascends up through a clearing in the sky, into and rising above a lining of clouds. These sensual realms are bracketed by two other textual zones: a substratum of code that reveals the actual software code underwriting the illusionistic spaces and the associated interaction with them, and a superstratum of text that hovers above the clouds representing excerpts from various sources that relate to technology, the body and nature.

As with Davies' *Osmose*, the over-arching perceptual focus and intense visual concentration involved in Luc Courchesne's *The Visitor: Living by Number* induces a disembodied, weightless sense of traversing through illusionistic image space.[3] Supported by an interactive viewing apparatus, which acts as a 'cupolaed' cinema into which the work's interactor must insert their head, the viewer's perceptual field is fully enveloped by a collection of panoramic images that can be imaginatively entered and navigated through using a series of audible cues. Integral to encouraging the effect of full immersion in this virtual geography is the correlative withdrawal from an awareness of being physically present and literally fixed, stationed to a real space. While on the one hand the armature of the viewing edifice presents a most imposing, highly self-conscious bodily experience that verges on the claustrophobic, the resulting viewing experience transcends the 'imposition' exerted upon the subject's body associated with its constriction by the viewing apparatus. The paradox that arises from this dialogue between states of suspended disbelief (immersion) and residual awareness has been described as follows:

> In the case of *The Visitor: Living by Number* the subject/object membrane is semi-permeable; the positions are never fixed. Whether inside or outside the artwork, the visitor moves effortlessly between the status of both active subject and passive object. (Crimmings 2001, p. 23)

Eavesdrop is a collaborative work by Jeffrey Shaw with David Pledger that draws on the exhibition platform employed by Shaw in a number of previous works using the Advanced Visualization and Interaction Environment (AVIE).[4] The creation of experiences of a virtual nature achieved by overlapping expanses of space evidences an enduring preoccupation that continues to sustain Jeffrey Shaw's work and research into immersive visualisation systems. The deployment of this juxtapositional strategy goes back at least as far as Shaw's early photo installation *Viewpoint* (exhibited at the Paris Biennale in 1975) wherein pre-recorded fictional events and actual situations in museum space seamlessly superimpose upon each other.[5] As a means of inducing the necessary viewing conditions, in the case of *Eavesdrop* the viewer is provided with the opportunity to control their movement in and through a series of virtual scenes by manipulating controls of a video camera mounted to a rotating, robotic platform located in the centre of the exhibition space. Correlating the spatial configuration of the installation with the design of the 360-degree camera views of the virtual environments, the respective spaces of image and screen are made contiguous. Derived from the interactions of a single, embodied user the work offers an illustration of a model of aesthetic transcription.[6]

The seduction of interactive virtual environments such as these is precipitated by framing the subject's perceptual participation and imaginative identification within the enclosure of the illusion. The contemporary relevance of Benjamin's interest in the phantasmagoria recognises, on one level, that new technologies and media pose a significant threat to the construction of a safe-guarded, private world that delineates itself by foreclosing its 'interiority' from external influences. Media, according to Charles Rice, 'open the interior up to an array of forces and influences beyond its apparently strict boundaries' (2004, p. 284). Interiority, as it relates to the conventions of gallery architecture, establishes an uninterrupted, homogenous viewing space supporting the aesthetic effect of immersion. The construction of 'interiority' is accompanied by a matching critical formulation, highlighted in both artist statements and critical writings about these aforementioned artworks. Such interpretations primarily concentrate upon the works' expression as it is directly communicated for maximal impact, leading to their subsequent immersion, upon a single, punctually focused and highly concentrated viewing subject.

The merging of virtual image with technological apparatus, however, establishes an intriguing kind of structural double-distancing, wherein the manipulative effects of illusion are conjured up even while the means of its production are exposed. In such synthetic spaces, the viewer is complicit in pulling the strings of their own imaginative capture. Rosalind Krauss identifies this as a form of modern viewing experience that becomes associated with proto-cinematic optical devices, or 'philosophical toys', such as the *phenakistiscope* and *zootrope*. This double-vantage might also be shown as equally applicable to the affect of estrangement as with the experience of dreams: the sensation of occupying the place of dreamer simultaneously with the experience of 'watching oneself have it from outside' (Krauss 1999, p. 58). In the techno-psychological configuration of the phantasmagoria, the viewer 'toggles' between being immersed as a protagonist within the dreamlike space of the virtual image and witnessing themselves have this experience from a critical distance at one remove. These mechanics of fascination propose a dialectical movement that reverberates between the extended stretch of a macroscopic, critical vantage and the contractive, immersive capture by the fully encompassing, or up-close 'deep space' effect.

So considered, virtuality might thus be characterised as crucially having a dialectical nature: its cross-referencing of what is being experienced through imaginative immersion 'within' the artwork with what remains 'without'. Elements said to fall outside of what might conventionally be referred to as the artwork proper – the viewer's corporeal body and *proprioceptive*[7] sense, the influence of the spatial environment or conditions in which the experience is being staged, the transitional zones in between – establish an interplay between the sensory presence of synthetic images in a particular, real space and the apparent 'event' that presents itself to perceptual reception.

The staging of these individual works has highlighted the indispensable part that the viewing subject plays in a 'complex, inter-related performance in a total synaesthetic environment' (Grau 2003, p. 193). For the most part, viewing engagement with synthetic systems, such as those created by Davies, Courchesne and Shaw, privileges the first-person experience of the viewing subject, immersant or interactor and overlooks what can be argued is actually the predominant mode of interaction with such works under exhibition conditions: that of third-person observers, onlookers or interlopers.

While their respective intentions and formal strategies differ, it should be acknowledged that the artists discussed do make some accommodation for the spectatorship of a more loosely defined public audience. In *Osmose*, the virtual-reality experience took place within a customised gallery space that insulated the work to all outside influence. This black box enclosure incorporated two screen surfaces: one that transmitted projected imagery of the virtual environments that the immersant of the work sees within their field of vision, and a second, adjacent rear projection that put the wired-up interactor on display, theatrically presenting their silhouetted, bodily contortions. The complicity of this cyborg puppet, functioning as a mechanism within the construction of its own perceptually-induced dreaming was thus revealed. Both Courchesne and Shaw also have constructed highly focalised viewing experiences that base themselves instrumentally upon sole occupants. Their works also point towards a more open, dialectical integration of art and exhibition. For his part, Shaw's continued use of the AVIE visualisation environment enables the work to be viewable from either inside or outside its parameter. Dispensing with the 'black box' gallery and instead presenting the work on a surface that can be taken in from either side of the screen allows the work to be approached from multiple angles; this porousness thwarts any sense that closure or completeness of the artwork is a possibility, and instead opens the work to the virtual.

The viewer's encounter with the artwork in the expanded context of the exhibition cannot be predicated exclusively to an intensive immersive experience of the self-contained work.[8] Reducing the aesthetic experience of such a work to a single viewing order or mode significantly limits the discourse to the part that illusion and immersion plays in critical formulation of virtual art. The revelation of the performance of the work through its cinematic and theatrical presentation for interlopers in the exhibition space is a dialectical strategy that enriches such an engagement with the work beyond the terms limited by restricting their discussion solely according to the terms of immersion. Inevitably, under exhibition conditions the work finds itself unmoored in an expanded field of relations that are native to the exhibition at large.

Since its inaugural exhibition in 2001, the Australian Centre for the Moving Image has employed an extremely varied range of installation strategies. Observed through exhibitions developed by ACMI, the analysis of the art of exhibition points beyond the architectural towards an engagement with the cultural positioning (the institutional, embedded, habitual properties) of the virtual artwork's interiorised spaces (as enclosed, contained and insulated). ACMI's inaugural exhibition, *Deep Space: Sensation & Immersion*, announced that it would offer its visitors a 'transformative experience' of being immersed in the totality (kinaesthetic visual, aural and informational) of virtual artworks. As introduced by curator Victoria Lynn: 'The audience is invited to immerse themselves in the wonder of spaces, to explore their physical construction, their digital presence, their filmic pulse and their spatial expanses of colour and light' (2001, p. 17).[9]

In selected cases illustrated by exhibitions developed in the years that have intervened since, the dialectical opportunities of exhibition space have been embraced. On one hand, this has been signalled in exhibition designs that have formally minimised their reliance on the type of gallery cubical and light-trapped interiors that predominated earlier, 'first-generation' exhibitions. In *World Without End*, for example, rather than being hermetically sealed off, cloistered or quarantined, the inventory of artworks was distributed and 'mixed' in an open-ended space where interrelationships were favoured over servicing immersive experience.[10] While retaining their innate character as individuated systems, works were interconnected by curatorial decision-making that facilitated an overall sense of flow throughout the entire space. In the case of *White Noise* – which arguably still represents one of the most ambitious exhibition designs realized in ACMI's Screen Gallery to date – space and artwork were thoroughly integrated as sensory environments. Their fusion in exhibition space was heightened by an overwhelming sense of spatial disorientation reinforced by the exhibition's distinctive interior architecture.[11] Caught up from the first step into the gallery space by the sweep and wash of stimuli, the viewer's perceptual 'free fall' challenged the traditional separation of art from space and the viewer's expectations of abstract art. Included in the exhibition was Ryoji Ikeda's *data.spectra* (2005), which was commissioned by ACMI. This work involved the exploration of the materiality of data through moving image and sound's encounter in physical space. [*Figure 6*] Accompanying this new production was the restaging of *spectra II* (2002) as an architectural installation designed for a single viewer. The piece was constructed as a narrow,

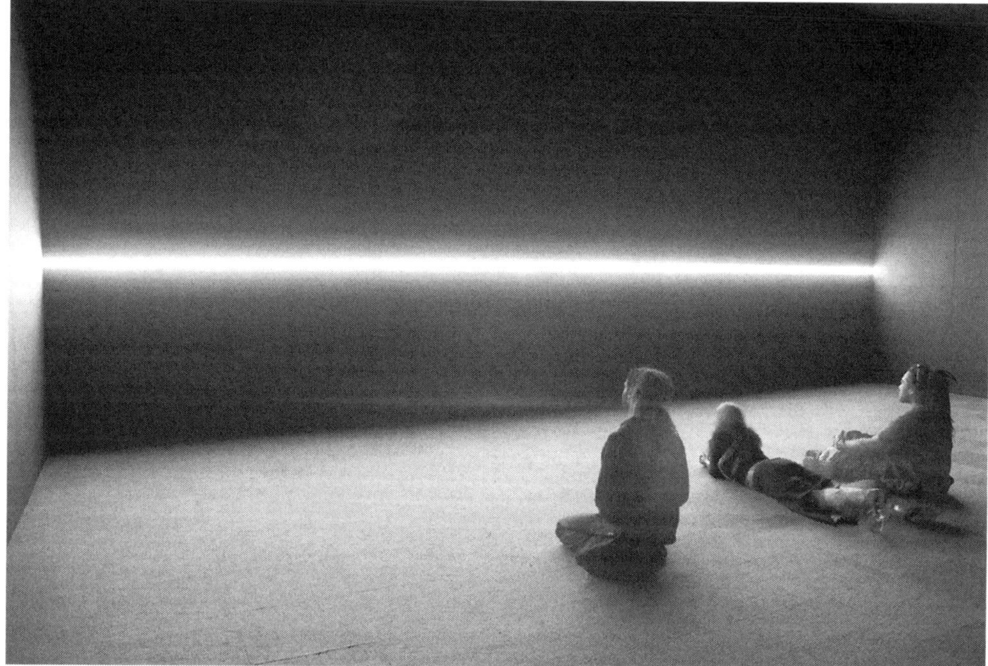

Figure 6: Installation view of Ryoji Ikeda, *data.spectra* (2005). Video installation with multiple projectors, mirrors and four-channel sound. The work was commissioned by the Australian Centre for the Moving Image. Produced by forma. Supported by the Arts Council England and the Japan Foundation (*White Noise*, ACMI: Melbourne, 2005). Photo credit: Christian Capurro.

enclosed corridor whose dimensions are experienced acoustically, by subtle, oscillating sound frequencies, and visually, through bursts of light that would interrupt the pervading darkness.

The integral relationship between the artworks and the mediated space of the exhibition was described by curator Mike Stubbs:

> *White Noise* is an exhibition in real-time. With varying degrees of luminosity, tempo and volume the artworks invite the audience into a space that is both physical and reflective: not to view pictorial representations of something, or document another time or place, but to invite us into the here and now. (2006, p. 49)

Stubbs goes on to explain the evolution of the distinctive exhibition design. Initially influenced by the idea of a Japanese bath, the design aspired to produce the conditions associated with its process of cleansing that follows strict protocols for purification that involves passing through a series of pools of water at different temperatures. Translated through sound and image scapes, across both virtual and physically-experienced space, the attentiveness paid to designing the exhibition's conditions served the purpose of establishing 'a default or reference point where the viewer might re-set their perception in between artworks, through noise and light cancellation' (Stubbs 2006, p. 49).

Reflecting a broadening of its curatorial agenda, ACMI has in more recent years begun to move away from its initial emphasis on media-based presentation towards a hybrid form of museological display incorporating physical artefacts alongside screen-based media. The possibilities offered by negotiating the combination of media and objects in a hybridised environment was broached most completely in *Eyes, Lies & Illusion*.[12] Developed initially by the Hayward Gallery in London, the exhibition was restaged at ACMI by creating a seamless mixed-media presentation of over 500 optical devices, objects and images along with specially selected contemporaneous artworks that explore the illusory potentials of the moving image. The exhibition was composed of different modes of exposition, ranging from vitrines to screens, informational display to experiential environments. Adopting both conventional display methods along with modes of media presentation, the exhibition's hybrid solution offered a preview of an integrative form of exhibition that will likely become increasingly commonplace in the future.

At the core of this critique has been the issue of how the overlaps and exchanges that characterise the integration of digital media in real space might lead to a reconsideration of the exhibition interface. By way of encapsulating a number of the ideas raised in the preceding discussion, I would like to conclude by drawing upon ACMI's staging of the monographic exhibition of Christian Marclay in order to illustrate how audio-visual experiences are symptomatic of their site of exhibition.[13]

With the installation of *Crossfire* (2007), the spectacular quality of its iconic source footage from films like *Pulp Fiction*, *Scarface* and *Bullet in the Head* is amplified. Finding him- or herself confronted by the work in a claustrophobic, enclosed 'black box' situation, the viewer is quite literally trapped in the crossfire of four synchronised video projections.[14]

Visually assaulted by the repetitive motif of fragmented images of gun blasts, this sensory overload is synaesthetically reinforced by the associated sound of triggers cocking and guns firing. However, this description betrays the work's actual spatial practice. In an exhibition context, the work is likely to be experienced with a group of other viewers. In this case, rather than locating themselves in the central, focal point of the space, the viewer's tendency (so it seems to me based on my first-hand observation of the work) is to gravitate to one of the four available corners of the room. If space has a subconscious, it reveals itself in this manoeuvre. From being a victim, fixed in the crosshairs of the work's mediated space, the viewer instead becomes a participant in the drama that unfolds in exhibition space: as an actor in a potential shootout with the others in the room, standing apart in their respective corners 'at five paces'.

This presentation of *Crossfire* contrasted with the curatorial design involved in exhibiting *Shake Rattle and Roll (Fluxmix)* from 2004. Produced from a series of videos recording the artist's handling of artefacts from the Walker Art Center's collection of Fluxus objects, the resulting multi-part installation presents these media sources on individuated monitors mounted atop freestanding plinths arranged in an inward-facing circle. Exhibited in this format, the installation offers an extremely effective example of successful *spatial calibration:* the attuning of work and space. The sensory experience of the viewer oscillates between levels of concentration: at one moment their perceptual focus is induced to distinguish discrete stimuli (such as the opening and closing of a box, scratching surfaces, rubbing materials together), while in the next they are synthesising these instances within the encompassing cacophony. Most interestingly, the work's spatial practice reveals how the viewer's engagement is motivated: from centring him- or herself within the interior demarcated by the ring of display units to moving to the periphery of the space, circulating all the while. Moving closer one moment (in order to focus, concentrate on an action, gesture or incidental sound), pulling back the next (to scan across an arc of images, to sweep their gaze over the whole space, to sense the enveloping atmosphere).

The conceptual framework for curatorial design draws upon an integrative approach to digital mediation and spatial practice. The examples focused upon in this chapter traverse the dialectical relationships that weave together artwork and viewer through mediated exhibition environments, extending the narrative and communicational possibilities for aesthetic experiences in the multimedial museum. The dialectical predisposition of curatorial design senses the implications that virtuality brings to a fuller conceptualisation of the art of exhibition.

Notes

1. The *Arcades Project* offers an historical backdrop for an integrative reading of audiovisual media. As part of his incomplete quest towards a materialist philosophy of the history of the nineteenth century, Benjamin inventories a kaleidoscopic array of related technologies and effects:

Panoramas, dioramas, cosmoramas, diaphanoramas, navaloramas, pleoramas (*pleo*, 'I sail', 'I go by water'), fantoscopes, fantasm-paratases, phantasmagorical and fantasmaparastatic experiences, picturesque journeys in a room, georamas, optical picturesques, cineoramas, phanoramas, stereoramas, cycloramas, panorama dramatique. (1999, p. 527)

2. *Osmose* was exhibited in *Transfigure* (8 December 2003–9 May 2004), curated by Alessio Cavallaro. *Transfigure* explored 'transformations of perception, body, movement, space and landscape to reveal tensions and wonder between technology and nature, identity and image' [http://www.acmi.net.au/transfigure.aspx].

3. *The Visitor: Living by Number* was exhibited in *Deep Space* (16 October 2002–27 January 2003), a major exhibition of Australian and international artworks where viewers were invited to 'interact with ghostly figures, engage with virtual worlds and be submerged in the wonder of space' [http://www.acmi.net.au/deepspace/].

4. *Eavesdrop* was exhibited in *SenseSurround* (7 October–7 November 2004). The exhibition, presenting 'exhilarating sensory environments by renowned Australian and international media artists that immerse the viewer', was curated by Alessio Cavallaro [http://www.acmi.net.au/sensesurround.aspx].

5. More recently, Shaw was involved in the co-production of *PLACE-Hampi*, a major cultural heritage project that enables the viewer to explore audio-visual scapes depicting significant archaeological, historical, sacred locations found at the Vijayanagara (Hampi) World Heritage site in southern India. In this work three kinds of narrative space are conjoined. These relate to the visuals (augmented high-resolution stereoscopic panoramas recorded at the heritage site), simulated events (enacted by a range of animated, mythological characters that have been composited into the three-dimensional landscapes) and sound (spatialised aural fields produced from ambisonic 360-degree recordings). When combined with a tracking system of infrared cameras and real-time software, audience participation is enabled to direct the course of the cinematic narrative. Conceived as a total interactive narrative system, the viewer experiences a sense of deep connectivity with the cinematic visuals presented in the augmented space. In so doing, the work aspires to 'articulate an unprecedented level of viewer co-presence in the narrative exploration of a virtual cultural landscape' [http://www.icinema.unsw.edu.au/projects/prj_hampi.html].

6. Relating modes of cinematic capture with subsequent informational processing by the viewer in a virtual environment, *aesthetic transcription* is proposed as a model for the production of interactive narrative within digital cinema (Brown et al., 2003).

7. Proprioception (from the Latin *proprius*, meaning 'one's own' and perception) is the sense of the relative position of parts of the body to each other. Used in the context of the discussion of exhibition space, the proprioceptive relationship involves a relational sense of 'positioning' in space and self-reflexive awareness in response to sensory stimuli offering narratives, representational spaces and dimensions separate to the subject's immediate spatial and temporal location.

8. Petran Kockelkoren discusses how technological mediation is based on a process of decentring/recentring by drawing upon philosophical anthropologist Helmuth Plessner's philosophy of human 'ex-centricty'. An advocate of philosophical anthropology, Plessner argued that because the human senses are always culturally mediated (by language, technology or art), ex-centricity is an *a priori* of the human condition:

Technology cannot alienate people from their naturalness, because they are already alienated by virtue of their very condition. Language, technology and art teach people how to articulate and even to celebrate their ineradicable alienation (Kockelkoren 2002, p. 27).

9. Inaugural creative director Ross Gibson exerted a significant influence on the centre's initial development. Amongst Gibson's credits was the curation of *Remembrance + The Moving Image*, which was exhibited over two instalments (*Persistence of Vision*, from 21 March–25 May 2003, and *Reverberations*, from 27 June–31 August 2003). Kevin Murray recognises Gibson's critical influence on ACMI's early programming reflected through the privileging of media art's relationship to cinema:

> ACMI is in the unusual position of evolving its own context: it takes the moving image out of the cinema and into the gallery. Rather than experiencing film while trapped in the dark by comfortable seats, conspiratorial silence and ushers, ACMI brings this ritual into the public domain. (Murray 2003)

10. *World Without End* (14 April–17 July 2005) was co-curated by Alessio Cavallaro and Alexie Glass. The exhibition aspired to a poetics of time, place and phenomena through presenting works that represent experiences of 'dramatic forces of nature, the energies and rhythms of cities, and the elastic time of global travel and instant communication networks' [http://www.acmi.net.au/world_without_end.aspx].

11. Curated by Mike Stubbs, *White Noise* (18 August–23 October 2005) was a major international exhibition exploring abstraction in a digital age. The realisation of the installation environments involved project coordination by Chris Harris, exhibition design by Studio 505 and lighting design by Flaming Beacon.

12. The inventory of *Eyes, Lies & Illusions* (2 November 2006–11 February 2007) combined 'spectacular new illusions with four centuries of rare optical toys and puzzles' in order to illustrate 'how the moving image captivated us before cinema was even invented' [http://www.acmi.net.au/eyes_lies_illusions.aspx].

13. *Replay Marclay* (15 November 2007–3 February 2008) was curated by Emma Lavigne from the Cité de la Musique, Paris. The first solo exhibition held in the Screen Gallery at ACMI, *Replay Marclay* surveyed the artist's work across the 'overlapping of realms of image and sound through video, film, sculpture, photography, installation, collage, music and DJ performances' [http://www.acmi.net.au/replay_marclay.aspx].

14. It is interesting for comparative purposes to consider different readings of this work. Jean-Pierre Criqui acknowledges the work's relation to earlier pieces such as *Telephones* (1995) or *Video Quartet* (2002) while distinguishing the character of its viewing experience: 'the viewer is completely caught in the crossfire, surrounded by a stunning ballet of appearances and disappearances' (2007, pp. 35–6). However, it is worth pointing out that Criqui concedes that his interpretation of the work is anticipatory; that the piece itself was 'still being edited when these lines were written'. Whereas, curator Emma Lavigne interprets the work in the cultural context of punk aesthetics:

> *Crossfire* offers no way out, and the protagonists literally fire on the spectator. It is a ring marked out by the four screens, from floor to ceiling, which impose a litany of flashes of light and gunshots on the viewer, with such a variety of sound to captivate them. (2007, p. 92)

PART II: EXHIBITIONS

Chapter 7

The Synthetic Image: Digital Technologies and the Image

Synopsis

My critical investigation into virtuality and the art of exhibition was initiated with the curatorial project, *The Synthetic Image*. In addition to practice-based creative production involved in its realization, the project was also articulated through a curator's essay elaborating on the central theme of the digital image. While published initially in the catalogue accompanying the exhibition, this text was subsequently modified for publication in the August 2002 issue of the electronic journal *Media/Culture* (*M/C*) as 'The Synthetic Image and the Theme of the Loop: Image, Exhibition and Networkability', where it was repurposed as an interactive digital publication whose format significantly extended the critique of the base text.

Together, the production of artwork, scenography and critical expansion encompass the combined critical and creative dimensions of the project. Following an introduction to the curatorial philosophy, primary sources – relating to the development of the contributed artwork, organisation of the exhibition space and articulation of main thematics from the perspective of the curator's essay – will be presented in this chapter. These sub-sections will be presented in a manner that highlights the focused, self-contained nature of their content and retains the integrity of the original documents. Particularly in the case of the curator's essay, the character of the writing reflects the hypertext structure of its publication format as originally intended. Repurposed here, these episodes will be bracketed by an overview of the exhibition's curatorial philosophy and subsequent reflective analysis that will illuminate aspects of the curatorial design approach illustrated by the project.

Curatorial Philosophy

T*he Synthetic Image: Digital Technologies and the Image* was an exhibition about the evolving state of digital imaging practices. The exhibition presented a survey of selected artworks by contemporary Australian practitioners whose works, when viewed together, described the contours of image art practices informed by new technologies. Exploring the hybrid nature of the digital image, the selected artists and artworks exemplify the crossover between digital and interactive media and the remediation of other artistic traditions, such as photography and video. These 13 established and emerging artists represent decidedly individual positions on the current role of the image in representing, simulating or creating realities.

New technologies of visualisation dramatically extend aesthetic possibilities. Recent innovations related to digital imaging technologies have transformed how images are generated and produced. Beyond the immediate loss of uniqueness through means of reproduction, the digital facture of images frays the threads that tenuously connect the image to an unravelling reality. The perspective of this project viewed the relationship between digital technologies and the image as a synthetic one. By recognising the ability to double and fold in the malleability of the material from which the digital image is composed, the dichotomy of inside and outside collapses. Instead of thinking of pixels as a solid, impenetrable grid, this conceptualization, rather, recognises in this resulting surface the qualities of a fabric, as a mesh of interpenetrating, weaving fibres. Instead of the content of the image being contained in pixel blocks, it is implied in the threads of the screen holding together the field of relationships, looping like a closed electrical or magnetic circuit. Reconceived as a *meshwork* – a term inspired by the writing of Manuel De Landa (1997) – the digital image embodies how the image's virtual (representational) content is interlaced with its material support. Whether fibres of paper or raster of pixels, the material base for the digital image offers a particularly malleable constitution to the image that extends the scope of intervention possible with the analogue photograph.

Underpinning this thematic was my own curatorial *projection* of the digital image – using the term as it is articulated by Ron Burnett to describe an active interpenetration of the processes of vision, representation, technology and the imagination that enmeshes the notion of the image within a network of relations. In his contribution to the anthology, *The Digital Dialectic*, George P. Landow (2000) offered an inventory of characteristics that define digital media. These traits result from a hybrid mixture of ideas relating hypertext writing to the visual language of collage. Included in this list is the quality of networkability.[1] It is through reading into this particular element that I was able to focus on the character of the digital image itself as multi-dimensional and how, by extension, this enmeshes notions of the image within a wider network of relations: of image to the imaginary, of vision to visuality, and of artwork to exhibition.

In many ways my approach to this topic as curator drew inspiration from Jonathan Crary's definition of synthesis as a 'rhythmic coexistence of radically heterogeneous and temporally dispersed elements' (1999, p. 297). In this exhibition the space of the gallery was approached as a narrative space. The curatorial role that was adopted made apparent the subtext of diverse strands connecting respective artworks and artists into a constellation through their juxtaposition in exhibition space. The installation operated by gathering together disparate components into what was as much a context as a physical and spatial realisation. Conceived from the outset as a survey exhibition, the curatorial approach set out to synthesise a variety of image art practices through its exhibition design. The nature of its curatorial design sought to connect, or 'loop', the diverse, idiosyncratic and individual approaches into an encompassing framework which drew them together by difference as much as by similarity. Operating as a loop structure that encircles and incorporates its contents, the exhibition made evident the subtext of diverse strands connecting respective works and artists with each other.

Reflected in this curatorial process were a variety of concerns relating to how creative approaches to the image arts have been influenced by advancements in digital imaging technology within the last generation. These included relating artists with an established pre-digital photographic basis to their practice (i.e. Phil George, Lynne Roberts-Goodwin) alongside 'native' new media artists (i.e. Troy Innocent, Patricia Piccinini) and demonstrating aesthetics that proceed from iterative processes involved in the facture of still images (i.e. Marcus Fajl, Murray McKeich, Trinh Vu) that contrast with those employing a mode of production predicated on a cinematic model (i.e. Matthew Perkins, Daniel von Sturmer). In addition, explorations involving presentation were showcased, whether related to manipulation of the material image (i.e. Marcus Bunyan, Gerard Minogue) or to extending the mixed media qualities of the luminous and animate image (i.e. Megan Evans, along with my own contribution to the inventory, *From Catalogue – Museum*, which will be discussed more directly as part of the Documentation section found later in this chapter).

Applied Curatorial Design

Each of the curated projects documented in the Exhibitions section of the book are characterised by their distinct, individualized applications of *curatorial design*. In practical terms, this approach involves modelling the desired relationship between the project's thematics and curating methodology adopted at the curatorial level, with strategies being instigated through applied design to establish the relationship between installation considerations, on the one hand, and the mode of discourse, or 'trope', being employed for communication effect on the other. The following section reflects upon how the trope employed directly in *The Synthetic Image* – and that I describe as 'choreographic' – was used as part of the exhibition's spatial rhetoric, directing how curatorial concerns related to theme and method were translated through the designing of its resulting exhibition space. The role played by a series of such choreographed spatial events will conclude this reflective analysis.

Choreography as an approach to curatorial design

As introduced above, the 'model' viewer's movement through the exhibition space was relatively choreographed. My use of the expression *model viewer* borrows from Umberto Eco's *model reader* and his influential work on semiotics. How the addressee is actively involved in the production of a work is central to Eco's theorization of the dialectic between what he has defined as open and closed texts. As he has described:

> To organize a text, its author has to rely upon a series of codes that assign given contents to the expressions he uses. To make his text communicative, the author has to assume that the ensemble of codes he relies upon is the same as that shared by his possible reader. The author has this to foresee a model of the possible reader (hereafter Model Reader) supposedly able to deal interpretively with the expressions in the same way as the author deals generatively with them. (Eco 1979, p. 7)

In the case of this exhibition, undoubtedly, the architectural plan, or 'footprint' of the venue contributed to the natural flow, circulation and progression made possible through the space itself. [*Figure 7*] The close interrelation – indeed synthesis – between considerations involving the coordination of exhibition design and curatorial selection on the other is a defining feature of the curatorial design process.[2] This integrated approach provided the means of directing the project from initial conceptualisation through to the realization of all aspects involved in publishing the exhibition. Working in this fashion was instrumental to the coordination of its selection process, particularly given the survey-based nature of the exhibition. As such, the curatorial narrative was developed in close alignment with considerations related to the exhibition's evolving form and structure.

In order to address the crossovers and intersections that make the topic of the image and digital technologies an intriguingly nuanced subject, representative properties associated with the image arts – such as the binary relationships of print and screen; still image or moving image – were subsequently extrapolated from a guiding schematic structure of themes and their interrelationships: *Mesh / Weave / Wire frame / Map / Moire / Screen*. Ultimately, the curatorial design solution would incorporate these 'gamuts' by creating overlapping zones, thereby enabling works to be combined in more open-ended groupings.

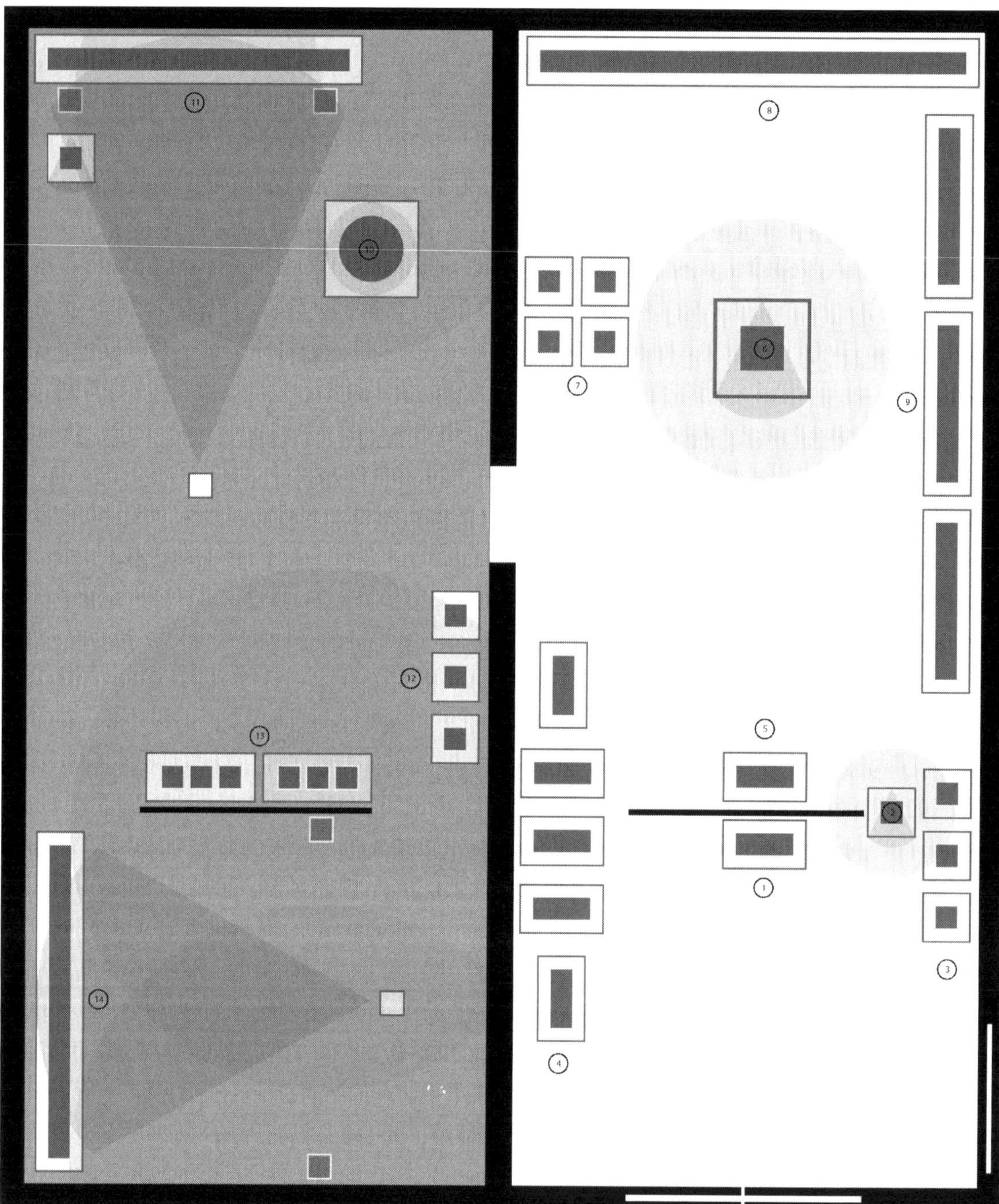

Figure 7: Installation schematic of *The Synthetic Image* (Faculty Gallery: Melbourne, 2002).

the**synthetic**image

Faculty Gallery, Monash University, Melbourne, Victoria, Australia, 8 July–4 August 2002

1. Patricia Piccinnini, *Lumpland* (1995). Computer-generated digiprint. 1270 × 2300 mm. Edition of 3. Monash University Collection.

2. Patricia Piccinnini, *Lustre* (1999). Video. 2.20 minutes. Unlimited edition. Monash University Collection.

3. Marcus Fajl, *Untitled* series (2002). Photographic prints. 1200 × 1200 mm each. Collection of the artist.

4. Lynne Roberts-Goodwin, *Bad Bird* series (2001-2). Digital giclée archival photographic prints. 117.5 × 86.5 cm each (framed). Collection of the artist.

5. Trinh Vu, *Polygonmania* (2001). Digtal print. 1500 × 1500 mm. Private Collection.

6. Daniel Von Sturmer, *Material From Another Medium* (2001). DVD projection on acrylic screen. 900 × 1200 mm. Collection of the artist.

7. Murray McKeich, *Memory Trade 01* (1998). Digital image. 58 × 62.5 cm.
    Murray McKeich, *Memory Trade 09* (1998). Digital image. 58 × 62.5 cm.
    Murray McKeich, *Memory Trade 10* (1998). Digital image. 58 × 62.5 cm.
    Murray McKeich, *Memory Trade 19* (1998). Digital image. 58 × 62.5 cm. All works collection of the artist.

8. Marcus Bunyan, *Chronos/ome* (2002). Mixed media. Various dimensions. All works collection of the artist.

9. Phil George, *Liquid World 1,2,3* (2002). C-type laser prints. 750 × 1800 mms. All works collection of the artist.

10. Megan Evans, *Vanishing virtually* (2002). Video installation. 1880 × 670 × 670 mms. Collection of the artist.

11. Matthew Perkins, *Thump/Smash* (2002). Video / Sound installation. Variable dimensions. Collection of the artist.

12. Gerard Minogue, *Candy 1,2,3* (2002). Mixed media: digital image rendered/printed in confectionary. 800 by 1250 mm. Collection of the artist.

13. Vince Dziekan, *From Catalogue-Museum* (2002). Mixed media. 6 units. 300 × 370 × 100 mms each. Variable Installation. Collection of the artist.

14. Troy Innocent, *au-vector* (2001). Interactive sound installation. Data projector. 5:1 speaker system. Custom interface. Collection of the Artist.

This dialectical strategy would come to characterize the resulting curatorial narrative and exhibition design.

In order to manifest this curatorial philosophy, it was integral that the potential of the exhibition site be explored. The Faculty Gallery is a highly flexible space made up of two adjoining galleries. Each space is approximately three times as deep as it is wide. The prospect of separating the space into two equally sized and self-contained enclosures is made possible by a sliding wall system. Access is made possible to each gallery through separate entrances off a main concourse. 'Light trapping' these spaces is problematic, given their glass frontage onto this public area. Early in the development process, it was decided to structure the installation around the trope of contrasting 'dark' and 'light' rooms, which, in turn, thematically refer to the production paradigms informing the nature of analogue and digital imaging practices, respectively. Practically, the gallery space was easily divided into two main halves, each further divided into a smaller annex and larger display area. Adjusting the wall dividers to leave a doorway-sized gap between them allowed for passage between the spaces, enacting the transition from light into dark environments. The structural division of the exhibition along these lines proved to be an effective way of resolving technical issues associated with presenting screen and projection work. The darkroom has been long established as the primary site of production for analogue photography. Emphasising the value of the image as print, it is doctrinaire to an approach to photographic image-making premised on the medium's material support or base. In comparison, the term *light room* alludes to the virtual workspaces of computer software. Characteristic of digital imaging, this workflow is associated with how manipulations actually occurring at the level of code are visualized through representative means on a screen-surface. Digital practice extends the possibility of the image both spatially (through screen-based display and projection) and temporally (the moving image).

Choreographed spatial events

The exhibition's scenography – functioning as a coordination of curatorial intention translated through the organization of gallery space – sought to produce an effective and compelling narrative in its own right. The characteristic of its unfolding narrative was built primarily out of setting works into meaningful relationships with each other. Occurring across different scales or registers, the viewer's encounter with each spatial arrangement, and in turn each element within its grouping, might be construed as organic.

The realization of the exhibition *actually* in space brought out a number of surprising effects that could not be fully pre-planned. These *incidents* had the potential to enrich the spatial narrative and viewing experience of the exhibition. Neither didactic nor forced, these *spatial events* emerged as part of the exhibition experience, particularly as they can be said to operate a more intuitive, even subconscious level of audience engagement.

The model viewer's choreography through the space followed a predetermined – if not fully prescribed – progression or course. This path was reinforced by the way that the exhibition space itself was organized (architectural division of two main galleries and their sub-division, position of aperture acting as conduit between light and dark spaces, placement of individual works within their arenas (a descriptive account of the intended movement of the viewer through the exhibition space follows later in this chapter)). While the spatial arrangement of works from the inventory primarily served to propel the curatorial narrative forward, opportunities to instil more indirect interventions were identified as part of the installation process. For the purpose of explication I have chosen to refer to the first such spatial event, here, as the *Red/Green/Blue (triadic arrangement)*.

It occurred as follows: The entrance annex was constructed in such a way that it effectively masked off the remainder of the gallery space from view. The primary route for the viewer to move from the first gallery to the second was along the right-hand side of the gallery, past Piccinini's monitor-based display. Therefore, when the viewer proceeded past the false wall along which the two Piccinini works are displayed they entered an arena that appeared surprisingly expansive. Compounding this impression, the viewer was granted a sightline that projected through the opening in the main wall that bisected the gallery into the depths of the *Dark Room* space. Unknowingly, the viewer is situated in space at the ideal vantage point to triangulate a set of visual elements that taken together compose a mixture of red, green and blue details. This spatial composition was created by linking (proceeding from right to left) a predominantly red square-framed print by Bunyan, the green-cast transmission of von Sturmer's video and the blue reflection of Perkins' small video monitor glimpsed from the darkened depths of the adjacent second gallery. While not intentional in the same way as other 'higher-level' considerations involved with presenting the exhibited works, this piece of curatorial design introduces a 'touch' that conceptually galvanized the structure of the entire exhibition – and for the perceptive (or fortunate) viewer, this incidental event brought with it the potential to enrich their experience, attuning their perception to seek out other relationships that 'might' exist throughout the rest of the exhibition.

The second incidental event created an unsettling experience that, when perceived by the viewer, might be said to have attuned or calibrated their sensibilities (indeed sensitivities) to make the most of the exhibition. The exhibition was composed of a mixture of artworks: some were static and still, other elements were animated and moving; some were reflective (in a physical sense), others were emissive (whether light, sound, even smell – as in the case of Gerard Minogue's candy-covered panels). Some works were introspective and required close, detailed inspection while others quite literally jumped out at you. Moving image works were deployed as components that punctuate the space. In aesthetic terms, the curatorial selection evidenced a preference for video works that were relatively ambient in content. This preference took into account that the curatorial design approach to the exhibition would compromise the effective presentation of more cinematic, narrative-driven works. In their place, the episodic and looping nature of the works selected became a driving feature of the exhibition. Whether as pulsing, light-emitting screens or as an animate wall surface, works involving dynamic media project themselves into their surroundings. Most works, however, elicited a conventional form of engagement from their viewers: the viewer was encouraged to approach, inspect and immerse him or herself in the content presented within the image's frame. This was especially prevalent in the *Light Room* space, given its predominant emphasis on print-media works. However, in relation to the viewing experience of this space, such focused attentiveness was broken by a visual disturbance: a *Phantom Presence*.

To explain: as the viewer moved through the *Light Room* space, their concentrated viewing was disturbed by the unsettling impression of something or someone occupying the adjacent *Dark Room* gallery. At intermittent junctures the pounding sound of footfalls would seem to emanate from the other space. Reinforcing this impression, a fleeting visual presence was sensed. This unfocused sensation was the result of peripherally catching a glimpse of the figure appearing (and disappearing) at random, off-register intervals across the eight fragmented frames that make up the wall-sized mosaic of Perkins' video installation. While actually only taking up half of the full wall space available, this projection filled the field of view that was granted from the restricted vantage of the *Light Room* gallery through the narrow wall opening. This slit or aperture was designed intentionally to reference a curtain-shutter of a conventional camera. This phenomenological effect was particularly pronounced when these short burst of visualised motion or energy were combined with the ambulating movement of the viewing subject.

This impression was reinforced by the role sound played in supporting spatial effects. It cannot be understated how influential sound can be in any media-based installation. For the most part, sounds associated with the moving image works included in the *Synthetic Image* were of an 'occasional' variety, more like sound effects as compared to narrative-driving dialogue or emotive soundtrack. Distinguishing where any particular sound event was emitted from, and to which visual event they were related, was an exercise for the viewer to piece together. In the *Synthetic Image* there were five pieces that included sound components. As such, the exhibition design ran the risk of creating a cacophony of indiscriminate and conflicting sound scapes that not only intervene with the presentation of other works, but also could potentially pollute the overall exhibition environment. Other than Innocent's *au_ vector* – which is a unique example given the primary role that sound plays in its realization – the sound associated with the media works by Piccinini, von Sturmer, Perkins and Evans are considerably more ambient, and therefore far more amenable to this type of group exhibition. Technically, the works presented through conventional monitors all emitted sound through inbuilt speakers that significantly limited their range, whereas Innocent's installation framed the interactor by the stereophonic quality of its acoustic space.

Patricia Piccinini's video was accompanied by an ambient track played at a low volume (so that the viewer only picked up the influence of the sound at the level of their immediate engagement with the work). In contrast, Evans' soundtrack for *Vanishing Virtually* operated as more of a score, rising and falling over the duration of its narrative cycle. As such, the louder passages of the soundtrack seduced the viewer, attracting their attention and drawing them to inspect the work and its miniature anamorphic *trompe l'oeil* more intimately. In the case of von Sturmer's video work, the amplified sound effects associated with the recorded material manipulations are exaggerated and heighten the absurdity of the different caricaturised scenarios. Each intermittent 'crumble' exuded from the isolated black monitor in the centre of the gallery seemed to ripple like a current through its surrounding space (this soundtrack added an extra dimension as an overlay to other works; this was most effective in relation to the visual staccato of rippling forms in Bunyan's digital photograms that were displayed immediately behind von Sturmer's piece).

Perkins' *Thump/Smash* installation was framed by two floor-bound speakers. Its occasional sound was registered with the visual events represented (running feet, shattering glass). As discussed previously, these sound effects punctuated the surrounding space at intervals. While Evans' piece was relatively insular and introverted in character, Perkins' work competed more directly for the acoustic space of the *Dark Room* with Innocent's *au_vector*. Because of the central role of sound in this piece, the furthest section of the available gallery space was given over to it as a way of minimizing the potential for it to have an overexerted influence on other works. The character of its soundtrack was influenced by its form: a library of computer-generated sound samples. This subset of sound events would be triggered from direct interaction by the viewer using the work's custom keyboard interface. As with other works by Innocent, the piece involved the viewer in an aesthetic exploration of game play to become familiar with certain languages and rules in operation. As this type of involvement requires the viewer to learn how to influence the simulated virtual environment represented on screen more meaningfully, for the most part the sounds emitted by it were more likely to sound like random 'blips' and 'burps' than a cohesively structured composition. In fact, when the work was running in 'idle' mode an automated script would draw sound fragments randomly. This feature had the effect of making it seem like there was always an interlocutor haunting the exhibition space.

Summary

New technologies of visualization dramatically extend aesthetic possibilities of representation. They also challenge conventional forms and approaches to their exhibition. Guiding the selection of artists and artworks that exemplify the crossover between digital and interactive media and the remediation of other artistic traditions was my own curatorial projection of how aesthetic appreciation of the digital image is enmeshed within a network of expanded relations. For its part, the artwork *From Catalogue-Museum* offered its own speculation on virtual art. Acting as a *chronotopos*, this piece acknowledged how its interpretation and apperception as art was influenced by factors external to it as an object.

Gallery space was approached as a narrative space. The exhibition's curatorial design synthesized disparate elements by arranging works together in a context as much as through physical and spatial realization. The close interrelation between curatorial selection and the coordination of exhibition design was instrumental given the survey-based nature of the exhibition and the resulting curatorial narrative was developed in close alignment with considerations related to the exhibition's form and structure.

As a result, the viewer's movement through the exhibition space was choreographed as part of the installation plan. While spatial arrangement served primarily to propel the curatorial narrative forward, opportunities did exist to indirectly choreograph a series of relatively inconspicuous spatial events. And while not operating in the same way as other high-level considerations involved with presenting the exhibited works, these incidental events enriched the viewer's experience by attuning their perception by way of encouraging their appreciation of the considered relationships established by the curatorial design throughout the rest of the exhibition.

Documentation

Artwork – Vince Dziekan, *From Catalogue-Museum*

Complimenting my role as curator, this exhibition also presented the opportunity to produce an artwork designed explicitly for inclusion in the inventory. *From Catalogue – Museum* (2002) was conceived as an exploration of the relationship of images and objects displayed within the gallery environment as (inter-, hyper-, meta- and para-) textual. Alluding to a larger creative project, the work prompts questions relating to legitimacy and conventional expectations placed upon artworks. Indicative of my interest in the adaptation and integration of digital media within museological practice, this work was conceived as a speculation upon notions of virtuality on the viewing experience of art. Described supplementarily as 'an artwork about an artwork in an exhibition', *From Catalogue-Museum* points away from itself, deflecting attention to virtually everything else, to what isn't to be found within its immediate presence (contained within an image, secured to a wall, installed in a gallery space). Frustrating in its apparent embodiment as an art object, the artwork operates as a *chronotopos* – a coordination that 'performs a meeting between (aesthetic) art(ifice) and (social) reality' (Bal 2002, p. 97) – that redirects attention to its unattainability.

The background inspiration for the work drew upon an indiscriminate collection of random printed materials (notebooks, photocopies, clippings). These 'remainders' – documenting seeds of inspiration and detailing plans for unrealised artworks filed indiscriminately along with outdated press clippings and sundry technical notes – lead me to think about how artistic inspiration might translate into an artefact and how tenuous this connection can end up being. What was it that made some specific elements resonate more meaningfully, while others remain only 'ordinary'?

Art does not exist in a vacuum. Rather, it operates within a field of practices dependent upon protocols of viewing and institutional rules of engagement. This latter point was developed by Pierre Bourdieu in his sociological critique of the cultural field, where he uses the term *habitus* to describe:

> Durable, transposable dispositions, structured structures predisposed to function as structuring structures, that is, as principles which generate and organise practices and representations that can be objectively adapted to their outcomes without presupposing a conscious aiming at ends or an express mastery of the operations necessary in order to attain them. Objectively regulated and 'regular' without in any way being the product of obedience to rules, they can be collectively orchestrated without being the product of the organising actions of a conductor. (1993, p. 5)

Embodied through formal constructs such as the consolidated art object, the bounded cubic environment of the gallery and the enclosure of the museum (whether literally as architecture or figuratively by its archival nature), these institutionalised manifestations are largely reliant upon a program of cultural 'freeze-framing' that runs counter to the more fluid and dynamic properties of the art field. The artefact, gallery and museum apparatus are powerful spatial representations that shape our perceptions and understanding of art. The influence of such received ideas on the form – and resulting conformity – of the cultural field should not be underestimated.

From Catalogue-Museum acknowledges its own impossibility and how, in the process of becoming art, the establishing influence of the work's coordinating field must be taken into account. In this case it did so formally by drawing attention to its reliance on the gallery wall, the planar surface upon which the exposition of the artwork was played out. As an exercise in framing, the presentation of the collected boxes on a freestanding wall unit further emphasised the separation of spaces through architectural division. When installed for exhibition, the resulting wall assembly is comprised of six boxes arranged in a row. [*Figure 8*] Half of these units trail power cords down along the wall. Those particular units are internally illuminated, while the others are lit by the only spotlight in the otherwise darkened gallery. The three left-most boxes present backlight transparencies. The remaining units display a disassembled brown-paper package and its contents. Through this understated formalist play with juxtaposition, the work's spatial coordination expressed a kind of organization attitude that relates to the discipline of museology.

These meditations led me to artistically explore this collection as a visual metaphor for the archiving practices or operations of the museum. Extending upon this, how might an artefact properly reveal everything that goes into its realization? How is it possible for an art object to show the intersection of ideas and tangents of thoughts that end up taking shape through its final expression in physical form? Such metaphysical ruminations over the nature of the artefact drew me to consider the properties of the package directly: its brown-paper skin, enclosing a stratified collection of leaves of paper; of ink and carbon on filaments of paper; of words (embodying ideas and concepts) and images (that as reproductions, represent other images) that point somewhere else, beyond themselves. Imagining the

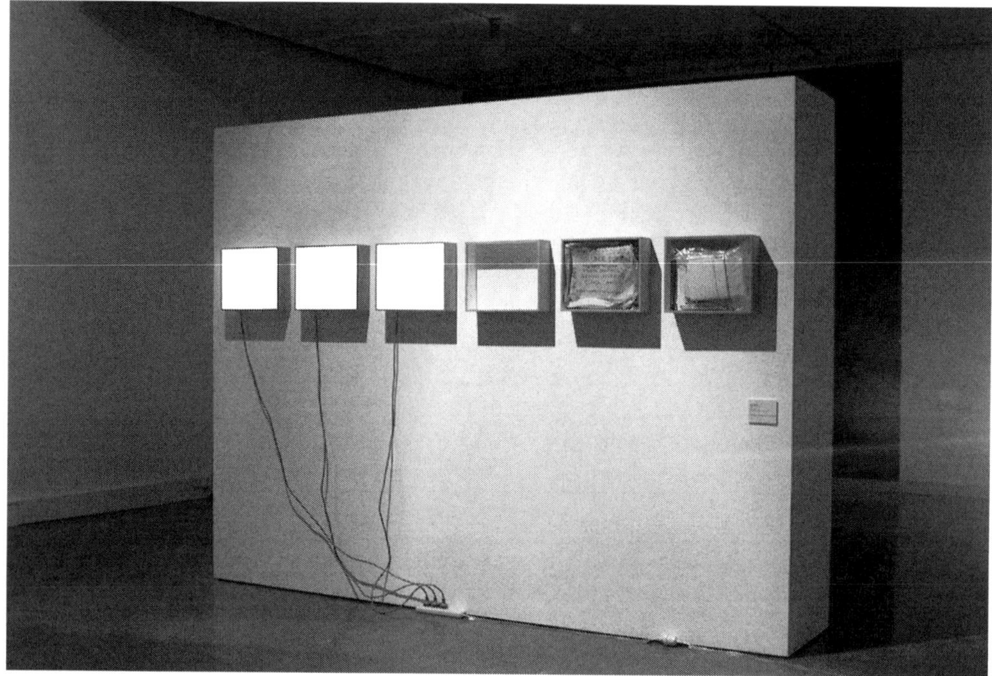

Figure 8: Installation view of Vince Dziekan, *From Catalogue-Museum* (*The Synthetic Image*: Melbourne, 2002). Mixed media, 6 units, 300 × 370 × 100 mm each. Variable installation.

contents of the package at my disposal as a museum archive of sorts drew me to undertake an initial exercise in cataloguing and organizing its contents. Next, this lead me to apply the most primal of photographic concepts – that of light passing through a medium and striking a sensitised surface – to their digitisation and to further aesthetic exploration.

In this regard it would be remiss to not directly acknowledge the inspiration of Marcel Duchamp's portable museum, or *Boite-en-valise*. This multiple artwork was a natural extension of Duchamp's earlier explorations with the idea of the facsimile as a work of art, such as the *Boite Verte* of 1934, which acted as a compendium of notes, pictures, photographs and diagrams related to the genesis of the *Large Glass* or *Grand Verre* between 1912–17.[3] In his authoritative text on the subject, Ecke Bonk has described this portable museum as:

Not only a convenient epitome of his work in miniature: it is also the synthesis of his paradoxical principles, of his apparently – but only apparently – contradictory rationale. The manifold overlaps and cross-references in his work as a whole are reflected in the spatial construction of the *Boite*, as well as in the arrangement of the reproductions. His artistic statements and achievements, in all their heterogeneous and many-sided profusion, are presented here by Duchamp as a carefully ordered whole. (1989, p. 9)

This album ('of approximately all the things I produced' according to the Duchamp) offers itself as the virtual artwork par excellence! Instead of presenting its contents in the conventional linear sequence of a book, Duchamp constructed an ingenious system for displaying both flat reproductions and miniaturized objects. The folding exhibition space simulates the horizontals and verticals of a room, perfectly to scale. Underlining the inaccessibility of many of the originals – not the least being the *Grand Verre*, which was awaiting restoration during the production of the *Boite* – this project acted as a catalyst for generating wider public interest in the artist's work. Not until 1954, with the permanent installation of the Arensberg Collection in Philadelphia, 'was it possible to accomplish with the originals what had already been achieved in miniature' (Bonk 1989, p. 21).[4]

In *From Catalogue-Museum* – and other works such as *Nature-History*, which will be discussed in the context of the *Small Worlds: A Romance* exhibition project – the oeuvre of another influential artist, Marcel Broodthaers, functions as part of a culturally shared visual vocabulary. Most directly in the case under discussion, intertextual cross-referencing was directed to the plastic plaques he referred to as 'rebuses' (Broodthaers 1988, p. 41). This group of works produced between 1968–70 was entitled *Poemes Industriels* and employed visual and textual strategies that exemplify the early phase of Broodthaers' transformation from poet to artist.[5] According to Buchloh, these works, executed as vacuum-formed plastic castings of moulded reliefs usually from letters and cut-out shapes, demonstrate what Broodthaers detected as the 'profound insincerity of the work of art' and challenge the 'universal domination of objects' (Buchloh 1988, p. 75). For Broodthaers the work of art no longer operated in terms of its inherited and quintessentially modernist dialectic: 'to be simultaneously the exemplary object of all commodity production and the exceptional object which denied and resisted the universality of that reign' (p. 72). Through these *Industrial Poems*, Broodthaers comments on 'their manufacturing technology, the meaning of that technology, and the historical context in which the choice of this procedure situated itself' (p. 81). Through this technical process:

> Poetic text, artistic object, discursive classification, and institutional demarcation are all literally made 'of a piece', and of one material; in their final format they are framed as mere advertisement, and in their final form, they are contained as mere object (pp. 88–9).

Transformed into 'mute plasticity and objecthood' (p. 74), these image-objects: 'engage in precisely that modernist strategy of hermetic resistance by which the visual or linguistic sign constitutes itself to refuse the visual or semantic data which the viewer demands' (p. 73). The resulting presence of language as a 'spatial construct was acquired at the price of a loss of narrativity and representation, temporality and referentiality' (p. 76).

There is a correlation between this body of work and the museum fictions that Broodthaers would subsequently move his attention towards later in his career. Under the title of the *Musée d'Art Moderne*, this project, commenced with the installation of packing crates in his apartment in Brussels (*Musée d'Art Moderne, Section XIX Siecle*, 1968) and reached its apogee in the museological arrangement of some 266 examples of eagles – the symbol and name used by Broodthaers to identify his museum department – in Dusseldorf (*Musée d'Art Moderne, Section des Figures*, 1972). The relationship between the singular qualities of individual works and their displacement within the overarching museum collection has been described by Rainer Borgemeister accordingly:

There was neither an immediately recognizable systematic order nor chronological or geographical sequence, although categories and classifications remained partially discernable. Present-day eagles found themselves next to historical examples (for instance, a plastic kite in the shape of an eagle next to a nineteenth-century parade banner), military eagles occupied a vitrine together with objects of natural history (thus: the trumpet ornament of a dragoon regiment alongside three preserved eagle eggs with their scientific labels). The historical entity 'eagle' was traced as an erratic process of transformation, and thus it seemed as if the exhibition was organized around the fundamental aspect of distance. (1988, p. 139)

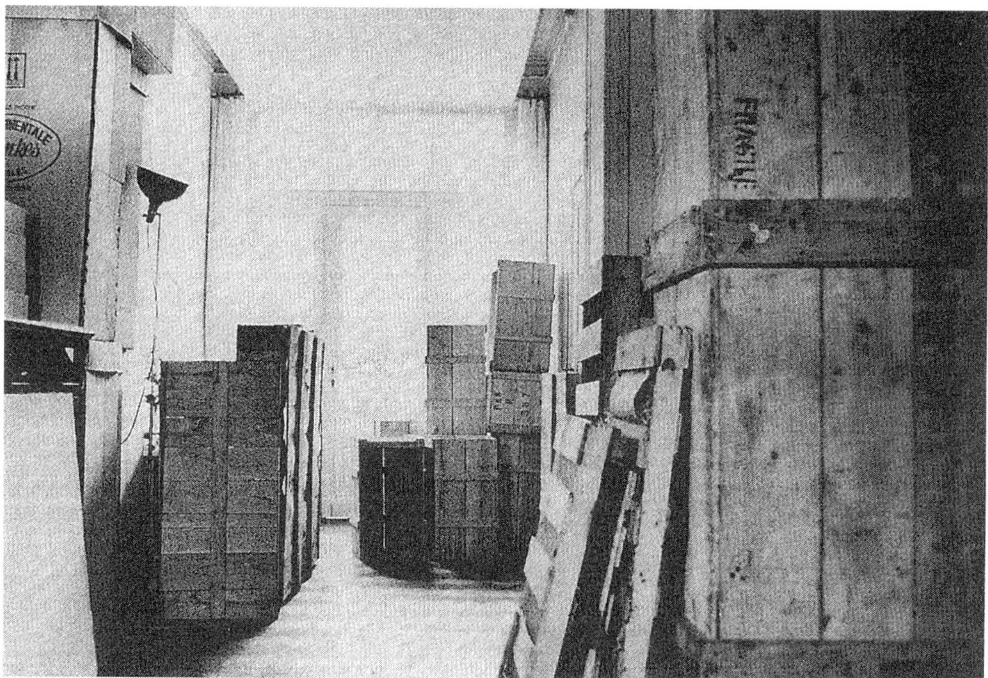

Figure 9: Installation documentation of Marcel Broodthaers, *Musée d'Art Moderne, Département des Aigles, Section XIXe siecle* (1968). Installation at 30, Rue de la Pepiniere, Brussels, 1968. Photo credit: Maria Glissen. © Marcel Louis Broodthaers/SABAM. Licensed by Viscopy, 2011.

An early set of plaques, which included the aptly titled *Museum* (1968), illustrates the parallelism that Broodthaers acknowledged in an artist statement written that same year:

> The atmosphere of this museum is also that of the plastic panels. These plaques (85 × 125 cm), fabricated in the manner of industrially produced signs, occupy the border between object and image. According to their mechanical production they seem to deny their status as art objects, or rather I should say, they tend to prove art and its reality by means of 'negativity'. These plaques express irrelevance; they refer to something other than themselves. (cited in Buchloh 1988, p. 96)

As a studio investigation, *From Catalogue-Museum* was approached from the outset as a preliminary experiment or exercise. The obligation to seek some form of ultimate resolution ran counter to my aspiration to create what would be effectively an unresolved artwork. Producing an artwork that would be considered complete, self-contained or fulfilled was anathema to the nature of the project, premised as it was on the notion of incompleteness. So in the end, this catalogue of the contents of an imagined museum archive would become *From Catalogue-Museum*, an artwork about a missing artwork in an exhibition.

Choreography of the Exhibition Space (for a Model Viewer)

The viewer first enters into what is designated as the *Light Room* area of the exhibition. The space is subdivided into two distinct areas: a small entrance annex, which leads onto a larger main display area. The entrance annex is designed around the hanging of Patricia Piccinini's *Lumpland*. [*Figure 10*] This canonical work by one of Australia's foremost artists

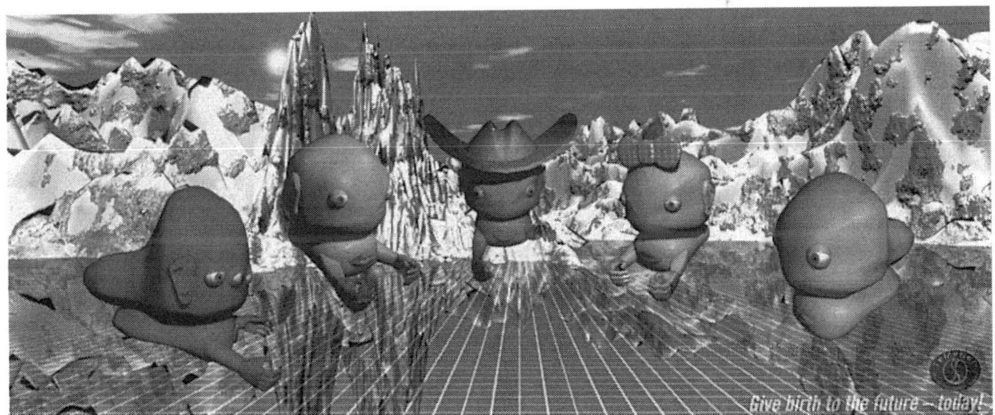

Figure 10: Patricia Piccinini, *Lumpland* (1995). Computer-generated digiprint, 1270 × 2300 mm. Edition of 3. Monash University Collection.

is given prominence, on one level, because it marks the acceptance of digitally mediated artistic practice into the museum. As such, it anchors the remainder of the inventory. The iconic status of the work – and its representational content of caricaturised 3D-modeled figures floating in a computer-simulated landscape – appears strangely out-moded for a work of relatively recent vintage. *Lumpland* acts as a counterpoint to the highly detailed, photographic images of Lynne Roberts-Goodwin and the computer-generated abstractions of Marcus Fajl. These two series effectively frame the works by Piccinini, which includes the seductively lulling surface play of her video piece, *Lustre*. By oscillating between the extremes of representational or abstract practices, these works are indicative of contrasting orientations to digital imaging. Coordinated in such a way, a spatial dialogue on the topic of *nature* (the representation of natural forms, as well as the nature of digital imaging) is set in motion between these works.

Befitting the overarching theme of the *Light Room*, the adjoining main gallery space is given over to a collection of works exemplifying practices that involve artistic interventions that focus on various materialities of the digital image. [*Figure 11*] As with the focal point provided by the established practice of Piccinini's work encountered previously, the works assembled in this area all turn upon the emerging media practice exemplified by Daniel von Sturmer's video piece, *Materials from Another Medium*. Panning across this arena,

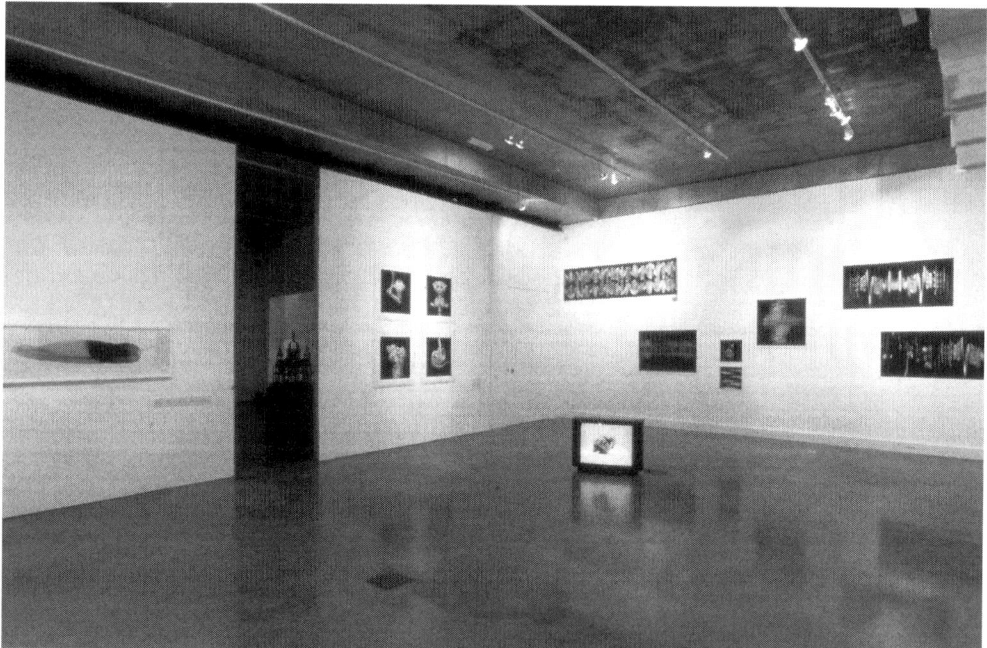

Figure 11: Installation view of *The Synthetic Image – Light Room* (Faculty Gallery: Melbourne, 2002). Featured works by Marcus Bunyan, Murray McKeich, Lynne Roberts-Goodwin and Daniel Von Sturmer.

the viewer's attention turns from Trinh Vu's digital drawings of flora to Murray McKeich's anthropomorphic digital collages. Next, Marcus Bunyan's digital reinterpretation of the rayogram juxtapose with the process employed by McKeich in producing his amalgams from his archive of miscellaneous found objects and textures. Bunyan's linear arrangement of printed sections reinforces their fluid constitution and sense of morphing seamlessly from one state of existence into another. These qualities segue into the row of three luscious prints from Phil George's *Liquid Worlds* series. Formally installed to continue the horizontality registered on the back wall of the gallery space by Bunyan's presentation, these images draw the viewer into an exploration of the play of their seductive surfaces and depths.

In contrast to these works, which are print based and variously presented using an array of presentation methods (single framing, gridded square, wall assembly of various fragmentary elements, image sequence), von Sturmer's installation is exaggeratedly sculptural. Reinforced by its presentation on a large, bulky monitor placed directly on the gallery floor, its image content involves a sequence of short episodes involving different tactile manipulations of mundane, everyday materials. These short scenarios all take place in the reductive space of a small cubic enclosure that is reinforced by the perspectival effect of projecting this virtual space behind the screen surface of the monitor. The work's influence on the overall space is further reinforced by the incidental sound effects associated with the crumpling a ball of paper or rustling of a plastic bag.

In stark contrast to the *Light Room* environment, the *Dark Room* was designed to provide a darkened space for the projection or screening of media artworks. However, as with the inclusion of two monitor-based pieces presented under standard lighting conditions in the adjoining *Light Room* space, the *Dark Room* also negotiated the challenge of integrating non-luminous works into a 'black box' environment. [*Figure 12*]

The main display area involved a diverse mixture of works that each in their own way respond to ideas associated with *visualization*. Matthew Perkins' *Thump/Crash* explores the phenomenology of visual phenomena. A disorienting projection of a person running across the frame plays dramatically across the main wall of the space and acts as a backdrop to the other events occurring in its vicinity. This footage is shot from above, which adds to its disorientating effect when projected onto a wall surface. Further, as revealed by the floor surface in this scene, the real (actual) and virtual (represented) spaces are found

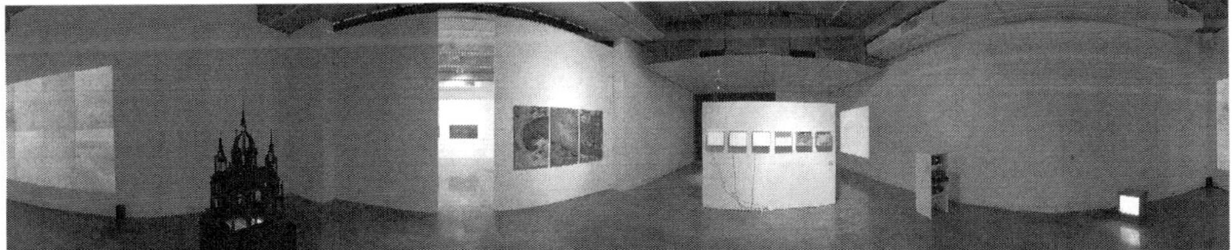

Figure 12: Installation view of *The Synthetic Image – Dark Room* (Faculty Gallery: Melbourne, 2002). Featured works by Megan Evans, Troy Innocent, Gerard Minogue, Matthew Perkins and Vince Dziekan.

to be contiguous (the represented action takes place in the same site as its screening). A small monitor juxtaposing the recording of a light bulb smashing on the floor is situated in the corner of this arena. Alongside, Megan Evans' theatrically presented animation work is all about the act of conjuring. Like Perkins' installation, the work coerces its viewer by controlling the scale of images and the viewer's proximity and mode of address. The viewer's expectations are further manipulated by *From Catalogue-Museum* (discussed earlier) and its pseudo-museological assembly of light boxes whose imagery alludes to x-rays or magnetic resonance imaging techniques used to produce a visualization of what lies under or behind the surface of things. Contrasting with the media presentation that connects these works, Gerard Minogue's three-panel composition is set off to one side and spot lit. While contrary in form, it is nonetheless in keeping with the over-riding thematic that connects the works found in this space. His work emphasises how the senses (not exclusive to the visual) are used to create mental pictures.

The exhibition reaches its conclusion in a final anteroom created at the far end of this gallery. In this area Troy Innocent's interactive artwork *au_vector* is installed. This work is highly abstract in its imaging content, recalling the visual quality of Piccinini's works, which, coincidentally, would be found located immediately on the other side of the gallery wall. This work is explicitly interactive and the viewer becomes an active participant in the act of triggering image and sound events. The work extends the definition of the digital image, giving it a decidedly new media inflection.

Curator's Essay – *The Synthetic Image and the Theme of the Loop: Image, Exhibition and Networkability*

The presentation of this expository text is a composite of two previous versions. The text was first published in the exhibition catalogue for the exhibition hosted in the Faculty Gallery, Monash University in June 2002. Adopting a novel approach to its publication design (developed in collaboration with graphic designer Wendy Ellerton), this text along with an accompanying commissioned essay provided by Dr. Anne Marsh was presented on the back side of a series of small cards that reproduced details of selected artworks from the exhibition.

In response to the opportunity to expand upon the existing text in the August 2002 issue of *Media/Culture (M/C)* based on the editorial theme of 'Loop', I decided to adapt my original curator's essay in order to maximise the potential offered by re-presenting the text in a multimedia format. As a result the text was worked into a set of short narrative sections, or lexias. Given the restrictions of conventional writing – with its inevitable beginning and end – the narrative composition of the argument was also redeveloped to take advantage of a hypertext format. This made it possible for each self-contained packet of text to be explored by the reader in a non-linear fashion. These discrete 'samples' were incorporated into a new interactive form of presentation that innovatively juxtaposed text and image. This visualization significantly extended the discursivity of the argument, overlaying a layer of associations that exist between any single text or image element and the larger contextual environment. The publication's graphical interface design was developed in collaboration with multimedia designer Leon Meyer.

This approach more fully brings out the cyclical, looping character of the argument in an effort to align the interactive reading experience of the text with that of the viewer attending the exhibition and experiencing the works presented through the installation. In describing the qualities this visual feature brings to the editorial theme, Mitchell and Rintel (2002) introduce the piece accordingly:

'The Synthetic Image' is an astounding interactive exhibition/installation which the user is invited to explore via a kind of looped nodal map. Indeed, 'The Synthetic Image' immerses the user in three kinds of loops. First, art and critique are drawn together into interlinking loops. Second, a centrifugal hypertextual structure is used to both create and display a narrative space. Third, the metaphor of the loop is used to discuss the synthetic nature of digital art that explores the relationship between the real and the virtual.

Introduction 1 – Transformations and shifting grounds

The transformation wrought by the innovation of imaging technologies have (always) altered not only the ways that images are fabricated, but further, reconfigured the very structural base that we use to interpret and understand visuality itself. This dismantling opens the process of representation to the larger intellectual investigation of embodiment and the nature of cognition and perception. What is characteristic of the perspective of contemporary theorists on the archaeology of technological imaging is the recognition that perception, and our understanding of the process of seeing, is more dramatically extended even than modes of representation by the introduction of new technologies of visualization. Paul Virilio writes: 'every vehicle or technical vector as an idea, as a vision of the universe, more than its image' (1994, p. 29). According to Jonathan Crary, new techniques of vision act as 'a nervous system interfacing with a continually transforming external environment' by a 'sweeping destabilization of previously what had constituted an "image", resulting in 'conceptualisations of reality as a dynamic aggregate of sensations' (1999, p. 344). As a consequence of these technological developments across the field of imaging is the shifting ground of subjectivity itself. Beyond the immediate loss of uniqueness and authenticity and the frayed thread connecting the image to an unravelling real, digital imaging technologies are intertwined with the dismantling of a unified model of spectatorship. The digital facture of images seem (seam) to satisfy the innate restlessness on which technologically mediated spectatorship is grounded.

Introduction 2 – Visualization of the synthetic image

When visualizing the qualities of the image itself, our perception gravitates towards notions of flatness and rectalinearity. This resulting 'window' of classical Renaissance perspective uses transparency to induce the effect of looking through the represented image into its illusionistic spaces. The digital image instead offers an alternative view, a sideways glance. If we rotate and skew the axis of the imaginary picture plane in our mind's eye, so as to animate it and view it from all sides (including faces and profiles, managing for an instant to reduce the three-dimensional plane to a two-dimensional line), we glimpse two distinctive aspects of the synthetic image coming fleetingly into focus: its fluid topographicality (left/right, top/bottom) and indeterminate dimensionality (front/back, inside/outside). Dynamically enacting these two properties is a third, a malleable morphological force that acts to pull the image together from its constituted parts, but which also pulses away, restless and reverberating, inside the image.

Mesh 1 – Veil/unveil

I will decide to use a veil of sheer diaphanous material to conjure up the photographic image; just as an image of a curtain introduces Roland Barthes' personal reflections on photography in *Camera Lucida*[6], and, according to Ron Burnett, operates to 'highlight the levels of mediation that both encourage the imaginary and prevent us from looking outside' (1995, p. 34). It is intended that this metaphor be identifiable in the way the pictorial components constituting the representational content is interlaced with a substrate acting as its support: the evanescent image evaporating on the deceptive transparency of the screen; as a site confusing surface and depth, object and image, projected light and its material support. While vaporous and fugitive, the mesh-like quality of the fabric (whether fibres of paper, weave of threads, raster of pixels) lends its support to the creating of an image – acting as framework, a lattice-like structure which paradoxically blocks and reveals, hides and unveils, mediates between seeing and understanding, from physiological optics to projection. The digital image manifests such paradoxical materiality all the more so, in that these differences seem to integrate within itself.

Mesh 2 – Surface and support

It is on these two inter-dimensional levels, simultaneously surface and support, as 'fabric', that the synthetic image is materialized (and imagined acting like a magician's handkerchief waved in front of an object about to reappear). Such an elusion of the image in the act of forming is to be found in Marcus Bunyan's *Chrono/some*. The wrapping, curling and draping of lengths of photographic prints alludes to an indeterminate corporeality, 'the emersion of the body into the depth of field of the reality of technology'.[7] Their installation, by creating a confusion of coordinates and vectors, a wrought torsion that enables inside to meet outside, recalls the contortions of the Mobius strip.[8] The digital photographs of Murray McKeich show his interest in bodies in the act of forming. At times seeming to emerge like sculptural forms out of marble, or vaporizing out the ether at others, McKeich's practice is a meeting of the tactile and the virtual, a perfect embodiment of the synthetic.

Mesh 3 – Fabric of synthetic image

If we visualize the digital image as a meshwork of pixels, the regularity of the grid discloses a much less predetermined ground; their meta-properties, bits, bytes and colour numbers operate in a far more flexible way, flickering away energetically under the skin of the image. This matrix rather than being fixed is ideally suited for the modifying relationships found within the processes of image production and reception. The term *fixed* calls up numerous meanings, including Sir John Herschel's discovery, which married the chemical components necessary for photography with the applied physics of the *camera obscura*. By coalescing and condensing the fleeting image and fusing it permanently to its base, this concept opens onto a range of positionings of photography premised on immobilizing, arresting and capturing.[9] This conceptualisation of the material base for the image offers a far more fleeting, fluid constitution. Herschel's 'solution' enacts the original, morphogenic site; the domain of the image as transient and variable, one that is visually articulated in the mirage-like qualities of Phil George's *Liquid Worlds*.

Weave 1 – Distortion and the projective process

'The camera is woven on the eye.' This aphoristic remark, attributed to the productivist artist László Moholy-Nagy, cuts like a vector intersecting with the act of picture-making, the image, the processes of vision and thought. Standing in contrast to the predominating optical primacy of the image, the fabric-like nature of the synthetic image relates to a more haptic (non-optic) constitution. The topographical revisiting of vision possesses qualities that weave opticality with (in) the bodily. The fiction of a luminous and transparent optical experience of vision made with omnipotent rays of light blinds us from seeing the physicality of vision. This intrusion of the bodily is already betrayed in this model by the over-looking of the mediation enacted by the lens, a deceptive transparency that furtively distorts what it portrays. The lens, envisaged as a thickness of glass, is integral to the forming of images, by bending and shaping light. Through this mediation distortion is woven into the projective process. As Crary points out:

> Unlike an eighteenth-century diagram of the eye in which light rays enter as if through a transparent lens to transmit an image, Helmholtz's drawing makes clear that the passage

of light into the eye is anything but unmediated. When light enters this opaque 'apparatus', it is no longer as part of a geometrical optics, as rectilinear rays travelling from point to point, but as a form of luminous energy that strikes a dense mosaic of receptors, setting off a complex of processes in this compound organ that culminate in visual perception. (1999, p. 153)

Weave 2 – Phantasmagoria

Consider the phantasmagoria as the product of such suggestive light. The phantasmagoria comes from the same ilk as the *phenakistiscope* and the *stereoscope*, pre-cinematic devices that produced the spectacular from an interplay of both optical (specular) and haptic (embodied, tactile, even synaesthetic) qualities of the image. It is this alternate lineage that we recognize in immersive work such as that of Troy Innocent. In his interactive environment, entitled *au_vector*, he continues his exploration of immersion and the interface of the human and machine, and the systems of art and language. Focusing on the interaction of sound and image, the manipulation of virtual objects is employed towards producing a multisensory experience. This work prompts a musing on artificial contemplation and the apprehension that since we can manipulate an image, it, in turn, can control us.

Weave 3 – Retina to monitor

Developing as an alternative to the seemingly transparent nature of the perspectival image, the model of the muscular component of vision and the elastic character of the eye as organ of the body, finds expression as an opaque, topographical field on which the various processes of projection play themselves out. As Crary notes in his analysis of nineteenth-century investigations into vision by the likes of Helmholtz, Muller and Sherrington:

Human vision could not be considered in isolation from the intricate relation of motor behaviour to the '137 million separate seeing elements spread out in the sheet of the retina'. The eye moving across a visual field was, he showed, dynamically interconnected 'with wide tracts of musculature as a whole'. (1999, p. 351)

For us at the start of the twenty-first century, this surface also finds parallel expression in the mosaic of light producing elements and receptive sheet of pixels that comprise the digital image and monitor screen.

Wireframe 1 – Information to out-formation

The synthetic image is among the most recent manifestations in the evolution of 'machine vision', advancing through a merging of photography with other machinic and increasingly industrial forms of image production. The computer forces us to think of the image as information (and which my own personal, artistic contribution explores). Image formation, in digital media, operates as in/formation turning into out/formation; the exposure of invisible, internal machinations searching for a surface on which to perform visually. With information being the 'real' stuff of digital imaging – the condition has been convulsed so that volume is no longer the measure of the reality of objects; this solidity is found in the apparition of 'flat figures'[10] activated into visualization on computer screens. This confusion is explored by Florian Rotzer, who observes that it has become possible 'through the digital code, to reduce all forms of information-representation into an unspecific language than can be translated into the various forms of representation' (1993, p. 69). As a result of digitisation, any form of image can be considered as the 'peripheral surface phenomena of the digital code' (p. 69).

Wireframe 2 – Wireframe structure and construction

New media artist John Maeda attests that today objects:

> Are not space-oriented on the outside but space-oriented on the inside, at incredibly tiny scales. This inner space is a consequence of the successive miniaturization of integrated circuit technology, which can realize topological complexities equivalent to entire cities within raindrop-sized volumes. (2000, pp. 24–5)

Trinh Vu's *Polygon Mania* realizes this non-objective world; the natural world previously only glimpsed through the thinking eyes of a visionary like Paul Klee. Herein, botanical specimens are gestated in a computer program, their lightness of touch and delicacy of structure built out of 'number crunching'; the mind-meeting of hardware and software whirling and sparking into ideation, creating mutations, variations upon zeros and ones. The wireframe construction (lattice-like, spindly) of each form becomes exoskeleton. The ensuing spline curves and polygon faces, the contour maps and faceting of these simulations, is recognized as a paradigmatic structure for realising images; and the structure is virtual.

Wireframe 3 – Virtual

The simulated model is an incident which instantiates the virtual. N. Katherine Hayles describes virtuality as 'the cultural perception that material objects are interpenetrated by information patterns' (2000, p. 69). An extension of this is what happens when the image, in its digital form, becomes capable of not only articulating information but also develops an appetite for information. Being responsive to input from a user (activated in immersive multimedia in such characteristics as interactivity and agency) forces a rethink of what we are actually looking at, represented or depicted in/by/through the image; and to ponder, in turn, what the image thinks of us!

Map 1 – Topographicality

Evolving from the horizon line to the image plane of Cartesian perspectivalism, and beyond, from picture plane to screen, the space of the synthetic image can increasingly be characterised as topographical.[11] Initially intended to provide the structural foundation for the classical image, the destabilizing of the perspectival grid not only affects the relationship of figure/ground, but also decentres the relation of spectator to image. The planar quality of the mapped image can be self-organising and projective. Responsive to touch, capable of reverberating, of giving as good as it gets, this type of animated space is suited to the mobile, embodied, interacting observer rather than the abstraction of the reduced, stable, disembodied eye.

Map 2 – Anamorphic deconstruction of space and seeing

The technique of anamorphosis literally uses techniques of perspective against itself. As such, it can be used as a means of turning embedded paradigms of space and meaning inside out. In Megan Evans' *Visualizing Virtually*, the plastic quality of space is convoluted and distorted. The window frame that is looked through is transformed into a Baroque mirror that we look at, and which looks back at us, if we catch the unstable image just right, revealing the image's unconscious subtext. As an instance of what the artist refers to as 'subjectivization of the viewing process', spectatorship is revealed as productive in nature rather than passive.[12] Such making-into-image explores the relation of physicality to the virtual and focuses on the image as an artificial product, a fictional reality.

Map 3 – Hypertext as surface and depth

While anamorphosis manipulates the relation of image and observer, hypertext plays with producing meaning through the interaction of reader and text. Hypertext writer Michael Joyce has described virtual writing as being 'topographical', using the term to emphasise the plasticity of the text, while for N. Katherine Hayles, hypertext possesses both surface and depth.[13]

Anticipated by his namesake a century, the illusory passage of time in literary narrative has increasingly been worked as a tactile surface. In a work such as *Ulysses*, James Joyce employed a radical, collage-like aesthetic informed by the photomontage experiments of his artistic contemporaries. Recognizing the linkage of representational modes and technology in modernity, Timothy Druckrey finds in montage 'the crisis of a respatialized image merging with a multi-faceted, one might say pre temporal, representation' (1993, p. 21). Exploring time in both synchronic and diachronic terms, Joyce connected represented episodes, meandering events, thoughts, reminiscences and daydreams into an interwoven textual fabric that can best be appreciated as operating spatially. In an analogous way the synthetic image lends itself to spatio-temporal explorations and hybrid textual structures (the 'sun writing' of heliography having originally, albeit obliquely, announced the relationship of the photographic image to text).

Moire 1 – Dialectic of dualities

The collapsing of surface and depth in the synthetic image introduces an affective relationship wherein inside and outside work dialectically. Embedded notions of the image operate by holding these features in distinct, fixed relationship to each other. Digitization takes the image into the realm of information theory, which in contrast, relies on dualities (such as information and noise, signal and non-signal) not so much as dichotomies but as a dialectic. As articulated by Hayles: 'the condition of virtuality implies, then, a widespread perception that presence/absence is being displaced and pre-empted by pattern/randomness' (2000, pp. 77–8). Consider the screen. Conventionally operating as the surface 'on' which the visible image is formed, the cinema screen becomes invisible, an instantiation of absence. Contrary to physics in which a screen is designed to shield or prevent interference between effects, the synthetic image, with its film-like skin welcomes compound effects to play across its surface, producing interference (referred to as artefact) and moire. According to Burnett: 'Projections transform the observable and the seeable, making the screen not a site of depiction but the location for a play of interpretations and speculations' (1995, p. 160). In the digital realm, the screen operates as the shifting ground 'on' which the projected light is deformed; the framework 'through' which the virtual is formed.

Moire 2 – Skin dynamism and moire

These permutations go a small way towards illustrating Maeda's definition of *skin dynamism* as 'the ability of an object's surface to change, resulting in a shifting focus from an object's body (which once defined its function) to its outer skin (which was once simply an artefact)' (2000, pp. 24–5). The emphasis upon such surface qualities can be recognized in numerous works in the exhibition. The abstractions produced by Marcus Fajl result from rendering the virtual optical while Gerard Minogue's tongue-in-cheek gesture comments on our blindness to the physicality of pixels when confronted by the overwhelming surface effects associated with much digital imaging. The works of Patricia Piccinini and Lynne Roberts-Goodwin, in their own divergent ways, work with this shimmering surface to repel the eye across their radiant images. Piccinini's video work *Lustre* is enamoured with the quality of vaporous luminosity, basking virtual objects in the screen's plasmatic sheen. Whereas Piccinini's work simulates the organic, in contrast, the works of Lynne Roberts-Goodwin call on the natural iridescence of bird plumage. Her sensuous, metallic photographic prints vacillate between camouflage and display, between documentary fact and artifice.

Screen 1 – From freeze-frame to dynamic image

The synthetic image extends beyond the freeze-frame of the conventional photograph. Its dynamic surfaces transcend these restrictions through expression and expansion across the dimension of time. With reference to Virilio: 'With the decline in volumes and in the expanse of landscapes, reality becomes sequential and cinematic unfolding finally gets the jump on whatever is static and on the strength of materials' (1997, p. 27). Here a connection can be made between the formal play of dynamic images (projected, animated) and the lineage of pictorial spectacles of the panorama and Edison's Kinetoscope. In these various forms, which play with the processing of perception, it can be recognized that photography's frozen moment and cinema's linear narrative is replaced in digital media by the structure of the loop. Lev Manovich, writing on digital cinema, draws attention to the loop structure as being an essential characteristic of digital filmmaking. Besides making the connection backward to pre-cinematic optical devices and early filmmaking techniques, he also positions the loop metaphor within the context and trajectory of the language structures of computer programming, which involves using the loop structure to control and alter the flow of data.

Screen 2 – Aesthetics of the loop

Prevalent across the variety of time-based pieces in the exhibition is the prevailing aesthetic quality of repetition. In these works (by Piccinini, Matthew Perkins and Daniel von Sturmer), we can sense two subtly different impulses to the loop: the compulsive and the hypnotic. The compulsive, as manifest in Perkins' piece *Thump/Smash*, involves the body and triggers involuntary, spasmodic reaction to sound (the sharp burst of the meeting of glass and concrete) and light (the shattering shards of breaking light against darkness). In comparison, the closed circuit of the repetitive loop in Daniel von Sturmer's *Material from Another Medium* manages to evoke a state of endurance, a duration-less floating quality of 'recorded' time (as differentiated from 'real'). Through his subtle poetics, objects transform into images and visual tricks conjure a folding/unfolding of the material of space and time upon themselves. In a way illustrative of all of the works in the exhibition, the synthetic quality of digital visualization addresses such impossibilities, imperceptibilities and realizes the unrepresentable.

Notes

1. 'Digital words and images take the form of semiotic codes, and this fundamental fact about them leads to the characteristic, defining qualities of digital infotech: (1) virtuality, (2) fluidity, (3) adaptability, (4) openness (or existing without borders), (5) processability, (6) infinite duplicability, (7) capacity for being moved about rapidly, and (8) networkability' (Landow 2000, p. 166).
2. This approach to the design-based organization of the exhibition relates back to my earlier curatorial project, *Archival Permanence: Time and Timelessness in 100 Years of Australian Photography*, which was conceived in response to the centenary of the Geelong Art Gallery (Geelong, Australia) and toured regionally in Australia during 1996–97.
3. Marcel Duchamp's portable museum project commenced in 1936. Its first edition took five years to complete. Through his use of reproduction techniques that both required meticulous attention and were extremely time-consuming, Duchamp 'blurred the boundaries between the unique art object and the multiple, between the original and its mechanical reproducibility, and created a number of transitional stages that were hard to define or distinguish' (Bonk 1989, p. 20). Duchamp would continue to produce partial editions over the remainder of his life.
4. The influence of Duchamp on the conceptualization of curatorial design project cannot be understated. In particular, the reader is directed to the discussion broached in the chapter found in the Expositions section dedicated to *Spatial Practice*.
5. Dieter Schwarz (1988) identifies three distinct, but overlapping, phases of Marcel Broodthaers' 12-year artistic career. The first phase (between 1963 and 1967) was marked by his production of visual object assemblages and his *Industrial Poems*. Between1968 and 1972–73, Broodthaers 'directed' his fictional museum (*Musée d'Art Moderne*) under the auspices of which he variously produced and published books, 'open letters' and films. His final phase, from 1973 up till his death in 1976, was represented by the staging of a series of installation-based *Decors*.
6. In reference to the Polaroid photograph attributed to Daniel Boudinet that acts as a front-piece to the publication of Barthes' *Camera Lucida: reflections on photography* (1981).
7. Artist's statement, 2002.
8. The Moebius strip, according to Bernard Cache visualizes the possibility for imagining a 'radical exteriority that would not be the opposite of an interiority' (1995, p. 37). He elaborates:

   > The interest of this sort of figure lies rather in the fact that it offers us a set of images in which inside and outside are notions devoid of meaning. Perhaps it is the virtue of such paradoxes, whether spatial or logical, to allow us to see, if only for an instant, a universe with no top or bottom, right or left, inside or outside. (p. 37)

9. Sir John Herschel's discovery of a 'means of arresting the further action' with a solution of hyposulphite of soda was eagerly applied by both William Henry Fox Talbot and Louis Daguerre in 1839 to their respective processes which mark the invention of photography. According to Beaumont Newhall, the term *photography* was also proposed by Herschel and would eventually

replace Talbot's original, awkward phrase of *photogenic drawing*. (Newhall 1982, pp. 21–2) The linguistic meshing of terminology and concept that I've alluded to can also be recognized in Herschel's proposal of the terms 'positive' and 'negative' which instantiate the two aspects of the photographic process, replacing Talbot's 'reversed copy' and 're-reversed copy'.

10. '[V]olume is no longer the reality of things. This is now concealed in the flatness of figures [… The real is hidden in the reduction of images on the screen' (Virilio 1997, p. 26).

11. 'What is at stake here is a model of subjective experience, located in many different places in the 1880s and 1890s, in which consciousness is not a seamless sphere where a world is fully self-present to a subject but rather a disjunct space in which contents move between zones of varying levels of clarity and awareness, vagueness and responsiveness […] This so-called "topographical" model of the eye might seem to organize the visual field in terms of figure and ground, with a separation between the focussed center and peripheral background, but those distinctions had no permanence or stability. Perception was a process in which those terms were perpetually shifting into one another, in ceaseless reversals and displacements. Even though the foveal 'Blickpunkt' coincided with an anatomical center, the cognitive modalities at stake here are part of larger processes of decentering' (Crary 1999, p. 294).

12. Artist's statement, 2002.

13. N. Katherine Hayles outlines the key character traits found in hypertext as: '1. Writing is inwardly elastic; 2. The topology of the text is constructed rather than given; 3. Changes in a text can be superficial, corresponding to surface adjustments, or structural, corresponding to changes in topography […] embody the assumption that the text possesses both surface and depth' (2000, pp. 88–9).

Chapter 8

Small Worlds: A Romance

Synopsis

The following case study is based on a curatorial project that was commissioned by the UTS Gallery, Sydney, and staged there from 14 October to 7 November 2003. Over the course of this chapter, the curatorial philosophy and its translation into installation scenography are outlined. Particularly illustrative of a number of ideas central to the curatorial thematic, the creative production of a multimodal artwork, *Nature-History*, is also covered. The reflective analysis discusses how an 'orchestral' curatorial trope acted as a guiding principle, mediating the relationship between digital artwork and exhibition space.

I nflecting curatorial practice with the term *design* places an emphasis on how *curatorial design* exerts an influence over the form of aesthetic experience under exhibition conditions. The influence of design on art has become increasingly evident. Inspired by contemporary museum architecture, innovative strategies applied to exhibition design have produced aesthetic viewing experiences that create a continuum across external and interior architectures. Dramatic methods of display and presentation contribute to instilling a preparedness in the viewer to engage with the artwork as part of a performed process. Over the rest of this chapter, I will develop this discussion by focusing on the spatial association between digital media and exhibition space, and on how this relationship was mediated in a direct, applied way as part of the conceptual development and realization of the *Small Worlds: A Romance* exhibition.

Small Worlds adopted the new virtual arena, in recognition of hybrid practice and the increasingly complex ecology that supports and sustains it. Earlier in this book, I have referred to this situation as art's *exhibition complex* as it is constituted from artwork, gallery and museum.[1] This space offers a new and dynamic environment for art to function within. In the case of this particular exhibition, my curatorial design creatively responded to the challenge of integrating screen-based image spaces within an enveloping installation atmosphere.

The expanded field opened up by emergent technologies is a space composed of a variety of relationships (between subjects, objects, languages and institutional practices) along shifting vectors of exchange (including varied types of information flows, directions and multi-level connections). Inspired by philosopher Michel de Certeau, who identified the 'museum' as a type of institutional 'place in which gaps need to be opened for other practices of space' (Conley 2000, p. 59), the practice-based exploration undertaken as part of the *Small Worlds* project explored the relationship between virtuality and the art of exhibition. The curatorial design involved in realizing the exhibition was approached with a view to creatively explore how the nature of the digital domain transforms an understanding of the exhibition form. Conceived as operating across both physical and virtual spaces, this quality of the integrative exhibition as a whole was reinforced by the instrumental role played by my artwork *Nature-History*, which was developed explicitly for this purpose. This tripartite work draws upon the virtualities and site-specificities involved with its exhibition across both physical and digital spaces. The online virtual exhibition acted as a parallel universe that extended the work's coincident 'phases' occurring in the installations included as part of *Small Worlds* and its associated exhibition in *Zero Light* (CSA Gallery, Canberra). Conceived as a multimodal artwork reconstituted in three parts, it explored the aesthetics of the artwork as an extensive product of contributing processes rather than as an intensive, consolidated entity.

The theoretical background provided by site-specificity and distributed aesthetics have influenced the development and subsequent realisation of the exhibition. As such, *Small Worlds* presents an interpretation of distributed spatial practice. So combined, these influences lead towards a comprehensive re-evaluation of the form, practices and purposes that have traditionally constituted the artefact, gallery space and museum. It is within this multifaceted 'ecology', produced by the mixtures of artworks, curatorial design and installation space, that relational-sensitivity increasingly comes to be understood as the very *materiel* of the exhibition. The philosopher Henri Lefebvre introduced this term to account for the 'immaterial' conditions, directions, behaviours and agendas that together with basic materials used to construct social space. It is worth quoting this passage at length as he outlines this productive process:

> From the start of an activity so oriented towards an objective, spatial elements – the body, limbs, eyes – are mobilised, including both materials (stone, wood, bone, leather, etc.) and materiel (tools, arms, language, instructions, agendas). Relations based on an order to be followed – that is, on simultaneity and synchronicity – are this set up, by means of intellectual activity, between the component elements of the action undertaken on the physical plane. All productive activity is defined less by invariable or constant factors than by the incessant to-and-fro between temporality (succession, concatenation) and spatiality (simultaneity, synchronicity). This form is inseparable from orientation towards a goal – and thus also from functionality (the end and meaning of the action, the energy utilised for the satisfaction of a 'need') and from the structure set in motion (know-how, skills, gestures and co-operation in work, etc.). The formal relationships which allow separate actions to form a coherent whole cannot be detached from the material preconditions of individual and collective activity; and thus holds true whether the aim is to move a rock, to hunt game, or to make a simple or complex object. (Lefebvre 1991, p. 71)

Or, to make art for that matter…

It is the *materiel* of relational-sensitivity that was most evident in the curatorial and artistic tropes found in *Small Worlds*, and which in turn, offers a redefinition of exhibition praxis that is equally valid for negotiating the architecture of galleries or the online archi-textures of museums. Even though walls and floors are, and will inevitably continue to be, used to physically support and show artworks, the fixed, physical boundaries of the art object, the form of exhibition and the museum apparatus itself have already been substantially transformed by a variety of spatial practices, as supported by the institutional critique associated with site-specificity, new museology and, more recently, digital rhetoric.

Virtuality is practiced as the state of exchange, an enacted mediation between the notional and the real. It is my contention that it is the process of virtuality that has been transposed, reinterpreted and applied to the designed organisation and the construction of the exhibition as a rhetorical form. This approach is not restricted to the utilisation of digital technologies but rather is exercised as a conceptual strategy that accentuates the interrelationship of abstract and material events, and offers a structural ground on which to construct the foundations for the multimedial museum.

Applied Curatorial Design

As the case of *Small Worlds: A Romance* demonstrates, the viewer's experience of the artworks was orchestrated as part of the collected *ensemble* of the exhibition. Each work, whether audio, video or interactive in form, maintained an internal structure that enabled it to function within the 'ebb and flow' of the exhibition's total environment. The curatorial project was modelled from the outset using the exhibition form itself as a unifying principle or field in and through which the assembled works by the respective artists were activated. Included because of how they respond to the curatorial theme (the exploration of the relationship between the real and the virtual, new media and other artistic traditions), these artworks extended the exhibition experience through sound, image and interactivity using a range of digital media, including 3D modelling, digital audio and moving image projections. Bruce Mowson's sound art, Richard Brown's interactive 'painting', and the projected works by Csaba Szamosy, Joel Zika and the author transformed the gallery space by creating a sensory atmosphere that enmeshed the viewer in a techno-psychological experience.

Collectively, the resulting exhibition of artworks traced the spatio-temporal boundaries of the gallery space and the exhibition event. [*Figure 13*] I find the term 'ecology' resonates particularly well in describing such an arrangement, particularly in an effort to emphasise a relational basis to the various processes and interactions involved in the muscological arrangement of elements taking place in the spatial sphere of the gallery, museum or site of exhibition. At the project's inception, my curation drew inspiration from considering what parallels could be found between the network-like properties of exhibition design and the organisational design associated with the emerging science of networks, or 'Small World' theory, which according to Mark Buchanen: 'offers a deeper perspective on the critical importance of "connections" in our world' (2002, p. 22).

The principle guiding the overall installation plan was the creation of a virtual ecology: a sensory space of fluid, shifting and intermixing impressions and potentialities. To this end the gallery was realised as an animate space full of interference patterns and alternating passages rather than a fixed and static, hermetically-sealed enclosure. Richard Brown's interactive work *Mimesia* was activated when engaged with by the gallery visitor. The accompanying presentation of three projection pieces operated in overlapping cycles. At any one time all projections may have been on view or at varying stages of juxtaposition.

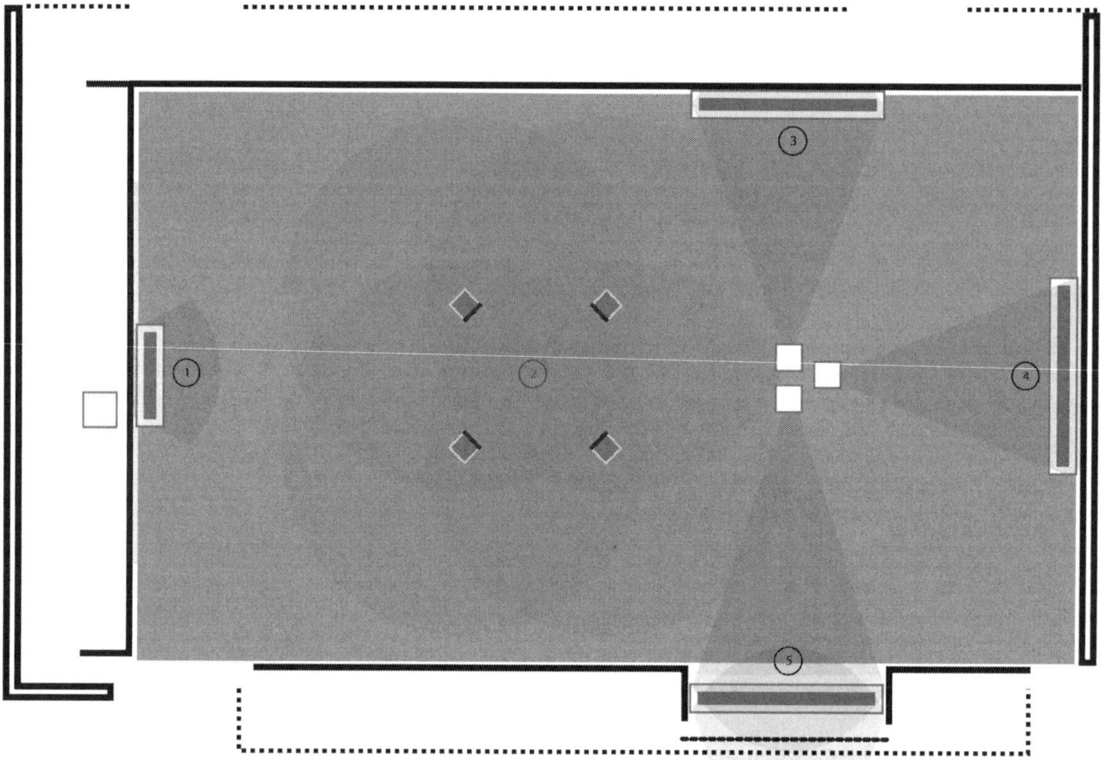

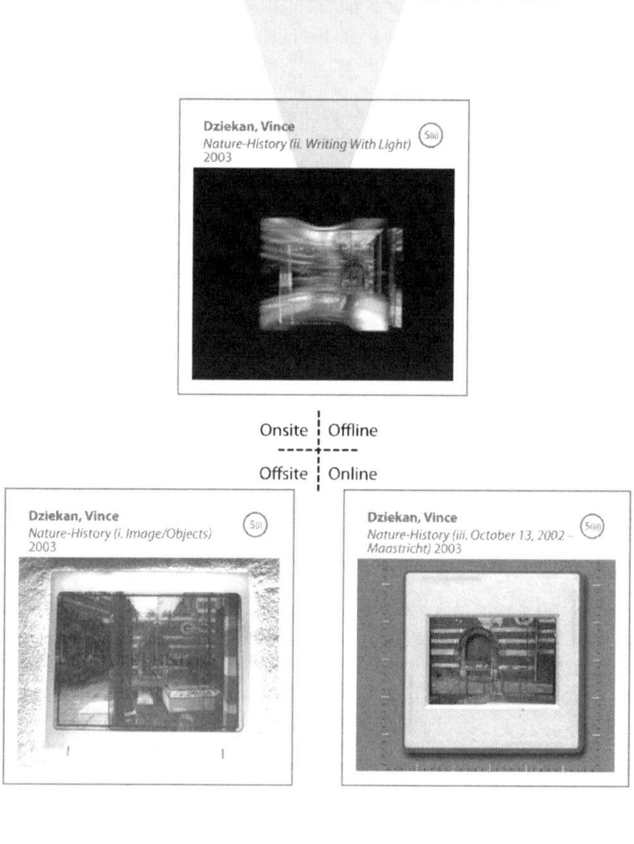

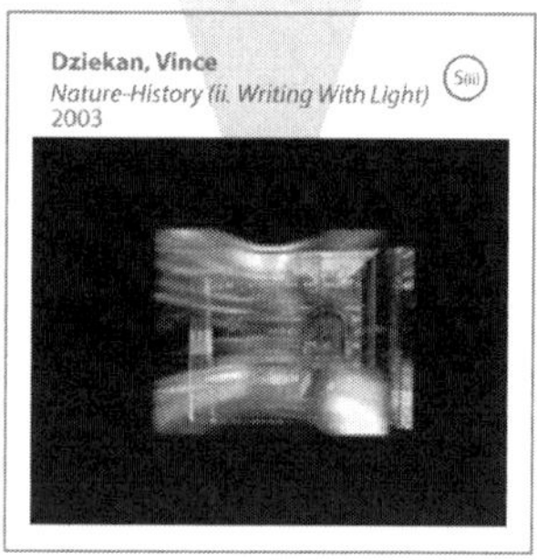

Onsite ┆ Offline
Offsite ┆ Online

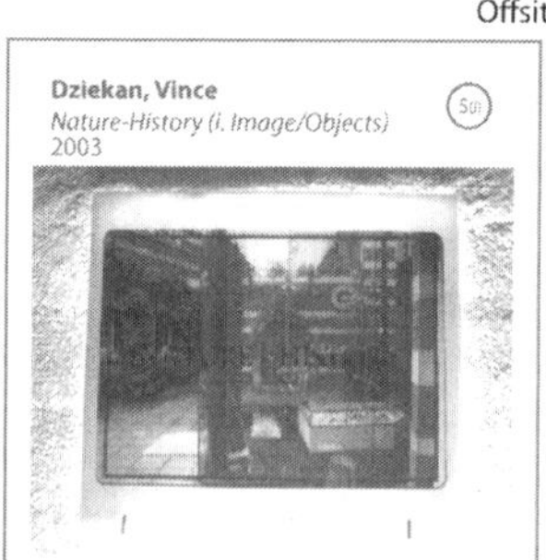

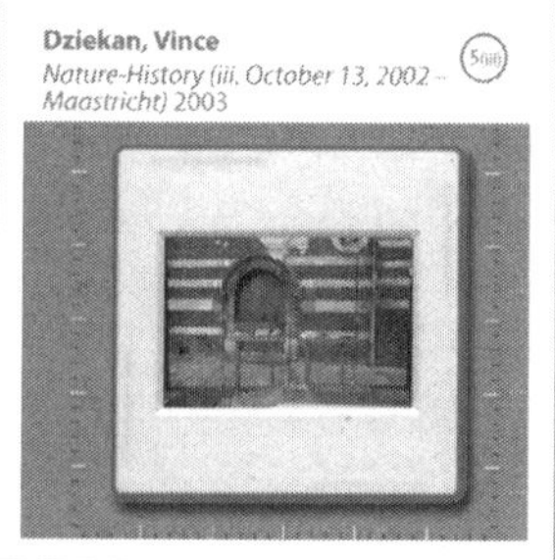

Figure 13: Installation schematic of *Small Worlds: A Romance* (UTS Gallery: Sydney, 2003).

Small Worlds: A Romance

small worlds : a romance

UTS Gallery, University of Technology Sydney, Sydney, New South Wales, Australia, 14 October–7 November 2003.

1.   Richard Brown, *Mimesia* (2003). Wall-mounted 'interactive painting'. Media/software: PowerRender (a games engine). Interactivity: VisualMouse. Collection of the artist.

2.   Bruce Mowson, *Untitled* (2003). Sound installation (digital audio). Collection of the artist.

3.   Csaba Szamosy, *Tree Loops* (2003). 3D animation (duration: 60 sec; loop). Collection of the artist.

4.   Joel Zika, *The Presence #1* (2003). Hybrid animation (duration: 5.00 min; loop). Collection of the artist.

5i.   Vince Dziekan, *Nature-History* (*i. Image/Object*) (2003). Mixed media: Digital transparencies. Fluorescent lighting. Image size: 29.5 x 360 mm each. Variable installation. Collection of the artist.

5ii.   Vince Dziekan, *Nature-History* (*ii. Writing with Light*) (2003). Digital animation (duration: 5.00 min; loop). Variable installation (projection, viewable from front and rear). Collection of the artist.

5iii. Vince Dziekan, *Nature-History* (*iii. October 13, 2002; Maastricht*) (2003). Website. Digital images. Interface design: 800 x 600 pixels. Collection of the artist.

The pervasive acoustic space designed by Bruce Mowson had the effect of defining the cubic area of the physical gallery. The soundscape enveloped the viewer and through this their subjective response to the other works on view. Composed to rise and fall in overlapping and recurrent waves (lighting up and fading down; appearing and disappearing), the viewer found themselves attuned to the durational qualities of their encounter with the exhibition as a performed event.

The exhibition's installation was conducted as an orchestral arrangement of 'tracks' rather than as an inventory of objects. Employing an orchestral trope led me to consider exhibition experiences I've had in which the arrangement of museological space had something of this character. The example of the installation of the Contemporary Collections Gallery at the Art Gallery of New South Wales, Sydney, from the mid-1990s still springs to mind, resonating as a particularly rich art experience. Even though operating as a conventional museum installation, this particular arrangement of works (combining pieces by Ian Burn, Ken Unsworth, Yves Klein, Gerhard Richter and Anselm Kiefer) illustratively accentuates the possibilities of intersecting the notional with the material. The relationship between individual pieces was rigorously considered. The ensemble (representing a range of works displaying conceptualist and expressionistic tendencies in postmodern work, which also placed contemporaneous Australian art in the same frame as its European counterparts) created an engaging, inventive and immersive multi-levelled narrative. The choreographed itinerary of the gallery visitor (conceived as a nomadic, travelling, mobile subject) was instrumental in moving the narrative along, collecting together the threads of the story as they unravelled across the space. The viewing experience, no longer exclusively modelled for the inspection of a disembodied spectatorial eye, played with the intricacies of seeing as spectatorship and performance. In this case, the resulting experience was definitely more than the sum of its individual parts. In deciding to approach my curatorial design of *Small Worlds* in a not dissimilar way, my use of this orchestral metaphor embraced interpretive associations to both its definition as an ensemble of different, contributing parts to a symphonic whole and the spatial notion of a theatrical 'parquet'.

The installation plan drew its inspiration from the site-specific features of the gallery space, which idiosyncratically presented transparent glass faces to both the inside (connoting architectural interiority) and outside (natural exteriority) spaces. The response to space also extended to the actual 'mixing' (in the sense of the term's usage in contemporary music production) of works taking the exhibition as a whole into account. Following this music analogy, in order to achieve the exhibition's curatorial philosophy, a level of direct creative intervention was required. This involved developing an ethos of co-production that applied in a number of cases. Save for Richard Brown's *Mimesia*, the remaining artworks were developed cooperatively with the artists as part of the project's evolution.

The production of the resulting triptych of video projections, for instance, was approached as a collaboration between the individual artists and myself. While each media element of the trio of works operated as self-contained episodes, my focus was directed at achieving a composition that wove these three pieces together. Viewed as such a unit, the arrangement expressed variations on the theme of nature. The omnipresence of foliage and the remediation of natural forms or motifs offered clues to this thematic overlay. Instrumental to this formation was the role played by my own piece, *Nature-History*. The virtual space it carved out – mapped by the imaginary circumference traced by the image's circuitous path around the centrally-stationed viewer – encompassed both works by Szamosy and Zika in its arc, like a sweeping searchlight defining the boundaries of its field of influence.

The production method applied to these works can be likened to 'sampling': the act of taking a portion of a piece of music and reusing it as an element in a new composition.[2] This approach was applied most illustratively to the production of *Tree Loops* by Csaba Szamosy. This work was based on an abbreviated media sample of a photo-realistic 3D-modelled animation sequence of only five seconds in duration. This base element was used as a loop and montaged into a longer segment that was subsequently post-produced. The post-production introduced the addition of a wipe transition that produced the effect of an opening venetian blind. The resulting projected image quite literally opened on the wall surface, starting as a thin strip of light and growing to reveal a full-framed vista before collapsing down again. The temporal pace associated with the other moving image works presented in its vicinity were taken into account when determining the duration of image in relation to black 'leader'.

In contrast, Joel Zika's *The Presence* was inspired by the visual language of scripted, cinematic narrative. Cinematic elements drawn from Gothic and horror films were reinterpreted and rendered through 3D animation. The artist's work process lent itself to co-production. Having first developed a series of short sequences, the work was then adapted as part of its editing. Informed by the compositional considerations related to its role within the cycle of moving image pieces, the resulting montage of the animation incorporated internal fade in/fade out transitions as part of its structure. These sections enhanced the spatiality of the work by introducing passages that helped to merge the projected images with the gallery wall, achieving the effect of the images rising and dissolving on its surface. Importantly, these expressions not only synthesised the work more totally within the total composition, or *Gesamtkunstwerk*,[3] of the exhibition, but also reinforced the artist's original intentions for the work.

These examples of co-production involved direct curatorial input during the process of creative production. In the case of the sound art work created by Bruce Mowson, this collaboration was handled slightly differently. This form of co-production entailed fully briefing the artist on the communicative intentions of the exhibition and on key factors being considered as part of its curatorial design. It was decided to incorporate the audio piece as an acoustic overlay that would act effectively as an exhibition soundtrack. Arriving at a mutual decision to explore an 'on/off' structure enabled sound to operate in two different ways: when active, the soundscape added a veneer to any of the time-based works on display; when off, the acoustic environment of the gallery fell silent and the works could be viewed as initially executed (as none of these works had native soundtracks). The work was executed onsite by the artist during the actual installation of the show. Drawing upon a subset of sound recordings that formed the basis of the work, the resulting composition was produced in response to the ambience and atmospheric qualities of the exhibition environment.

All works presented in *Small Worlds* exhibited a durational character. This was a consistent feature across the range of media employed. The full experience of the exhibition was composed as a presentation lasting, ideally, ten minutes. During this period, projected light and sound acted as the framework through which the virtual was formed, drawing upon the combined desires and imagination of the artist and the spectator. According to Freud: 'Everything that can be an object of our internal perception is virtual, like the image produced in a telescope by the passage of light rays' (Freud 1900, p. 611).

Their exhibition, naturally enough, broached a range of technical issues related directly to their presentation. Given the digital nature of these works, the central issue faced by their collective exhibition design revolved around addressing the visibility (or invisibility) of the technology involved in their delivery. It was decided early in the curatorial process that the technological apparatus should be as invisible as possible. For an exhibition of new media artwork, the resulting scenography was exceedingly minimalistic.

Richard Brown's work was activated through a sophisticated technical system that enables the viewer to control their movement through the virtual space through the combination of their proximity to the work and head movements. Brown has described his interactive installations as computer-based works involving 'real-time interactive 3D graphics' that respond to changing external parameters without any noticeable delay. He relates how:

All my installations make use of sensing technologies to create works that are transparent and immersive. The works are transparent as the body is intuitively used to interact with the work. They are immersive through the combination of large-scale video projection, ambient audio and engaging interactive content. (Brown 2003, p. 23)

The screen-based content of *Mimesia* was directly realised using a games engine, computer programming and 3D design software. [*Figure 14*] The viewer's passive interaction with the work was achieved by using sensing technology. A web camera was used to track the viewer's position in space and this information was processed using pattern-recognition software. This information was used to control the point of view of the virtual camera that framed the virtual world. However, this complexity is belied by the reductive simplicity of its presence in the gallery space: a conventionally-scaled monitor frame displayed at eye level in the centre of an otherwise unaltered expanse of wall space. As far as the viewer was concerned, their engagement with the work was seamless – and, as a result, fully compelling.

Creating the impression that the gallery was cycling through alternating states of emptiness and fullness was achieved without sophisticated technical programming. Rather, if a 'programme' as such existed, this was the result of applying a consistent design principle to the time-based audio/visual works. This principle related to the cyclically recurring, looping nature of the works. Without exception, each of these pieces was designed specifically or

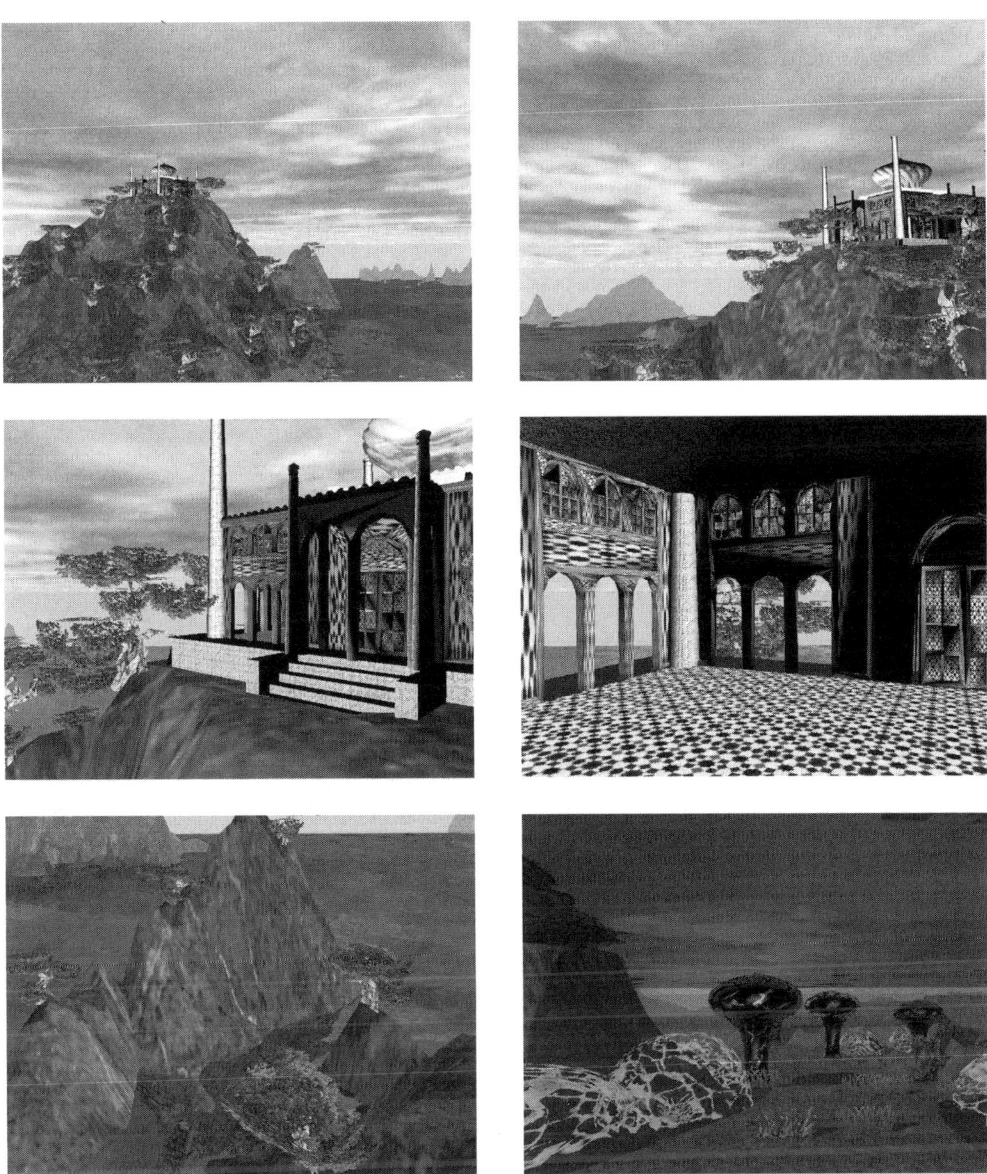

Figure 14: Frames from Richard Brown, *Mimesia* (2003). Wall-mounted 'interactive painting'. Media/software: PowerRender (a games engine). Interactivity: VisualMouse. Collection of the artist.

modified through the process of their co-production to incorporate alternating 'on/off' states. The motion graphic processing and montage editing that I employed in my production of *Nature-History* overtly built such a cycle into its structure. Zika's episodic scenes were stitched together with intervals of darkness. Szamosy's painstaking virtual representation of naturalistic phenomena loop repetitiously. The piece's transition between on and off states had the hypnotic effect of breathing. It was as if the wind rustling the leaves of simulated trees was inhaling and exhaling. The addition of Mowson's soundscape added a further overlay to the visual scenarios being played out across the space. Bruce Mowson's audio artwork existed as a static acoustic form, in that the discrete sound sample does not actually change over time. Rather, change is sensed as the listener's perception shifts across the surface of the sound. The artist's interest lies in the shift from music to noise and the idea that these two things can occupy the same space at the same time. The new piece commissioned specifically for *Small Worlds* incorporated recordings taken within the gallery space of sounds that generally go unnoticed and unheard in its composition (the hum of air conditioning, footsteps in the corridor). Interpretively, as a by-product of this acoustic overlay, the mechanism driving the wipe effect that swept over Szamosy's animation was given added resonance. The association with Gothic horror films to Zika's work was exaggerated as otherworldly (the sound of poltergeists permeating spaces that otherwise lacked any overt human presence: an empty room with lace curtains that is transformed by the camera zooming into motifs of the sheer fabric, blending with a screen of branches buffeted by a storm raging outside). With respect to *Nature-History*, the spinning movement of imagery sweeping across the viewer's field of view seemed to be propelled by an unseen engine.

These structures operated internally within each work. When thus composed across the composite space of the exhibition, their interplay produced a higher level of orchestration. Viewed in this way, certain scenes and passages seemed to mesh with each other. These moments of coincidence were fortuitous, but built into the design structure operating at the level of the artwork as well as exhibition. When so combined, artistic and curatorial practice amplified the possible relationships that could exist between artworks, and through this, the exhibition experience was fully animated.

For all intents and purposes, each viewer's experience of the exhibition was different. Given the differing time codes and lengths of each piece of media, a potentially limitless number of possible scenarios were produced in latency. The production of this effect was achieved without resort to computer-based programming or the kind of technical infrastructure required to trigger random sequences. Rather, through curatorial design, the artworks were integrated at a higher level of coordination, with their interplay and admixture resulting in varying patterns of synchrony and interference. As such the exhibition remained open to virtually limitless possibility and continuous renewal through the orchestrated combination of forms and the experience of their activators. The composite presentation emphasised latency, a pregnant state of immanence. Requiring imaginative activation, the curatorial design of *Small Worlds* sought to arouse in the viewer a sense of the sublime, of a *delightful stillness and amazement*.[4]

Summary

Inflecting curatorial practice with the term *design* emphasises how *curatorial design* exerts an influence over the form of aesthetic experience by focusing on the spatial association between digital media and exhibition space. *Small Worlds* creatively explored how the nature of the digital domain can transform an understanding of the exhibition form in order to respond to the challenge of integrating screen-bound image spaces within an enveloping installation atmosphere. Through activating artworks conceived as 'tracks' produced from direct creative intervention or co-production as part of a collected *ensemble*, this 'orchestral' approach to the curatorial design created a sensory atmosphere that enmeshed the viewer in a techno-psychological experience.

The curatorial project was modelled by using the exhibition as a unifying principle or field. The principle guiding the overall exhibition event was the creation of a virtual ecology: a sensory space of fluid, shifting and intermixing impressions and potentialities. The application of a 'programme' producing alternating states of emptiness and fullness transformed the gallery into an animate space open to virtually limitless possibility and continuous renewal through the recombination of forms and the experience of their activators rather than a fixed and static, hermetically-sealed enclosure. This state was reinforced by the particular qualities of the multimodal artwork *Nature-History*. In the end, virtuality was put into practice, activated as the state of exchange operating between the notional and the real. Importantly, the applicability of this approach to the exhibition *Small Worlds: A Romance* was not restricted to the utilisation of digital technologies but rather was exercised as a rhetorical strategy that accentuated the interrelationship of abstract and material events relevant to the aesthetic conditions of the multimedial museum.

Documentation

Artwork – Vince Dziekan, *Nature-History*

A pervading interest in much of my own work has involved the manipulation of its own framing as 'art'. Increasingly, this exploration has come to focus upon the concept of virtuality and the techniques associated with exhibition. As a result, the artwork *Nature-History* is caught up in this trajectory, measuring the artefact against the issue of excess and remainder, and the very contention of the artwork as the *presentation of a sublimity* that cannot be embodied in any sensible form.[5]

The work was composed out of three distinct phases: a projection piece (installed as part of the *Small Worlds* exhibition), an artwork (displayed concurrently in the *Zero Light*[6] exhibition) and the accompanying website archive. Each of these individuated parts was presented in a manner that coincided with its immediate site of exhibition while maintaining its relation to other iterations of the work. In effect, each of these three modes (physical,

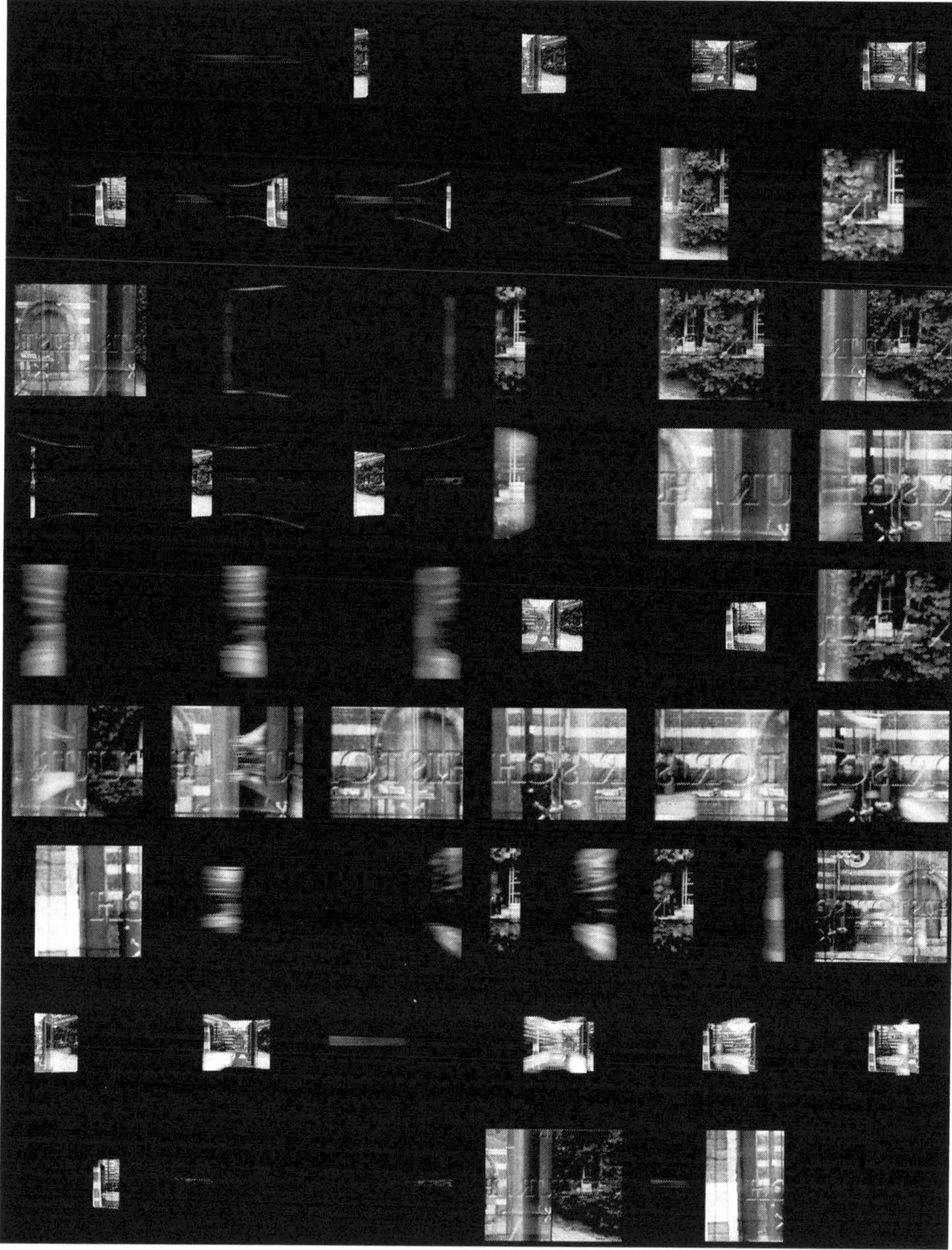

Figure 15: Storyboard version of Vince Dziekan, *Nature-History (ii. Writing with Light)* (2003). Digital animation. 5.00 min (loop).

ephemeral, virtual) served to locate the main photographic image – representing a moment of aesthetic contemplation in a Natural History Museum in Maastricht, Holland – at the fulcrum, the point of intersection, somewhere between latency and artefact, the fleetingness of everyday moments and their archival permanence as documents, immediate experience and memory – the 'hyphen' between nature and history. [*Figure 15*]

Inside a glass portico, a man and woman in respectful pose gaze down into a glass-encased crypt. Their attitudes are contrasting, reading as reverence on the one hand (the man's bowed head and clasped hands) and scepticism on the other (the woman's crossed arms). These figures are registered visually in the photograph by the cross-shaped architectural fitting that adorns the glass frontage of the gallery. The image involves a series of mirrorings that connect the artefact to its casing, the display to its viewers, the viewers in turn to their own glass-lined enclosure and this interior space to its external surrounds. A series of divisions occur across the surface of the image. Green ivy covers timeworn brickwork. Reflections on glass mix with details superimposed on the image surface. In contrast with this play of depth and surface, a closed arched doorway sits at centre of the image – a ghostly trace of a figure (the photographer's reflection) can barely be made out, standing alongside.

Acting as a motif of sorts throughout the piece, the image was subjected to further digital treatment. The photograph's presentation was simulated to represent a plaque, alluding in an intertextual manner to the work of Belgian artist Marcel Broodthaers. Emblazoned with text reading 'Natuur-Historisch', the surface effect of three-dimensionality was reinforced by its apparent embossing and translucence. In its object-based form as *Nature-History: i. Image/Object*, these surface effects lead to the viewer to read the images as mirrored *recto* and *verso* versions of the same image. This physical correlate was enhanced by the installation aspect of the work, and its presentation of the work as transparencies mounted to Perspex that are propped against the wall surface and illuminated by a fluorescent tube situated directly underneath. The associated time-based version (*Nature-History: ii. Writing with Light*) extended the image's manipulation through further distortion (convoluting the image as if it were wrapped across the inner surface of a drum) and animation (the image sweeps across the field of vision at different rates and proximity, creating a dizzying, vertiginous effect). The moving image implied a virtual circumference that was described by its trajectory across the gallery space, only revealing itself through the gap framed by the area of the projection surface. The resulting relationship of the artwork to gallery space was coincident, in the sense that the surface of projection was purposefully aligned with the wall of glass lining the length of the gallery's frontage. As a result, this instantiation of the work further convoluted the reading of interior and exterior. As the image moved across this field, its reading as inside/out or back-to-front alternated depending upon whether the viewer was situated in the gallery or their vantage was from the outside. [*Figure 16*]

Accompanying the projection piece shown in the context of gallery space was the presentation of a collection of images archived online. Just as the projection piece played with the frontier, the border space determining the gallery's interior from its exterior, so *Nature-History: iii. October 19, 2002 (Maastricht)* extended the work's narrativity and reading. The

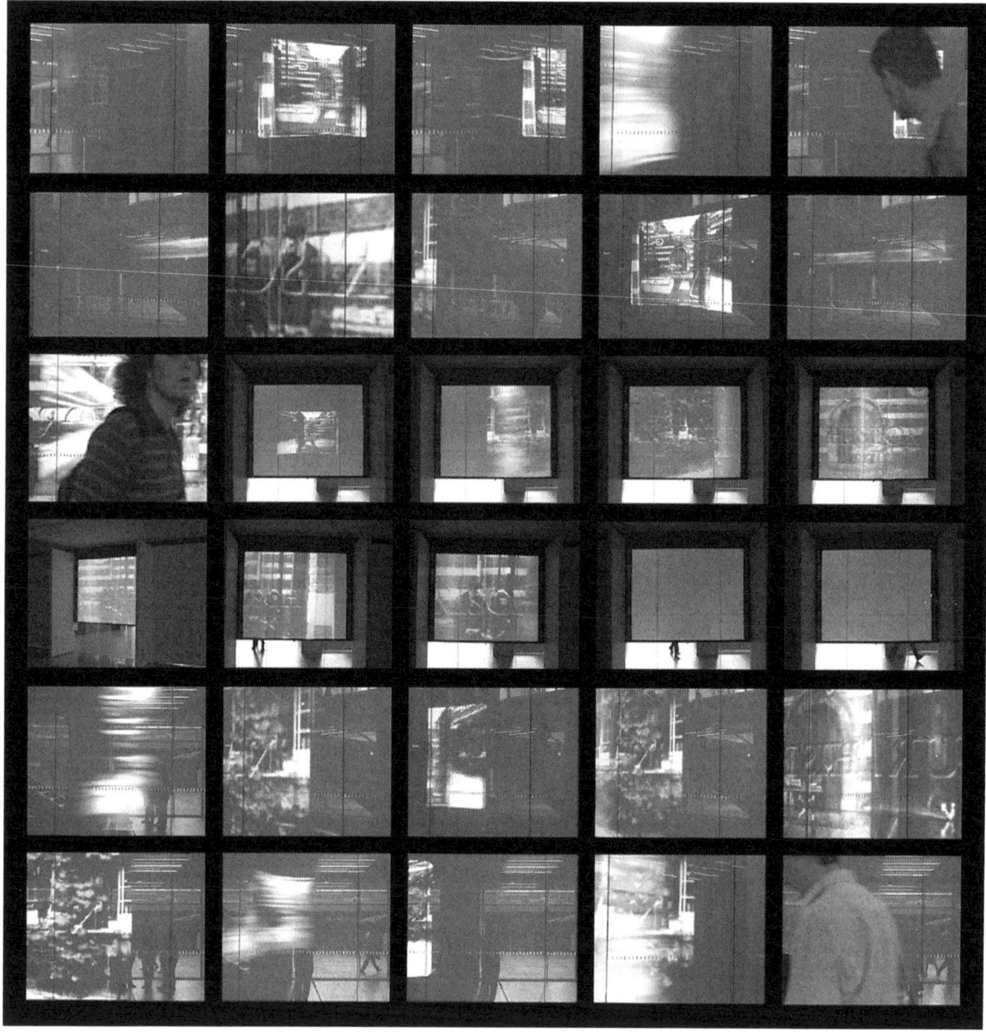

Figure 16: Installation views of Vince Dziekan, *Nature-History* (*ii. Writing with Light*) (*Small Worlds: A Romance*: Sydney, 2003). Digital animation. 5.00 min (loop). Variable installation (projection, viewable from front and rear).

virtual exhibition contextualised the main photographic motif used throughout by situating that particular image within an intertextual, pseudo-travelogue. Categorised as three sets of images, the work represented museum-based encounters contrasting viewing experience with 'behind-the-scenes' museological operations. Its centrepiece was the Natuur-historisch Museum Set, which involved the presentation of a room containing various natural specimens (stuffed swans and owls, legs of a horse) arranged in a manner associated with a classical European natural history museum. This selection of images contrasted markedly with the Bonnefantenmuseum Set, which presented candid documentation from the Bonnefantenmuseum in Maastricht and its collection archive related to Marcel Broodthaers and one of his most celebrated décors, *L'Entrée de l'Exposition* (*Exhibition Entrance*, 1974). Each set was organized into a series of self-contained collections. For the most part, these collections presented the means of accessing a series of still images that have been arranged in systematic fashion based on theme or location. Distinct from these images, three separate 'panoramas' presented QuickTime VR representations of various image scapes (tree-lined environ, museological room with wall-lined cupboards and taxidermy specimens, distorted exhibition space arranged with framed images and potted palms). These images located the visual experience within a cylindrical enclosure that could be explored through direct interaction by the viewer.

The suite of 36 images in total referenced the standard number of frames contained on a single roll of film. The images were categorised in a mock-archival fashion, with each assigned a file number and descriptive title. Upon closer detailed inspection of this cataloguing, the viewer would find that entry number 16 had been omitted from the list. Situated at the epicentre of this collected series of photographs, this missing entry referred back to the iconic image and the impossibility of reproducing its epiphanous moment of artistic revelation.

Descriptive 'Walkthrough' (for a Model Viewer)

The exhibition installation appears deceptively simple. [*Figure 17*] It may even seem initially that the gallery space is almost totally deserted. The room is eerily quiet and in the muted darkness of the unlit space, the walls appear bare. Only a centrally located seating unit surrounded on four sides by speaker stands indicate any presence in the otherwise empty room. But strangely, there is no sound emitted from within the space – only ambient noise and passing traffic in the building's concourse can be discerned at random intervals.

The sense of somehow having missed the exhibition (maybe the exhibition is still in a state of preparation or could it be in the process of being dismounted?) is soon dispelled as dissolving images slowly appear to emerge from the surfaces of the walls of the gallery. The subtlety of these visuals is in stark contrast to the disruption experienced as a loud, rumbling burst of sound fills the gallery. This shrill soundscape has the effect of totally enveloping the viewer in an acoustic cocoon. However, no sooner has it started than it jarringly halts and silence once again reigns.

Thus seduced into the exhibition environment, the viewer gravitates to what proves to be a focal position within the gallery arena. Having entered into this particular zone, the viewer's movements appear to be influencing an image found mounted to the side wall. As the only frame occupying this expanse of wall space, this screen slowly modulates a landscape scene. Richard Brown's *Mimesia* represents a simulated 3D landscape. Its visual character is reminiscent of the kind of virtual environment one finds in the context of a

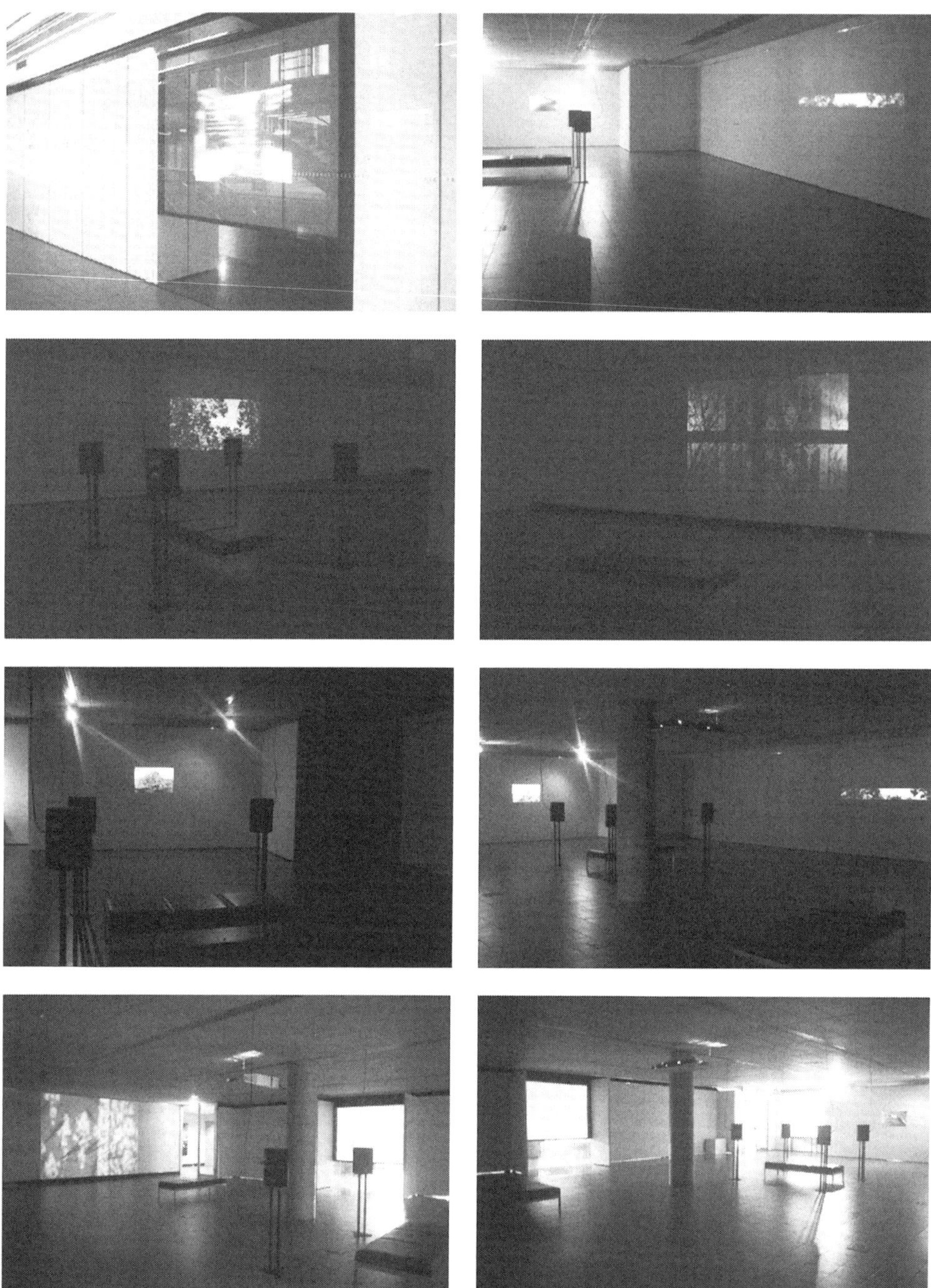

Figure 17: Installation view of *Small Worlds: A Romance* (UTS Gallery: Sydney, 2003). Featured works by Richard Brown, Csaba Czamosy, Bruce Mowson, Joel Zika and Vince Dziekan.

fantasy computer game. The image appears to taper and shift incrementally. The viewer soon comes to the realization that the image moves in concert with their own movement in the peripheral field or scope of the image itself (moving closer, the image appears to grow and more detail is revealed; moving laterally in front of the screen, the vantage onto the scene shifts in accordance).

The mesmerising effect of this interplay between viewer and virtual world is dispelled by the intrusion of the soundscape once again; their dreamlike dalliance is brought back to the reality, and they find themselves situated once again in the alien surrounds of the gallery itself.

Delving deeper into the exhibition space the viewer may choose to sit down on the seating provided in order to immerse him or herself within the soundscape designed by Bruce Mowson. This piece was custom designed by the sound artist to operate as the 'soundtrack' for the exhibition. Using sound recordings of hardware and fan noise produced by the processing of a computer, the composition is bracketed by expanses of silence that introduce a rhyming motif that relates the audio to the syncopated structure of the three moving image works playing in the far end of the gallery. The work was composed *in situ* during the period of the exhibition's installation.

The second half of the gallery presents three moving image pieces on three sides. All of these works are projected from the same focal point using a centrally located rig of ceiling-mounted projectors. Moving into this area, the viewer faces a large black-and-white projection that appears to emerge from the surface of the back wall of the gallery (Joel Zika's *The Presence #1*). To their immediate left, a thin narrow band of light grows to a full rectangular frame (Csaba Szamosy's *Tree Loops*). A canopy of leaves gently rustles before a horizontal 'wipe' effect narrows the image back to a thin line before it totally disappears.

Around to the opposite side, false walls have been erected to line the glass frontage of the gallery. These walls effectively black out the full interior. There is only one gap in the surface: a section has been extracted and a rear projection screen inserted. The screen occupies the upper portion of the aperture; below it the floor can be seen to continue out into the general thoroughfare.

A fleeting image blurs across the otherwise dark surface. This apparition appears again and continues to reappear at accelerating intervals. Likewise, the image grows, become larger and as a result more pictorial details can be discerned. Two other 'viewers' can be made out in this revolving scene. They appear to be located in a glass-enclosed space looking at something that, in turn, is interred in a glass case. The words 'Natuur' and 'Historisch' can be made out as the image sweeps past. This work, *Nature-History* defines the gallery's interior from its exterior. Viewable from both sides of the glass, its movement emphasises the image's fleeting coincidence with its viewing plane, the surface on which it appears before disappearing. Its arc of movement describes a circumference that reinforces the viewer's own position in relation to the screen and the gallery space more generally.

Throughout, while viewing this triptych of animated artworks the soundscape comes on without notice. Likewise, each of the moving images has their own cadence. The relative brevity of *Tree Loops* is compensated by its relatively frequent repetition. *The Presence*, in contrast, seems to fall into a lull and lingers on the surface. Its cinematic narrative plays itself out as a series of episodes framed by intervals of darkness acting as transitions. Meanwhile, *Nature-History* cycles incessantly, albeit at varying paces, slowing down before speeding up again. The images spiral forward, growing in size to fill the entire surface of the screen before shrinking back and appearing to sink into the impossible depth of the screen.

The sound of nothing reappears just as immediately.

Notes

1. The convenor of Tate's online programmes in 2006, Kelli Dipple, directed attention to my formulation of the *exhibition complex* in previous research to initiate discussion in the Tate's *Liquid Architectures* forum.
2. Sampling features in industrial or electronic music, which itself developed out of *musique concrète* (an avant-garde form of music pioneered in the 1940s that incorporates natural environmental sounds and other non-inherently-musical noises to create music). While commonly associated with DJ-ing, the use of 'samples' has become a familiar feature in much contemporary music.
3. *Gesamtkunstwerk* – from German meaning 'total' or 'complete artwork' – is used to describe the integration of multiple art forms. Attributed to the German opera composer Richard Wagner, *Gesamtkunstwerk* relates to how opera encompasses music, theatre and the visual arts. Wagner was known for his revolutionary use of lighting techniques and sound effects to focus the audience's attention. These effects were employed at the service of creating an immersive experience of the imaginary world of the musical drama.
4. The italicized phrase references Joseph Addison's 'Essay on the Pleasures of the Imagination' cited in de Botton (2002, p. 165).
5. The italicized phrase is drawn from Jacques Derrida's (1987), 'The Parergon'.
6. *Zero Light*, CSA Gallery, Australian National University, Canberra (10 October – 2 November 2003), curated by Peter Fitzpatrick. The exhibition included works by 11 international artists inspired by the principle of 'zero light' – involving experimental research into photon science anticipating the development of teleportation and extended space travel – through video projection, photography and other light-generating artworks.

Chapter 9

Remote

Synopsis

This chapter provides an overview of the *Remote* exhibition, with a particular focus on selected artworks and their distributed properties. Reflective analysis relating to the curatorial theme (digital aesthetics associated with the transmitted image) and curatorial design (distributed spatial practice) are broached. An outline of the studio practice involved in realising the exhibition details the production of an artwork (*V. Travels in the Netherworld*) along with the creative production of the exhibition's scenography. This discussion is complimented by critical expansion in the form of the curator's essay, which contextualises the digital mediation associated with the 'tele-image'. In addition, practice-based considerations involved in my curatorial design of the exhibition will be discussed through case studies that detail how key works in the inventory were incorporated into the exhibition's 'itinerary'.

As a case study, the exhibition project demonstrates the influence that the digital has had on matters involving curatorial design and ways of dimensioning of the exhibition form itself. Through the applied practice of curatorial design – and its concentration on the ecological complex of relations that are synthesised by the exhibition form – the virtuality associated with the digital media is given expression.

Curatorial Philosophy

By recognising the close relation that coincided in the mid-nineteenth century between the invention of photography and advances in instantaneous telecommunications, the set of curatorial themes for *Remote* were developed as a means of focusing on the aesthetics associated with digital images that are mediated through forms of transmission. As a result, the curatorial philosophy used the medium of exhibition to give expression to the paradoxical relationship between proximity and distance. Amongst the earliest applications of the then-new technological process of photography, it involved the recording of images of exotic or uncharted places. Documented by intrepid photographers on scientific, archaeological or anthropological expeditions, these otherwise remote locales were subsequently made available to a geographically distributed audience by drawing upon the medium's own capacity to capture, collect and disseminate such scenes, thereby transporting the viewer of these images imaginatively to a vast array of otherwise distant times and places.

Illustratively, the correspondence between the earliest beginnings of photography with contemporary aesthetic considerations related to the digital image today was encapsulated for me by a fortuitous encounter with a deceptively innocuous work produced by British artist Chris Meigh-Andrews as part of a series of site-specific installations commissioned by the Victoria and Albert Museum between May 2002 and March 2003. The focal point of this small arrangement of sundry artefacts associated with early photographic technology was an original copy of William Henry Fox Talbot's book, *The Pencil of Nature*. It was there, in an unassuming side gallery adjacent to this otherwise stock standard cabinet-encased display, that I came unexpectedly upon a digital projection of an oriel window of the type immortalised by Fox Talbot in his earliest photographs dating back to August 1835. At first, it was easy to dismiss this fleeting projection as a case of the afternoon light being cast through the windows lining the length of this narrow gallery. Upon closer inspection, however, the shadow play seemed to uncannily re-enact the exact characteristics of this famous photographic image. To refer to this digital image as a representation is descriptively inadequate in that the image gently playing on the wall surface that I was standing before involved the direct transmission of the actual light passing at that very moment, not through the windows in the very room in which I found myself, but through the windows of Lacock Abbey in Wiltshire, near Bath in the west of England. Titled, *For William Henry Fox Talbot (The Pencil of Nature)*, the work entailed the production of an exact re-composition of Fox Talbot's famous 'photogenic drawing' captured by a solar-powered digital camera and relayed 'live' via an ISDN phone line to the gallery in South Kensington, where it was presented at actual size and in 'real time'. Besides connecting these two geographically separate sites, Meigh-Andrews' work staged, through its uninterrupted image-flow, the connection that history maintains with the present, while also reasserting photography's origin as light (the image being the memory of light's act of writing, recalling Joseph Nicephore Niepce's earlier assignment of the term *heliography* to the medium).

As will become apparent through my discussion of the curatorial design involved in the *Remote* exhibition, this confluence was explored in a reciprocal direction by drawing upon the distinct qualities of online practices and adapting them to an offline application. How the digital contents of the selected works translated into real space informed the overarching exhibition plan. Acknowledging the hybrid character of this practice, and in response to the increasing infiltration of digital technologies shaping this field, the exhibition's 'cybridised' nature offered a new frontier for artistic and curatorial practice. The exhibition project was directly set out to explore the potential of this approach.

As a result, a strategy for how the curatorial philosophy would be realised was determined by designing how a series of different works would be both accommodated by their nominated physical sites and enacted through the context of the exhibition. My earliest curatorial concepts – developed during an intensive, onsite residency – recognised the potential for developing an expanded exhibition that would be realised through a combination of gallery-based installation and other modes of presentation enabling onsite/ offsite and online/offline dynamics to be negotiated. By recognising that the exhibition need not be restricted, delimited or bounded by the spatial domain of the gallery, the possibilities presented for its curation were extended significantly.

In the context of site-specificity and its challenge to the conception of the art object, unity is not to be found in the reductive idealisation of form. Rather, in the contemporary technologised context that gives rise to distributed aesthetics, the artwork emerges *from*; it is a formative by-product of how techno-social networks are involved in the relay and dispersal of meaningful experiences through interaction with media and communications. The relevance of a distributed aesthetics approach might then be effectively summarised as:

> A continuous emergent project, situated somewhere between the drift away from coherent form and the drift of aesthetics into relations with new formations, including social (networked) formations (Munster and Lovink 2005).

This allusion to drift can be likened to the slippery transitions involved in mediating between real and virtual, and is recognised in the relationship between architectural space and narrative. Drawing upon the enduring influence of the architectural design of processional passage through space, media artist Mark Meadows has developed this perspective as the basis of how architecture and interactive narrative share similar principles of interaction:

Architecture might be said to be interactive because, if designed for such, it allows visitors to participate in the key steps of interactivity: observation, exploration, modification and reciprocal change. (2003, p. 174)

Remote addressed the interface of informatic and physical spaces by not restricting the exhibition to the confines of the gallery itself. The artworks in *Remote* were assembled through the exhibition's connective tissue, which induced the experience and encounter with art dispersed across a broader ecology of spaces. Artworks were treated as 'nested' episodes or events within a larger, distributed set of relations.

As mentioned earlier, the paradoxical interplay between distance and proximity underpinned the thematic rationale of the exhibition. The curatorial design involved in developing the exhibition's particular spatial attributes realised this thematic through effecting the contiguous meeting of different times and places across a range of physical spaces including, but not exclusively restricted to, the conventional gallery space. For while *transcription* involves technological mediation – which in this case directly involved artworks that employ digital media and the application of multimedia communications, such as web streaming, and technologies such as GPS systems – the exhibition of these new media works also involved a translation of digital contents into real space in what otherwise might be described as a *transposition* of virtual spaces into (and – as in the case of the artwork contributed by Pete Gomes that will be illustrated shortly – *onto*) a subset of selected physical environments. The translation involved in distributing (locating, positioning) the selected inventory of artworks within the parameters established as exhibition space commingled both syntactical and site-specific tendencies. As argued by Nick Kaye in his discussion of site-specific art:

If one accepts the proposition that the meanings of utterances, actions and events are affected by their 'local position', by the situation of which they are a part, then a work of art, too, will be defined in relation to its place and position. (2000, p. 1)

The remainder of this chapter describes how curatorial design induced the exploration of art across this broader ecology of spaces and negotiated the tension between virtuality and site-specificity by taking into account the subset of conditions that are aggregated through the exhibition.

Applied Curatorial Design

Conceived and expressed through the medium of the exhibition, *Remote* is characterised first and foremost by its distributed form. Its distinctive *scenography* draws upon the particular characteristics of the Plimsoll Gallery, found at the University of Tasmania's waterfront campus in Hobart, and its local environment, incorporating them into the overall sweep of the expanded exhibition.

Crucially, the processes involved in curatorial selection and exhibition design – conventionally operating as separate, asynchronous stages in the project development process – were synthesised as part of the curatorial design approach. Preliminary research and development was facilitated directly by a curatorial residency organised by the Plimsoll Gallery and the Tasmanian School of Art at the University of Tasmania.[1] With regards to the selection process, the nature of the project offered the possibility of innovatively including 'local' Tasmania-based practitioners with 'remote' artists.[2] In an effort to compile an inventory through which a globalised view or zeitgeist could be sensed, it was my curatorial intent that the represented artists and their works would effectively blur the boundaries of location and acknowledge the liminality of borders in the digital age.

The curatorial design of *Remote* sought to engage the viewer with different ways and means through which the network, broadly understood, functions in determining the increasingly dispersed contours of art and aesthetics. The exhibition form was called upon to provide the infrastructure that locates the viewer simultaneously at the juncture and disjunction of here and there, structuring an experience of being dispersed between informatic and physical space. In so doing, the distributed spatial practice demonstrated through its curatorial design process addressed the paradoxical conditions of digitally-mediated experiences: experiences that are simultaneously dispersed and situated, that combine synchronous and asynchronous features that take place (somewhere, sometime) across a continuum of real and virtual spaces.

The works exhibited employed digital media in a variety of forms, with an emphasis upon screen and projection-based moving image work, webcast transmissions, site-specific interventions and locative media that drew upon or referenced televisual media and the application of tele-communications and global positioning systems. While a sub-set of the inventory would still occupy gallery space and exercise its language and potentials, these particular works effectively used the gallery in a more instrumental way – as a node in a wider network – by connecting dispersed, networked and superimposed components back to that space. Employing the gallery more instrumentally meant that artworks could be 'delivered' from the gallery but encountered and viewed in or through a number of supplementary, annexed spaces. Instead, the exhibition environment was expanded to include artworks that are made accessible in a variety of settings or situations spanning both the ground and first-floor levels of the Centre for the Arts building. Supporting the idea of the exhibition as 'itinerary', the audience/visitor was encouraged to explore 'other' spaces, including transit spaces such as the reception area and foyer and external environments such as the garden enclosure and courtyard. Because this strategy opened up the possibility of a multiplicity of entry points, there was no single, linear route through the exhibition.

The curatorial design process mediates the way in which a work is translated as part of its resulting exposition. These factors span the range of considerations occurring at the level of the exhibition between artwork, gallery and museum through what I have described as art's 'exhibition complex'. By way of explication:

Artwork – Formal concerns are defined as the design pre-conditions existing within the construct of the artwork itself.

Gallery – At the next level, architectural considerations involve transposing the formal qualities of the artefact to the particular attributes of the physical environment (such as the way the space itself functions, lighting conditions, surface characteristics, and scale). Related to this, spatial composition addresses the arrangement of elements or components that make up the artwork within the immediate architectural setting of its display.

Museum – Beyond this kind of design-based decision-making, the work's contextualisation within the larger context of the exhibition is negotiated by interfacing between the formal properties of the artefact or architectural conditions of gallery space and the set of spatio-temporal relations occurring within museological space. At this level factors influencing and guiding the spatial translation of the curatorial philosophy are addressed through the form of the exhibition. Aligned with these conceptual concerns are higher-level dialectical objectives expressed through the act of exposition, such as design strategies pertaining to context, exhibition design and resulting scenographic effects.

As mentioned previously, the guiding curatorial trope of *Remote* involved transforming the installation through distributed spatial practice into an itinerary. Fundamentally, this conceptual shift drew attention to the contingent nature of the artworks presented. It also placed added emphasis upon the active agency of the individual viewer. By encouraging the exploration of other spaces besides conventionally assigned gallery space, the peregrine quality of wandering or travelling was actualised through the organisation of the exhibition. The distribution of artworks across a widened range of locations enabled them to operate, in effect, as nodal points of reference that collectively would come to define the exhibition proper.

As will become apparent in the following discussion, the curatorial design process mediates the way in which an artwork is transposed under exhibition conditions. The cases of Pete Gomes' *Littoral Map (Tasmania)* and Derek Hart's *A Maravilha do Rio de Janeiro* offer effective illustrations of how the complex of relations that interconnect artwork, gallery and museum were negotiated as part of the curatorial design process applied to the *Remote* exhibition. As the installation of the locative media work developed in collaboration with London-based artist Pete Gomes demonstrates, site-specificity not only entails an artwork's relation to its particular physical site, but also its context (at a micro-level through its own mixed media and multimodal organisation, and at a macro-level by the encompassing exhibition).

The work under discussion is representative of Gomes' ongoing performative utilisation of GPS technology. The genesis of *Littoral Map* drew its inspiration from the artist's pre-visualisation of a tract of Madagascar coastline and its superimposition over the local precinct in Hobart in which it was to be transposed.[3] [*Figure 18*] This particular iteration

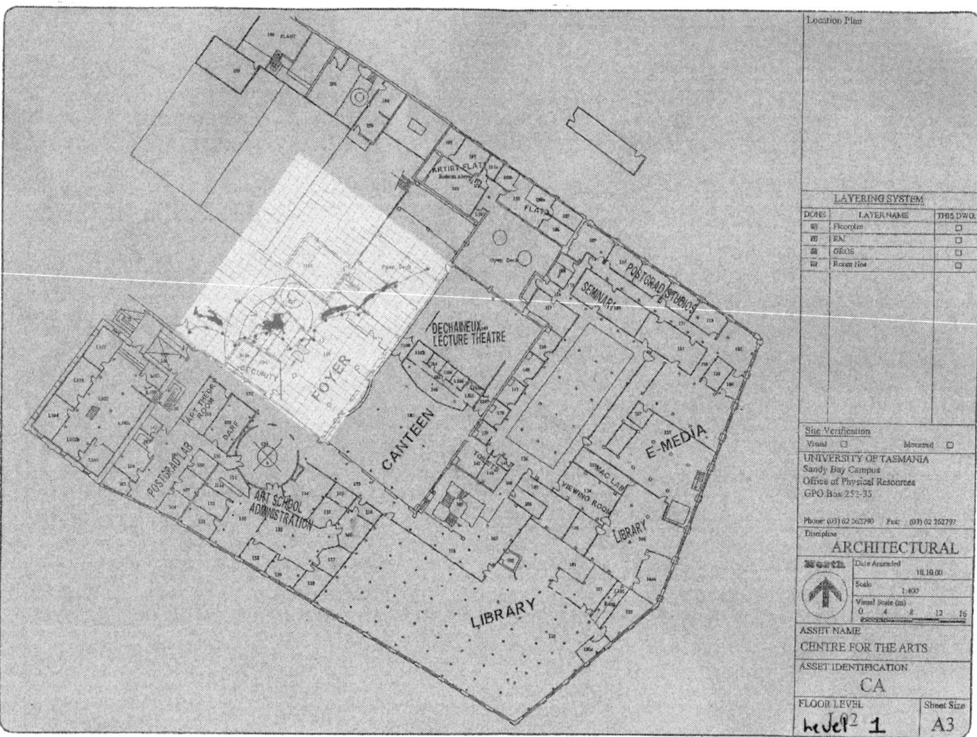

Figure 18: Transposition for Pete Gomes, *Littoral Map* (*Tasmania*) (Plimsoll Gallery: Hobart, 2006).

of the work employed a distinctive *multi*-media approach, with its centrepiece situated in the main entrance foyer of the Centre for the Arts. In this bustling public space, a series of four large prints were mounted into window recesses that line a glass wall opening onto an external courtyard. Upon closer inspection, these works presented a series of maps representing the island of Madagascar. Increasingly magnified details focused attention to a coastal area of littoral forest in southern Madagascar with the final frame superimposing this coastline over a floor plan of the Centre for the Arts.

To the right of this main arrangement – which is informed by the familiar language associated with information display – photocopied printouts found on a low podium offered information about the mineral ilmenite and its use in the production of titanium dioxide. Discernible through the adjacent set of access doors, the sound of assorted bird and animal calls filled the exterior courtyard. Blending in with the atmosphere of local sounds – ranging from seabirds to the sound of local heavy industry, plus conversations taking place in the social space frequented by staff and students of the art school – this soundscape leaked into the interior whenever traffic passed through the doorway.

At floor level, a white chalk line ran continuously from the exterior courtyard, coursed through the foyer and cascaded down the main staircase into the plaza below. The drawing directly transposed geographic coordinates of southern Madagascar onto these locations using chalk and toothpaste (in reference to the use of titanium dioxide as a whitening material found in paints, food and many toothpastes). Both ends of this path were exposed to the elements. The path itself was impermanent and eventually 'washed away' as a consequence of being exposed to Hobart's winter weather. As a result, over time only ephemeral tracings were left *in situ* to record the line and its marking of coordinates, whose notations indicated the GPS positioning of a series of selected points tracing the contour of the Madagascar coastline with that of the exact location of the Centre for the Arts.

Gomes' *Littoral Map* was thus assembled through the connective tissue of the exhibition. When its dispersed and apparently unrelated elements were actualised by the continuous chalk line that wove its way over, across and through a variety of sites, the work's resulting effect was put to the service of visualising the invisible streams of information that pervade, permeate and envelope any geo-political sense of the interconnection of local and global spaces.

Turning attention next to the redevelopment of Derek Hart's *A Maravilha do Rio de Janeiro*: the main expression of this project involved its distillation into a single-channel video piece that presented a linear series of aerial sequences of the six most popular scenic locations in Rio edited from footage shot by helicopter under direction of the artist. This re-enactment was inspired by an original television survey and feature produced by Brazilian TV of the same name – which translates as 'the marvel (or wonder) of Rio de Janeiro'. The artist initially conceived of the work as six separate projections. Presenting the locations simultaneously in this way would allow the work to be understood more directly as a continuation of the original survey in which viewers were able to participate by registering votes. For *Remote*, however, a single-screen projection version was produced to show the six locations in the hierarchical order of the results of the public survey. This decision was determined by installation considerations and presented a new challenge for the artist to interpret the work in a generously apportioned space using a ceiling-mounted projector and hanging screen. With this mode of presentation, the work's more implicit social commentary was not as pronounced. Rather, by adapting to the context of the show, the artistic focus was trained on the continuum of spatial relationships proceeding from artwork to gallery space, from virtual image to more phenomenological, sensory experience, wherein the helicopter's perspective became a body with vision suspended in the air, manoeuvring in a space shared with the viewer.

This way of screening the work warranted a revised exploration of the artist's project to determine the most effective mode of presentation, projection method and technique. This reconsideration extended to other dimensions of the project that would not normally be immediately available to the viewer, and renegotiating these features helped contextualise the overarching socio-cultural aspect of the artistic project. They included selected sequences originally screened on television and the uninterrupted source recording of the helicopter's entire flight. Both of these aspects of the work were more fully integrated as a result of the artist and curator entering into a process of collaborative development, which led to the work adopting a distributed model of exposition. Ultimately, it was decided to present the work as three distinct episodes in three different locations situated across the exhibition site. As already indicated, in the first place, the original video artwork was presented as a projection in gallery setting. Secondly, the actual television feature as shown on *TV Globo* was screened in the gallery's reception foyer. Finally, a monitor-based installation was situated in the main public area of the Centre for the Arts showing extracted 'outtakes' from the flight path over one of Rio's notorious *favelas*, or shanty towns.

The work's translation through curatorial design can be summarised by outlining a number of factors that were negotiated in response to its exhibition complex:

Artwork – Formally, *A Maravilha do Rio de Janeiro* adopted the contentions associated with a screen-based video artwork. Projection method was used in its gallery installation, whereas monitor-based screening was used for the non-gallery iterations developed for *Remote*. With respect to this presentation method, aesthetic considerations were employed in determining the appropriate type and character of hardware and plinths used. As an audio/visual artwork, sound plays a key role. In this case, the sound varies from Portuguese soundtrack drawn from the repurposed television footage to ambient sound recordings sourced from the raw footage captured by helicopter.

Gallery – Transposing the work to the gallery space entailed three separate installations presented across both controlled and uncontrolled environments. In each case, the design qualities and functions of the space were addressed. This involved positioning the artwork in relation to its wall/backdrop in the main foyer for maximal effect. The placement of the monitor adjacent to the gallery entrance effectively framed the entrance to the gallery proper. The most aestheticised response involved determining the optimum aspect and vantage to the hanging projection screen for its gallery-based installation. These architectural considerations sought to maximise the potential of each species of space (i.e. exhibition gallery, social or public spaces).

In representational terms, each of the three works was tailored to the characteristics of their respective exhibition space. As case in point, the black box setting for the projection of aerial footage framed the most aesthetic part of the work. Projected onto a suspended screen situated in the centre of a larger, empty cubic space, this content was presented in a manner which utilised the preconditions of the gallery space itself to support its reading as a moving image artwork. This highly aestheticised presentation was further amplified by contrasting its character with that of its two companion pieces, which were both displayed in non-gallery spaces in conventional manners associated with a more general form of public address or 'infotainment'. Representationally, the quality of the sound component of the gallery-based projection was purely atmospheric and emotive, in contrast to the narrative voice-over of the piece immediately outside the gallery, which connoted the presentation of information.

Played back in Portuguese, this soundscape transformed its apparent descriptive content into unintelligible 'noise'.

Museum – The higher-level concerns of exhibition space are most clearly aligned with conceptual and dialectical objectives. Expressed through the act of exposition, these design strategies pertain to context, exhibition design and resulting scenographic effects. Dialectical considerations involved the application of various codes that influenced the interpretive reading along with factors determining viewer engagement with the work. For example, the resulting adaptation of *A Maravilha do Rio de Janeiro* drew upon a combination of both art/non-art and gallery/non-gallery conventions by presenting the work across mixed environments. For its part, the exhibition design operated as a multi-dimensional montage whose cumulative effect led to an enhanced, composite reading of the artwork. Through the spatial distribution of the three individuated episodes, relational connections were made across spatial divisions and contrasting types of spaces. The viewing order or sequence in which these self-contained iterations are encountered was variable. As a result, meaning was subjected to a more open reading or interpretation.

Museological and non-museological codes were juxtaposed. For example, the decision to display the video artwork as a hovering projection in the potentially boundless, expansive darkness of gallery space heightened the auratic qualities of the gallery-based presentation. This installation's aestheticisation was in stark contrast to the monitor display presented at the entrance to the gallery. Complete with voice-over narration, the presentation of the appropriated television featurette offered a didactic, informational supplement that confused the boundary between waiting room and gallery space. Prominently located immediately outside the main gallery entrance, the visual language associated with infotainment (accompanied by Portuguese voice-over which reinforced this reading purely by tone of voice alone) provided a disconcerting entrée to the exhibition galleries.

Finally, the exhibition scenography exerted its own contextual effects. In particular, the insertion of monitor and plinth display in the central foyer of the Centre for the Arts that presented the eerily suspended recording of a Brazilian *favela* or shanty town. A number of infamous *favelas* exist in Rio de Janeiro, even though the city itself does not legally recognise their existence. The artist's decision to present footage captured while flying over a *favela* during the filmed re-enactment of *A Maravilha do Rio de Janeiro* (which ostensibly focused on the most popular, iconic and picturesque locations of the city) introduced a form of social commentary to the work. This aerial footage was echoed by the viewer's experience of actually having ascended staircases from either the main public plaza or the lower gallery level.

In the context of these collected elements, the viewer must be prepared to be an active contributor to the work. First, this takes an immediate participatory form via the viewer's mobility. Second, once each of the distinct instances of the work has been encountered, the viewer must be capable of reassembling these spatially and temporally separated instances into an aggregated narrative whole. Overall, the viewer's appreciation and understanding of the artist's conception is elaborated incrementally by every new encounter with each successive episodic component.

The customization of these specific artworks for *Remote* as multimodal, distributed artworks can be appreciated as a means to direct and focus the exploration of networked spatial practice. Designed to explore the dimensionality of different places and times, both *Littoral Map* and *Maravilha do Rio de Janeiro's* hyperlinking and cross-referencing between separate but connected locales contributed to the transformation of the overall exhibition experience from its conventional installation in a distinct, enclosed, and clearly defined space. Instead by using the gallery itself more instrumentally to provide nodal meeting points in a wider network, their dispersed, interconnected, and superimposed components were connected back to that space. These representative works promoted the mobility and agency of the viewer by linking distributed media contents and situating their respective narratives across the exhibition's wider ecosystem.

Summary

The project's curatorial philosophy focused on the aesthetics associated with digital images that are mediated through forms of transmission. How the digital contents of such works could be translated into real space informed the overarching exhibition plan. Research and development led to the conception of an expanded exhibition in which the selected artworks would enter into a dialectical relation with their nominated physical sites and be enacted through a dialogical process framed by the context of the exhibition.

The curatorial design process was used to mediate the way in which each work was translated as part of its resulting exposition, taking into account ecological factors occurring at the exhibition level between artwork, gallery and museum. The guiding curatorial trope of *Remote* transformed the installation through distributed spatial practice into an itinerary. Fundamentally, this conceptual shift was designed to draw attention to the contingent nature of the artworks presented. It also placed added emphasis upon mobilising and promoting the active agency of the individual viewer.

The artworks in *Remote* were assembled through the exhibition's connective tissue. This approach – illustrated by the locative artwork that I designed specifically for this purpose, *V. Travels in the Netherworld*, and the collaborative redevelopment of key works tailored specifically to capitalise on their conditions of exhibition – encouraged the experience and encounter of art dispersed across a broader ecology of spaces.

By not restricting the exhibition to the confines of the gallery itself, *Remote* addressed the interface of informatic and physical spaces. The distributed spatial practice demonstrated through its curatorial design process illustrates the paradoxical conditions of digitally-mediated experiences.

Documentation

Artwork – Vince Dziekan, *V. Travels in the Netherworld*

The production of an artwork designed especially for *Remote* was seen as a way of inducing the viewer to explore the unconventional range of spaces that the exhibition would occupy. *V. Travels in The Netherworld* (1890–2006) afforded me the opportunity to apply emerging portable technologies for artistic purpose. The prototype version of *V. Travels in the Netherworld* ran exclusively from a handheld device (HP iPAQ hx4700 series Pocket PC) that was made available during the exhibition. [*Figure 19*] The device contained media contents comprised of five moving image sequences designed especially for small-screen display. Each of these short episodes were 'tagged' to one of five specific locations distributed across the University of Tasmania's Centre for the Arts. These locations were identified by graphic markers left in a particular locale, situation or context. Each marker coincided with a nominated piece of media intended to be launched by the viewer by navigating the PDA's straightforward graphical user interface.

The work promoted the mobility and agency of the viewer by cross-referencing media contents contained on a handheld PDA with a series of location markers found within the immediate proximity of the gallery. Alluding to the conventional role of a Gallery Guide, the psycho-geographic relation between these different real and virtual spaces was suggested

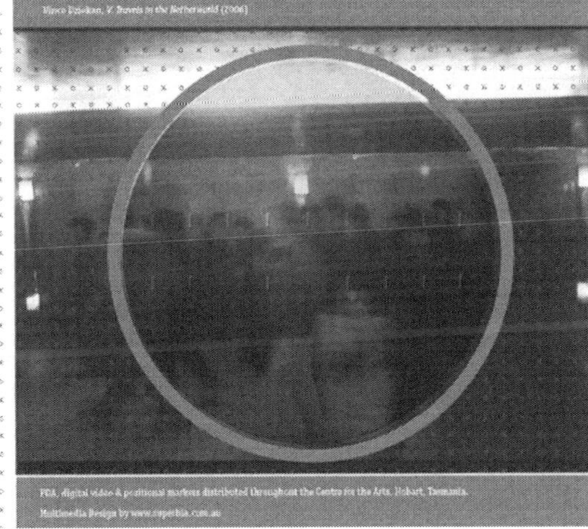

Figure 19: Interface designs for Vince Dziekan, *V. Travels in the Netherworld* (1890–2006). Digital imaging. Interface design: 320 x 240 pixels.

by the convergence of representational content with the place-based context in which these episodes were to be encountered. [*Figure 20*]

The media content was presented as short, episodic scenarios, variously portraying the movement of crowds against dark, subterranean backdrops. The media production drew principally upon video footage captured during Chinese New Year celebrations in Shanghai, China. Footage for two scenes (*IrisWall* and *StillLife*) was drawn from an underground pedestrian thoroughfare lined with backlit 'wallpaper' representing familiar motifs from the oeuvre of Vincent van Gogh, such as sunflowers and iris fields. The paired *TimeTravel* sequences offered two different 'first-person' views of propelled movement through a disconcertingly illuminated tunnel. In the first version, an uninterrupted view heightens the vertiginous quality of the abstract pulsing choreography of lights and lasers, whereas in the second, the vantage is masked by the profiles of two other onlookers. *GirlStar* contrasts with the fixed camera perspectives of these pieces by presenting a telescoping view that moves in towards its main subject – a girl caught in the midst of a surging night-time crowd wearing a flashing star-shaped brooch – before zooming back out, losing her back into the passing

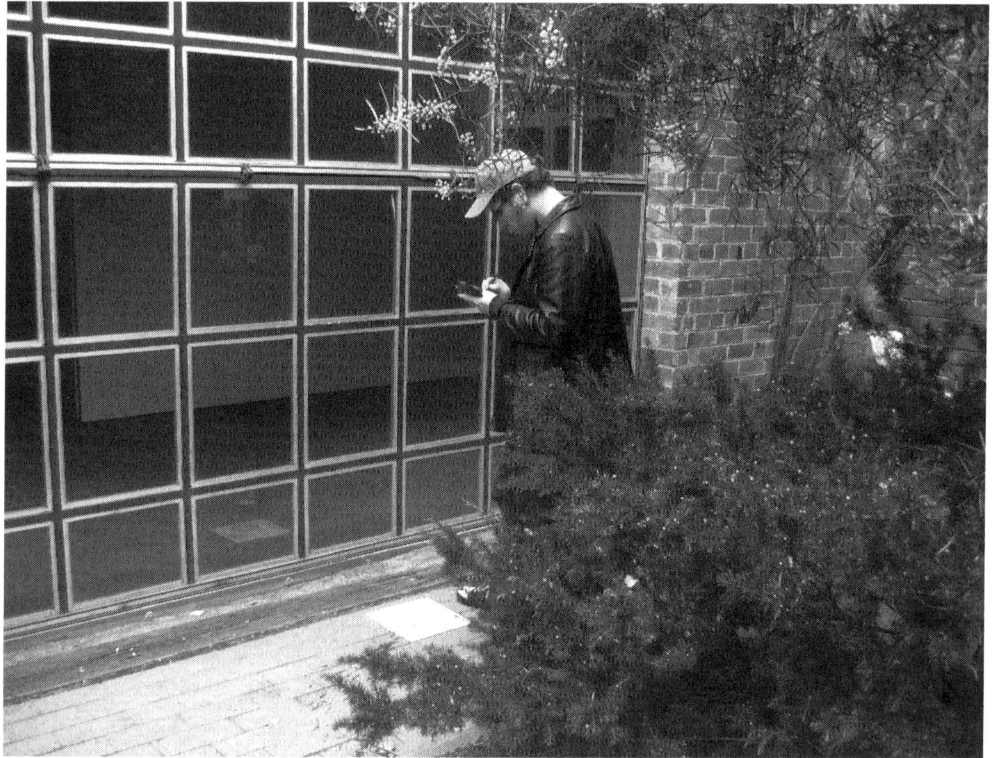

Figure 20: Installation view of *Vince Dziekan, V. Travels in the Netherworld* (Remote: Hobart, 2006). Mixed/locative media: PDA, digital content, graphic markers. Variable/site-specific installation.

crowd. The imagery was subjected to digital manipulation that heightened their dreamlike qualities through employing a combination of distortion (giving the appearance of a lens-affected view) and framing effects (scenes are viewed through the aperture of a round portal). Each piece explores different viewing experiences mediated by the camera's eye: fixed and situated in a flat frontal position exaggerates the 'sleepwalking' of pedestrians passing laterally across the picture plane (*IrisWall* and *StillLife*), being simultaneously stationary but transported through advancing and receding spaces (*TimeTravel 1 & 2*), or projecting into and out of its imaginary scene *(GirlStar)*. [*Figure 21*] Stop-frame animation was employed to propel the action at a slightly arrested, syncopated rate, and editing was used in numerous instances to loop and repeat certain frames, inducing further disorientation.

The nominated locations that the viewer was required to locate before activating the assigned media content were identified by a series of graphic markers. Numbered (1) through (5), each small adhesive panel contained additional text/graphic content, alluding to the 'chrono-graphic' diagram that adorned the cover screen of the mobile device. While apparently didactic in content, the role of this text/graphic content found on each locational marker was as much allusive as elusive. In each case, the juxtaposed informational content was intended to add a further contextual dimension to the viewer's interpretation. Visually designed to reference a graphical readout connoting a band of sweeping radar, the content of these markers related variously to the stratification of the Earth's geological core and outer atmosphere, references to elements and forces, and cities and towns identified with various stages of Vincent van Gogh's artistic career.

These markers were situated in a variety of locations. Distributed throughout the Centre for the Arts complex, they were positioned strategically, in the first instance, to establish the nominated setting for the viewing of the mobile media content. These viewing situations challenged the ideal of a properly contemplative viewing experience by instead embedding the aesthetic experience of the work in the midst of real, social space. These positions were found in non-conventional settings for viewing art (such as immediately outside the gallery in a small garden enclosure or in transitional spaces or 'passages' such as doorways and staircases).

More insidiously however, they effectively drew the viewer who was following the predetermined course of this work unknowingly through the expanded exhibition environment. As such, they were brought unwittingly into contact with other works that they may otherwise overlook or not 'connect' with the exhibition.

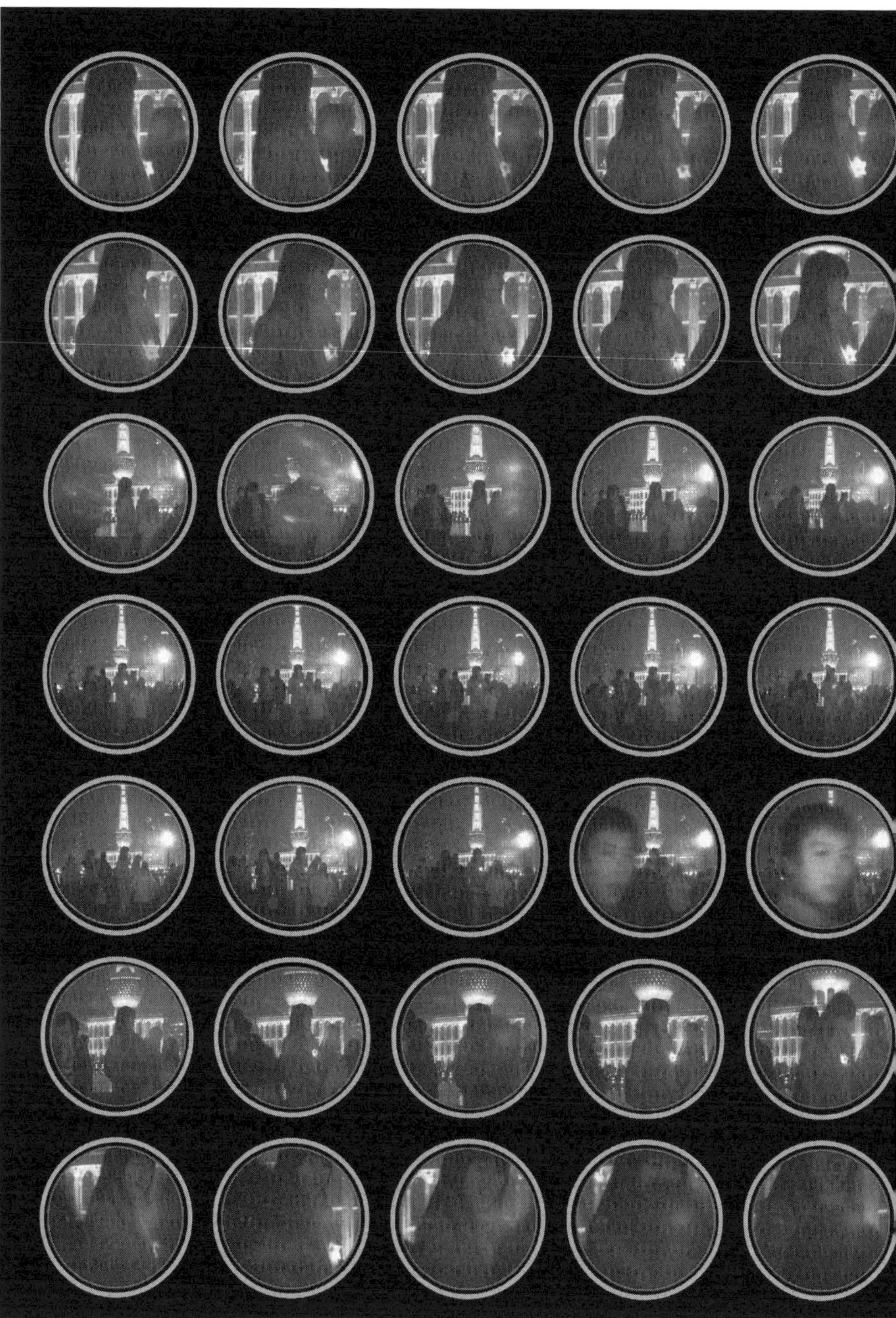

Figure 21: Vince Dziekan, *V. Travels in the Netherworld – GirlStar* (1890–2006). Digital animation, 2.00 min (loop), 320 × 240 pixels.

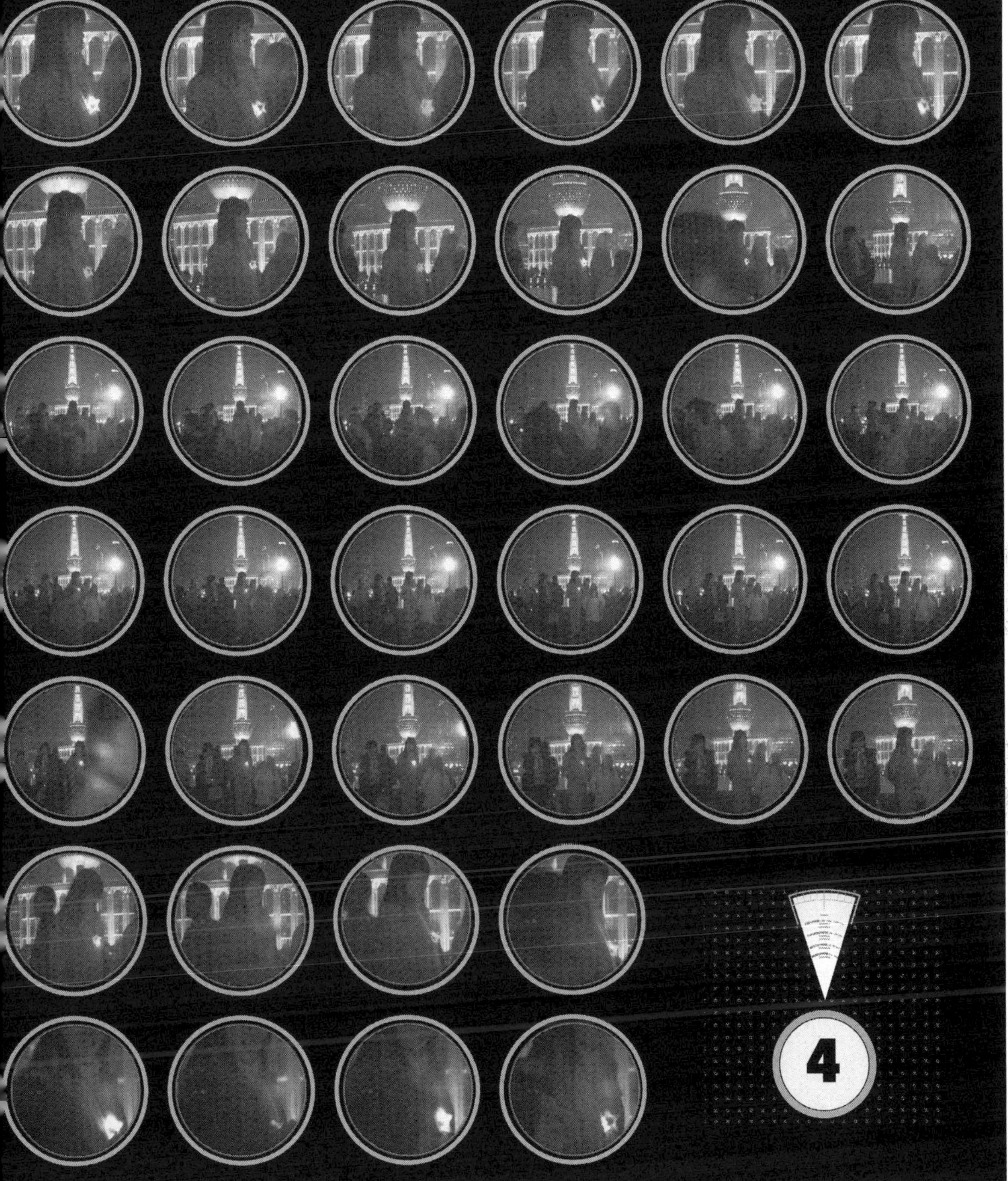

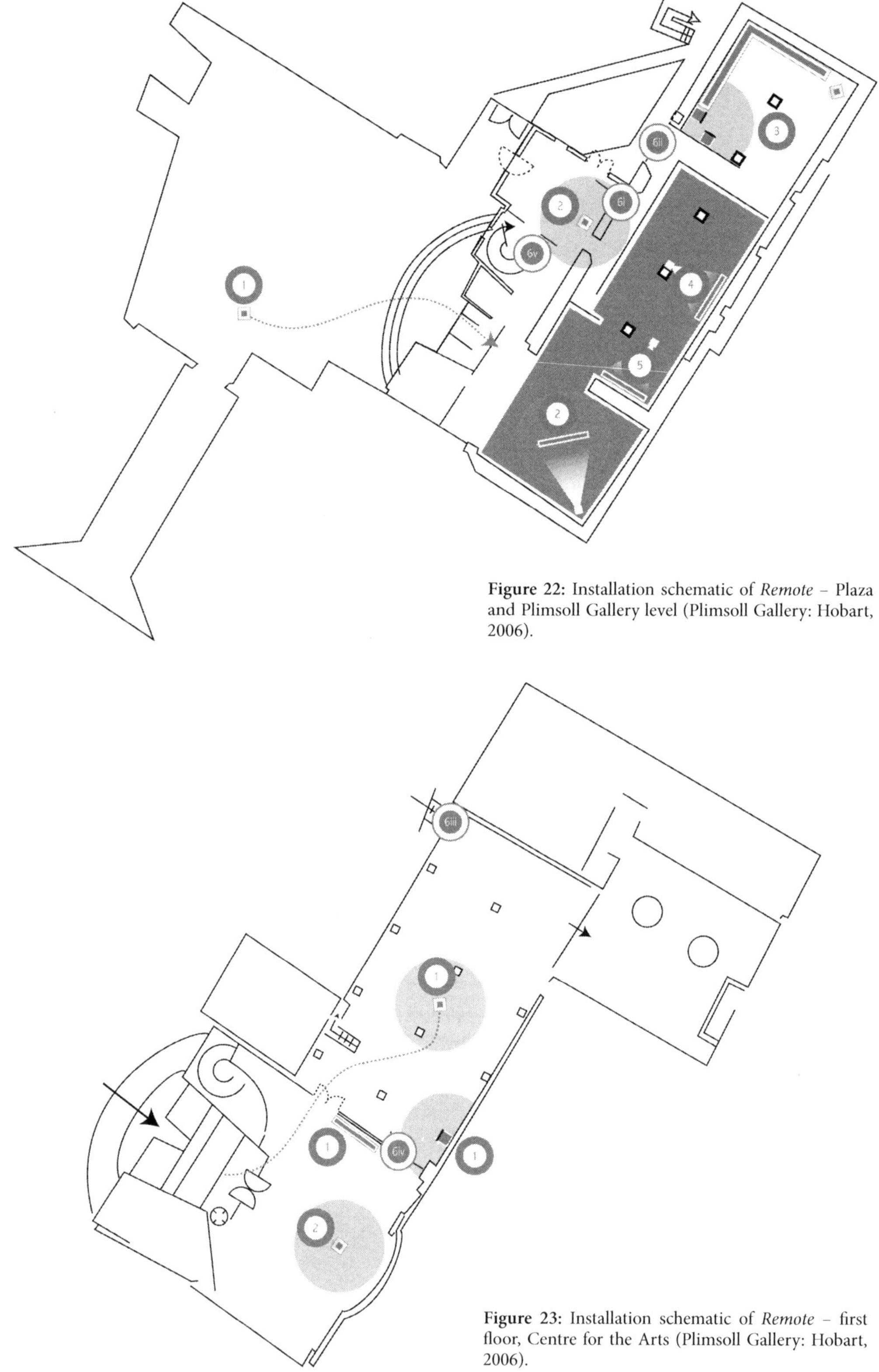

Figure 22: Installation schematic of *Remote* – Plaza and Plimsoll Gallery level (Plimsoll Gallery: Hobart, 2006).

Figure 23: Installation schematic of *Remote* – first floor, Centre for the Arts (Plimsoll Gallery: Hobart, 2006).

Remote

Plimsoll Gallery, University of Tasmania, Hobart, Tasmania, Australia, 3-23 June 2006

1. Pete Gomes, *Littoral Map* (*Tasmania*) (2006). Mixed media. Print media. Sound. Site-specific installation. Collection of the artist.

2. Derek Hart, *A Maravilha do Rio de Janeiro* (2002-6). Digital video (projection and monitors). Distributed installation. Collection of the artist.

3. Martin Walch, *Losing the Plot - XYZ/T v15-220206* (2006). Mixed media. Digital video. Sound. Variable installation. Collection of the artist.

4. Susan Collins, *Glenlandia* (2005-6). Web transmission. Projection. Variable dimensions. Collection of the artist.

5. Nancy Mauro-Flude, *Take Me There: Bring Me Back* (2005-6). Web transmission. Projection. Variable dimensions. Collection of the artist.

6i. Vince Dziekan, *V. Travels in the Netherworld - IrisWall* (1890-2006). Mixed/locative media: PDA, digital content, graphic markers. Variable/site-specific installation. Collection of the artist.

6ii. Vince Dziekan, *V. Travels in the Netherworld - StillLife* (1890-2006). Mixed/locative media: PDA, digital content, graphic markers. Variable/site-specific installation. Collection of the artist.

6iii. Vince Dziekan, *V. Travels in the Netherworld - TimeTravel1* (1890-2006). Mixed/locative media: PDA, digital content, graphic markers. Variable/site-specific installation. Collection of the artist.

6iv. Vince Dziekan, *V. Travels in the Netherworld - GirlStar* (1890-2006). Mixed/locative media: PDA, digital content, graphic markers. Variable/site-specific installation. Collection of the artist.

6v. Vince Dziekan, *V. Travels in the Netherworld - TimeTravel2* (1890-2006). Mixed/locative media: PDA, digital content, graphic markers. Variable/site-specific installation. Collection of the artist.

Scenographic Field Notes

In *Remote*, the exhibition was liberated from the spatial confines of the Plimsoll Gallery, located within the University of Tasmania's Centre for the Arts in Hobart. As a form of response to the blending of real and virtual spaces that has recently become characterised as *post-digital*, the exhibition was organised as an open structure that did not restrict the exhibition to the confines of the gallery. Conceived and expressed through the medium of exhibition, the scenography of *Remote* – understood as the exposition of curatorial thematics through spatial expression – drew upon a variety of ancillary spaces, including passageways, a gallery reception area and surrounding public spaces both internal and external to the Centre for the Arts building. These locations were incorporated into the overall sweep of the resulting 'distributed' exhibition. Most obviously, this approach to distributed spatial practice capitalised on the architectural footprint of the particular site, accentuating both the physical properties as well as the social conditions which sees the gallery function within the immediate centre, housing the premier art school in Tasmania, while also being publicly accessible to the greater cultural precinct situated along the Hobart waterfront.

As part of this strategy it was recognised early in the development process that it would not be particularly productive to attempt to configure a one-dimensional exhibition experience for a model viewer, or visitor. Rather, multiple points of access and trajectories of viewing across a number of spaces influenced the resulting design strategy. In addition, the mixture of different locations, each with their own site-specific qualities, was factored into how each of the artworks were situated, as was the case with Pete Gomes' *Littoral Map (Tasmania)* and Derek Hart's *A Maravilha do Rio de Janeiro*, discussed earlier.

The means to effectively mobilise the viewer's interaction across the exhibition's itinerary was supported in two different ways. In a straightforward fashion, didactic material was produced that graphically communicated the overall exhibition plan to the gallery visitor. In addition, as curator-artist, I produced a locative media artwork (*V. Travels in the Netherworld*). Utilising a handheld device, this interactive multimedia piece operated as a stand-alone, self-contained artwork that was woven into the main inventory. The mobile device was available for the use of visitors upon request. Using the artwork's own internal narrative structure, the viewer was compelled to find graphic markers that were situated in five different locations distributed throughout the exhibition. Upon reaching each position, they were directed to play the predetermined media contents assigned to each location. As a result, this 'travelogue' led the viewer unwittingly on a route whose overlapping trajectory intersected with the path interconnecting the dispersed collection of other artworks. Strategically, the five 'nodes' that comprise *V. Travels* were placed strategically in what might be classified as 'transit' zones situated in-between the fixed locations of the other works. For instance, the fifth node, featuring the media sample titled *TimeTravel2* was placed at the base of the staircase providing access between the ground floor and the first level of the building. This specific location connected the gallery with the main foyer of the Centre for the Arts. At the exhibition level, the strategic placement of the viewer-visitor at this point in space also set them on a course that would support their ability to connect the three separate iterations of Hart's *A Maravilha do Rio de Janeiro.*

In adopting a form of distributed spatial practice, the exhibition drew fundamentally upon the movement and passage through and between the discrete elements that constitute each of the artworks as dispersed throughout both gallery and non-gallery environs. Operating as counterpoints to the enveloping sense of the exhibition as transitory, ephemeral and contingent, these stationary, individuated instances of artworks provided anchors for distinct events, whether of a representational character (such as the continual updating of Nancy Mauro-Flude's webcam imagery, the almost imperceptible refresh-rate of Susan Collins' tele-images, and the suspended, semi-frozen quality of Hart's video footage) or spatially realised (the mixed media components brought together within Martin Walch's gallery installation or Gomes' sprawling locative media work which meanders through interior and exterior spaces). Each of these different iterations afforded the viewer moments of concentrated, reflective punctuation in the midst of a continuous flow of data. By distributing the exhibition across a range of spaces in this way, self-contained artworks were encountered as 'pauses' in the midst of passage (whether visualising the movement of data through networks or the viewer's travel through space) and flow (reinforcing the formal qualities of streaming media or drawing attention to the aggregative effect that duration and juxtaposition across time and space has on the interpretive meaning of the work itself). Accordingly, the exhibition as a whole was experienced as an 'itinerary' that, by definition, related highly focalised moments of engagement that were connected and collected through the convergence of relationally-constructed viewing or visiting paths and the active nature of migration between them in real space.

Curator's Essay – *Remote (Close up, from Afar)*[4]

> What is aura, actually? A strange weave of space and time: the unique appearance or semblance of distance, no matter how close the object may be.
>
> – Walter Benjamin

> Beauty changes quickly, much as a landscape constantly changes with the position of the sun.
>
> – Auguste Rodin

History has it that Samuel Morse successfully transmitted his first electric-telegraph message on 6 January 1838. Having become increasingly obsessed with the possibility of transmitting 'intelligence' at a distance by electricity, the artist and part-time inventor built a telegraph machine using a variety of materials that he found readily at hand, scattered throughout his workshop. Using bits of wire, cotton thread, sundry art materials and old clockwork mechanisms, he succeeded in sending a message – coded in the graphic language he devised especially for such a purpose – a distance amounting to some ten miles. Legend has it that this experiment was realised entirely within the four walls of his New Jersey studio by coiling the total length of copper wire used to conduct the sequencing of electrical pulses – a message written literally with light – around the interior of his studio.

The paradoxical interplay between distance and proximity that is realised through the contiguous meeting of different times and places in a physical space underpins the curatorial rationale of *Remote*. Conceived and expressed through the medium of the exhibition, *Remote* is characterised by its distributed form. Its distinctive scenography (as the interrelationship between curatorial thematics, which are expressed through the communicative act of exposition involving scenic design, and the exhibition as the writing of that space) draws upon the particular characteristics of the Plimsoll Gallery and its local environment, which has been incorporated into the overall sweep of the expanded exhibition. This inclusion of other locales in the immediate proximity of the Centre for the Arts – their hyperlinking and cross-referencing to the exhibition – transforms the experience of the exhibition from its basis as an installation in an enclosed, cubic space into something more likened to an itinerary. While naturally occupying gallery space and exercising its language and potential, the works by each of the five featured artists in their own way also utilise the gallery in more 'instrumental' ways – using the gallery itself as a node or meeting point in a wider network – by interweaving dispersed, interconnected and superimposed components back to that space.

These artists – Susan Collins, Pete Gomes, Derek Hart, Nancy Mauro-Flude and Martin Walch – explore certain 'transpositional' characteristics associated with the visualisation of virtual space. Each negotiates their relation to the real world and their works demonstrate how the transaction between reality and virtuality might be constituted today when any firm sense of presence (real space) and immediacy (real time) is exacerbated by technologies that problematise notions of nearness and remoteness, such as the televisual, telecommunications and satellite navigational systems. While represented through a diversity of expressions that include screen and projection-based moving image work, webcast transmissions, site-specific installation and locative media, a common point of departure for all is apparent: a confounded sense of place and proximity.

This transaction between times and places at once immediate (present, proximate, up close) and at a remove (absent, distanced, afar) is central to the modern industrialisation of the production and dissemination of visual images. This feature – which in its advanced form comes to distinguish the paradoxical logic of contemporary perception from its dialectical modern counterpart – is clearly present in the coincidental inventions of telecommunication and photography.[5] Both technologies were introduced in the early to mid nineteenth century and intersect the act of seeing with memory. Eduardo Cadava for one, in his wonderfully poetic meditation on Walter Benjamin and the intertwined relationship between words (history) and light (photography), alludes to the 'irreducible link between thought as memory and the technical dimension of memorisation, the techniques of material inscription' that was central to Benjamin's preoccupation with the beginnings of photography and technologies of reproduction (Cadava 1997, p. xviii). Proceeding from the transcription of the lived event into represented memory through technological means, such as the camera apparatus, our relationship to reality is paradoxically brought up close while simultaneously remaining afar: 'This oscillation between space and time, between distance and proximity, touches on the very nature of photographic and filmic media, whose structure consists in the simultaneous reduction and maximisation of distance' (p. xxv). More recently, the work of Paul Virilio has outlined the implications of instrumental seeing and the eradication of distance by the speed of instantaneous telecommunications – the telescoping of tenses or time frames past and present. According to Virilio, the increasing dependence of perception upon technological mediation entails the 'conveyance of sight that produce(s) a telescoping of near and far, a phenomenon of acceleration obliterating our experience of distances and dimensions' (1994, p. 4).

Perhaps through recognising the close relation that coincided in the mid-nineteenth century between the invention of photography and Samuel Morse's first electric-telegraph message or Cyrus Field's ambitious undertaking leading to the laying of the transatlantic cable (both of which in their own distinct ways contributed to creating a sense of connectivity between increasingly dispersed places through the power of instant telecommunications), some thoughts that focus on the aesthetics associated with digital images that are realised principally through transmission and relayed using the Internet might be developed.

As a contributing theme of the exhibition project, *Remote* entertains the kind of telescoping (alluded to by Virilio) of the relationship of the perceived, immediately experienced event and its transcription (through various ways and means of writing and representation). The dynamics involved in this open dialogue can be seen to operate across all works, included in the inventory, albeit manifesting itself in a variety of ways.

Artists Martin Walch and Pete Gomes share an interest in mapping the experiential, first-hand encounters with physical places. Both use global positioning system (GPS) derived data sets that are subsequently translated into visualised notation. This processing literally transcribes the traces of recorded passage through spaces both drawn from actual tracking in the natural environment (from Walch's earlier forays into the Mount Lyall wilderness on Tasmania's remote and rugged west coast, or, more recently, his excursions in the relatively accessible wilderness area of Tasman Island) and imaginatively filtered by the imposition of distance (London-based artist Gomes' pre-visualisation of a tract of Madagascar coastline that the artist will subsequently inhabit as part of his involvement in a community aid project there). Gomes has volunteered to spend time working in and around the last remaining stands of littoral forest in southeast Madagascar with the charity organisation Azafady. The staging of this particular iteration of this multi-dimensional work, which he has also 'performed' in London, is a response to the destruction of this distinctive feature of the local ecology where the rainforest grows to the edge of the sea. In particular, the artist intends to draw the viewer's attention to the impact that the mining of titanium dioxide is having on the local ecosystem there. Representative of his performative utilisation of locative media, Gomes' artistic process of mark-making raises to a level of visuality the invisible streams of information that pervade, course through and envelope any geographical (which also underpins Walch's *Losing the Plot – XYZ/T v15-220206*) or geopolitical sense of the interconnection of local and global spaces. This transient act of leaving behind traces as indicative of meaningful intervention contrasts with the way we normally take photographs of (and subsequent transport them from) a particular locale and transpose them into another place. Instead, such location-sensitive and aware artworks imbue the space in which these traces are left with a superimposed record or 'meta-tagged' meaning derived from another register of perception of that space. Recalling the classical mnemonic technique known as the 'Method of Loci', the works of both Walch and Gomes, memory and imaginative projection, technology and topography become fused (Virilio 1994, p. 3). The ordering of space and time through the sequential interconnection of locations is applied for the purpose of performing the reactivation of intangible histories, remembered stories or rites.

Derek Hart shares with these artists a practice that is characterised by active, participatory involvement, accumulative documentation and performative re-enactment. For his part, Hart presents a distributed artwork that has adapted itself flexibly to the expanded environmental conditions of the exhibition's distinctive scenography. *A Maravilha do Rio de Janeiro* is based on the televisual representation of six of the most scenic attributes of Rio de Janeiro, including Guanabara Bay, Maracanã football stadium, Sugarloaf Mountain and the Christ the Redeemer statue. Inspired by a populist survey that ranked these prominent, iconic locations, the artist directed the shooting of source footage, executed as an instructional relay between the English artist and the Brazilian pilot of a TV Globo news helicopter. Image-making in this example is reduced to that purest act of 'sighting' and 'targeting'. Creative visual subjectivity of the photographic medium is submitted to the production of ambient technical effect.

Tele-Image:
It is, however, in the transmission-based pieces of Nancy Mauro-Flude and Susan Collins that the movement of time as it is constituted in the photomedia image – as distinct from its 'arresting' in still photography – is most thoroughly addressed.

In the installation of *Remote*, Mauro-Flude's *Take Me There: Bring Me Back* (2006) and Collins' *Glenlandia* (2006) are presented adjacently in a darkened expanse of exhibition space. Intriguingly, because of the time zone difference between continental Europe and eastern Australia, the middle of the night coincides with the opening hours of the exhibition. This translates Mauro-Flude's relay of a live video feed from her window overlooking a canal in Amsterdam as a predominantly dark screen. Only the twin reflections of street lamps on the inky surface of water breaks the surface of the otherwise indiscernible image. Reprising her earlier webcast *Tradestream* (2005), the webcam image is refreshed at six-second intervals, not unlike the intermittent traffic along the watercourse; the open-channel transmission of the image's feed via the Internet likened to the steady passing of the ordinary time of life. Like the perpetual ebb and flow of the canal, it seems arbitrary to think of the work as having either beginning or end. The thorough immersion of the artist in the contemporary networked culture of the datasphere is exemplified in the work's continuous performative exchange – which is indicated by the insertion of intimate, personal aphorisms that are updated regularly ('Is starlight a wireless signal?'; 'The unruly has been censored') and the interjection of different visual tableaux that interrupt the otherwise steady image 'flow'. Acting like thoughts for the day, these phrases juxtapose with the insertion of information recording the transmission's time and date stamping. This set of textual excerpts are superimposed upon whatever incidental image 'happens' to be within the camera's field of view at the time (an ordered pair of seabirds frozen in centre frame, a dispersing flock amongst bare tree branches, a blue cargo ship whose name, truncated to read 'C–MAX' by the partial obliteration resulting from the fortuitous placement of a tree limb in the foreground, one can't help interpreting as 'CLIMAX'). Day and night, the artist's fleeting thoughts and impressions provide a tone that colours these 'slices of life', existing somewhere in-between ritual or routine, the happenstance of waking reality or nocturnal dream episodes. Intriguingly, dawn's rising in Amsterdam coincides with the closing of the exhibition's viewing hours in Hobart.

In contrast, British artist Susan Collins' transmitted image presents a stratification of time within the single image surface (the technicalities of this effect will be expanded upon shortly). In this jewel-like image that emanates from out of the expanse of the gallery's enveloping blackness the image is banded into horizontal strata that separate phases of daylight and night. The work entertains the possibility that the online world supersedes the dichotomy that separates notions of the real and virtual, and instead offers the means to be 'elsewhere'.

One way that this concern manifests itself in her practice involves the exploration of technologically-mediated exchange between geographically remote locations. Her work *Transporting Skies* (2002) introduced a number of the concerns that continue to resonate in her more recent webcam tele-artworks, including the 'attempt to make visible what it means to send information across time and place, and to expose the material that we use to do that with' (Collins 2005). *Transporting Skies* involved the transmission of images linking exhibition spaces 300 miles apart in Yorkshire and Cornwall (the choice of this particular location took its inspiration from the fact that Marconi transmitted the first transatlantic Morse code message from there). As with Morse's studio-centric transmission over 10 miles of coiled cabling, the actual distances involved become something of an irrelevance; the artist has commented how the work was initially conceived for a significantly larger scale involving different time zones. However, once attuned, the relative proximity of these two sites revealed unexpected but perceptible differences and subtleties between the urban Sheffield landscape and the Penzance seascape (differences such as the onset of dusk and the colour qualities of the night-time sky). In this work a video image of sky was captured in real time from each location and sent as streaming video to the opposite gallery location. An image of the sky relayed from Cornwall was presented as a large-scale projection on the wall of the Site Gallery in Sheffield, while the counterpart image from Sheffield was integrated into the lantern ceiling of the Newlyn Art Gallery in Penzance. An additional level of viewer interaction was incorporated into this part of the work by having the viewer's own attentive image captured and combined using chroma-key techniques with the live image of Yorkshire sky transferred to the ceiling projection in Penzance.

More recently, Collins' work has concentrated on producing (in actual fact 'propagating' might be a better word) artworks that elude temporal closure or the fixing of pictorial space in an image. One such 'pixelscape', *Glenlandia*, is exhibited as part of *Remote*. Constructed in a similar way to its 'sister' piece, *Fenlandia* (2004), these art projects involve observing the relationship between landscape and technology over greatly extended time spans; in the case of *Glenlandia*, the work is 'active' over the course of a full year. *Fenlandia* was situated in an area of East Anglia known as 'Silicon Fen', after the proliferation of new technology companies located in the region, which is known for its fens, or marshlands. In noting how technology had become literally embedded in the flat horizons of this reclaimed landscape, the artist has commented:

It seemed the perfect opportunity not only to marry the horizontality of my pixel landscapes to their subject, but also to develop the work further, distributing it live online as well as archiving (harvesting) images from the work over the course of a full year (Collins 2005).

Comparatively, in the case of *Glenlandia*, Collins has set up a webcam in Pitlochry to take in the view of what appears to be a quintessentially 'natural' Scottish scene. [*Figure 24*] However, Loch Faskally is actually a man-made loch and its water levels fluctuate according to demand on power generated from a nearby hydroelectric dam.

This tele-image endures as a continually refreshing image feed. Each pixel records a different second in time throughout the duration of the exhibition period, cascading from top left to bottom right corners of the continuously 'overwritten' single image frame. Time becomes the 'dynamic fabric of the work' as the total number of pixels captured by this 320×240 resolution image translates effectively into a single day, amounting to 76,800 seconds, or 21.33 hours (Collins 2004, p. 55). While digitally updating the techniques of the cinematic time-lapse or photographic long exposure, this method of image production also entails a conceptual shift in focus:

The image loses its characteristics of instantaneousness to become a stratification of the passing of time. It's an elaboration which involves a remarkable conceptual leap compared to the creative use of the shutter speed in classical photography and which contains one of the peculiar characteristics of digital technologies (the accumulation of information), applying it to the domain of time and of visual effects. (Ludovico 2004)

Any valorisation of the aestheticised instant proves irrelevant as the image's decisive moment shifts constantly: from when it was instrumentally captured, digitally archived or, as when viewing successive single pixels refresh, moving the image inexorably forward into

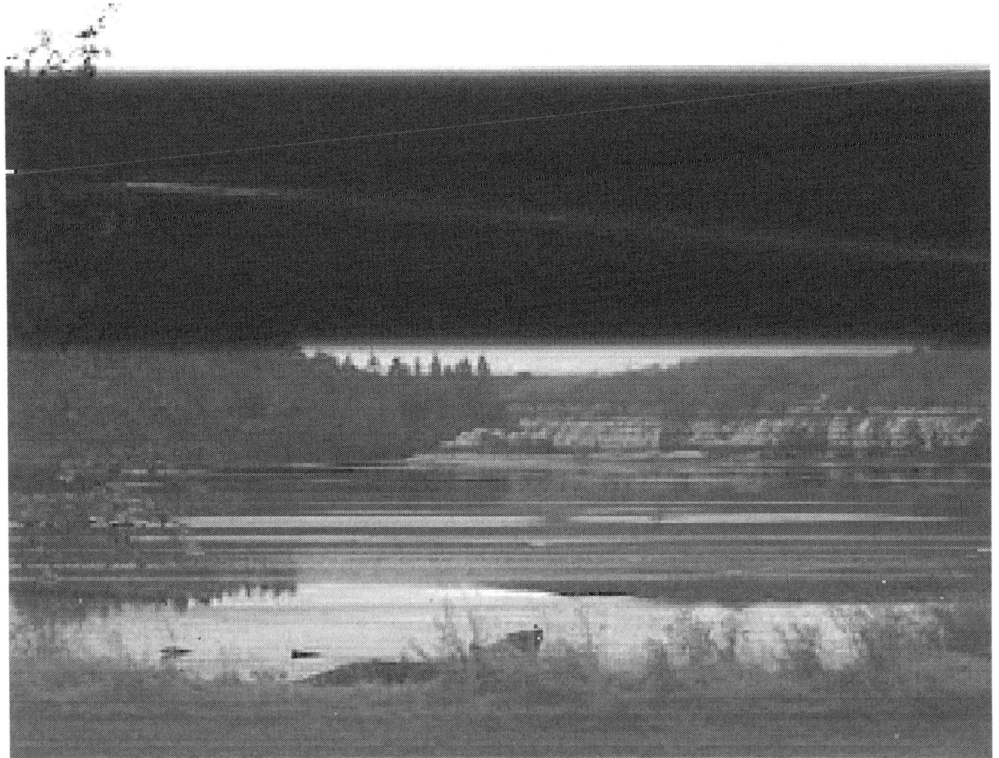

Figure 24: Susan Collins, *Glenlandia* (Live and online from 10 September 2005 until 10 September 2006). Web transmission. Projection. Variable dimensions. Collection of the artist.

the future. Yet, as both artists have acutely observed, it is through the pulse, the continuous disturbance of this 'time shift' that the image finds itself delicately poised between banality and epiphany. As Collins (2005) summarises, surprising revelations are found in the midst of the tele-image: 'for instance the occasions that a full moon is captured passing through the night sky, gives a real sense of planet/earth movement which serves to really consider nature in time and space'. In the midst of day passing into night and as light turns to darkness, 'stray' pixels capture presence in all its fleetingness – clouds pass and birds fly, human life intrudes, stops awhile before dissolving back into flux.

Duration:
Possibly the most apparent property of relayed, transmitted tele-images is that they perpetuate the passage of light. It is the camera – not the image – that is 'fixed' while reality continues to wander past its receptive wide-open lens. This stationary quality of the camera as recording device is exaggerated by Collins' continuous pixel-by-pixel acquisition of visual data over the extended period of a full year. Mauro-Flude's obstinate framing of the view

available from the vantage of her apartment window, echoes, in its own way, the earliest photographic facsimile produced by Niepce in 1827. The image endures, enabling the transposition of different times and places by creating a continuous connection between the site of origin and reception. Thus extended, the image oscillates actively between the two poles of here and there, now and then. Rather than arresting the transmission of light, as the 'incidental' image is translated into a transportable form (film plate, instant photographic print, image capture) and souvenired away from where it was first 'found' and replaced to another, remote from it, the image becomes somehow 'conductive', a channel or conduit through or along which the disturbance that is visual matter flows unabated. The visual world is perceived as a state of continuous becoming.

The transmitted or relayed image artworks of these two artists reintroduce the 'durational' character of photography, first revealed in the fluctuating luminosity and the blurs and wipes of vague amorphous form that characterise many early photographs due to the technical limitations that resulted in prolonged exposure. In a strange way, the long exposure times that are characteristic of such representative photographs of the era produced a coherence of illumination and atmosphere that resulted in a 'correspondence' between subject and technique. This short-lived period of 'congruence' would soon become 'incongruent' when, according to Benjamin, 'advances in optics made instruments available that put darkness entirely to flight and recorded appearances as faithfully as any mirror' (1979, p. 248).

In *The Vision Machine*, Virilio notes how at the inception of photography, the photograph was considered a 'false witness' by contemporaries such as the sculptor Rodin because 'in reality, time does not stand still' (1994, p. 2). Echoing the philosophy of Henri Bergson, Gilles Deleuze notes that movement was 'brought into concepts at precisely the same time that it was brought into images' (1992, p. 282). For, according to Bergson, whose thoughts on movement that are played out in *Matter and Memory* (originally published in 1896) took shape during the era in which cinema was invention, 'it is our duration that thinks, feels, sees' (quoted in Virilio 1994, p. 3). Reality, because it is continuity, inevitably exceeds its representation:

> We break up this continuity into elements laid side by side, which correspond in the one case to distinct words, in the other to independent objects. The unity of the original intuition of reality is broken into discrete units by its representation, a reconstruction of experience of real phenomena. (Bergson 2004, p. 239)

Duration is defeated, paralysed by technical advances leading progressively towards photographic instantaneity; and in turn, it promotes a general aesthetics of the instant photograph, or 'snapshot'. What Virilio refers to as the 'image-time-freeze' disrupts any sense of felt temporality for the photograph's witness. As Benjamin writes in 'A Small History of Photography' (the text that previews many of the themes that would continue to resonate in his 'The Work of Art in the Age of Mechanical Reproduction'): 'During the considerable period of the exposure, the subject as it were grew into the picture, in the sharpest contrast with appearances in a snapshot' (1979, p. 245).

It was just such wonder that brought together two of the great protagonists of the art and technology nexus: American inventor of the electric telegraph Samuel Morse and French photographic pioneer Louis Daguerre, after whom of one of the medium's first processes, the daguerreotype, was named. The anecdote that Morse recounted was based on his meeting with Daguerre soon after the public announcement of his photographic process to the French Academy of Sciences in Paris in March 1839.[6] Morse was to relay his first impressions of this new medium, contained in what might otherwise appear as an 'ordinary' photograph, in a letter to his brother:

> The effect of the lens upon the picture was in great degree like that of a telescope in nature. Objects moving are not impressed. The Boulevard, so constantly filled with a moving throng of pedestrians and carriages was perfectly solitary, except an individual who was having his boots brushed. His feet were compelled, of course, to be stationary for some time, one being on the box of the bootblack, and the other on the ground. Consequently, his boots and legs were well defined, but he is without body or head, because these were in motion. (quoted in Newhall 1982, p. 16).

In discussing the earliest photographic facsimiles that Niepce referred to as 'points of view', Virilio comments:

> Yet, when you look closely at these first 'solar writings', what you notice is not so much the scarcely discernable, colourless objects as a sort of luminance, the conduction surface of a luminous intensity. The main aim of the heliotrophic plate is not to reveal the assembled bodies so much as to let itself be 'impressed', to capture signals transmitted by the alteration of light and shade, day and night, good weather and bad, the 'feeble autumn luminosity' that hampers Niepce in his work. (1994, p. 19)

It should be remembered that Niepce's invention of heliography around 1827 helped in promoting ideas for nineteenth-century physicists investigating electricity and electromagnetism. The principle of electromagnetic induction, discovered by Michael Faraday in 1831, maintained that electric, magnetic and gravitational forces are able to be passed from one body to another through lines of force, or 'strains' in the area between two bodies. It was through such images, whose recordings took in the order of 30 minutes to expose, that a demonstration was provided of 'how objects and solid bodies are eclipsed as central subjects in representational system of the image by the sheer plenitude of light energy'. (Virilio 1994, p. 20–1)

Noting the implications of the transmitted image, Virilio signals the tele-image as effectively undoing the formalist logic that has governed the aesthetics of the representational image to date. Today, as decisive action (defined by the tripartite tenses past, present and future) is superseded by the distinction between 'real time' and 'delayed' time, Virilio notes: 'The past of the representation containing a bit of this media present, of this real-time "telepresence", the "live" recording preserving, like an echo, the real presence of the event' (1994, p. 67). This convergence (first drawing together, collapsing and then moving beyond) in the preserved recording of the 'live' event heralds a new paradoxical logic that, emerging from the relayed image's ambient technical effect, inevitably impacts on the viewer's identification, interpretation and participatory experience of place and time. The evolution of the analogue, photographic image into the digital image – as represented for instance by the tele-image – is one more indication that supports the ascendance of a distinctively contemporary logistics of perception, wherein:

> Today, the strategic value of speed's 'no place' has definitely outstripped the value of place. With the instantaneous ubiquity of teletopology, the immediate face-to-face of all refractory surfaces, the bringing into contact of all localities, the strong wandering of the gaze is at an end. (Virilio 1994, p. 31)

Closing Remarks:
The technologised interface between physical and virtual spaces has consequences for how communication and meaning is culturally negotiated and the act of involvement or participation is socially organised. Before concluding, it is worth briefly commenting upon how the relationship between perceptual experience and its aesthetic re-presentation might find material, media or mediated expression through visualisation, digital imaging and communications technologies.

The burgeoning of what has been termed a *distributed aesthetics*[7] is indicated by the highly individualised aesthetics of the artists that have been brought together, framed, by the curatorial and architectural parameters of the *Remote* exhibition. A number of positions currently developing within this genre are encompassed by terms such as 'net art', 'locative media' or 'networked narrative environments'. In terms of digital aesthetics, one commentator has observed:

> The exploratory movements of locative media lead to a convergence of geographical and data space, reversing the trend towards digital content being viewed as placeless, only encountered in the amorphous and other space of the internet' (Hemment 2004).

For instance, 'telepresence', or telematics, involves both performative and interactive exchanges that are enabled by 'bringing remote participants together in a shared telepresent environment' (Sermon 2004, p. 83). *Hole-in-Space* (1980) by Kit Galloway and Sherrie Rabinowitz acts as a forerunner of such a practice. Defined as a 'public communication sculpture', this art event connected East Coast and West Coast audiences – its pioneering of the genre of telematic art paralleling the cross-continent telegraph cable linking California with the East Coast in 1861 – relaying life-sized television images in Lincoln Center for the Performing Arts in New York City and a department store in the Century City shopping mall in Los Angeles. Today, British artist Paul Sermon is an exemplary representative who continues working in this lineage of networked narrative performance. The installation *Body of Water* (1999) was situated between two distanced sites in Germany: the Wilhelm Lehmbruck Museum in Duisberg and a shower room in a disused colliery in Herten. Combining archival footage and live relayed video feed, the work connected remote audiences via shared monitor screens and water projection interface achieved via Internet and video conferencing technologies. As commented by the work's collaborator Andrea Zapp, it is the distributive potential of the network that, by connecting digital media to the real spaces (in which they are encountered) or environments (to which they are interconnected), 'provides the technical backdrop that enables a remote and open-ended dialog between these spaces' (2004a, p. 12).

To capture elusive, fleeting images has long been the objective of representational art; it has been sought after since at least the technical invention of the *camera obscura*. Before the advent of the substantially more miniaturised, table-top *camera lucida*, the 'black box' had to be constructed in the selected location, placed to best frame the desired vantage upon the view to be transcribed by the artist – from within the camera's sealed walls. It is worth remembering, particularly in relation to *Remote*, that the first 'camera' was actually a room that the artist was required to erect and occupy *in situ*. For its own part, the curatorial design of *Remote* calls upon the exhibition form to provide the infrastructure that locates the viewer simultaneously at the juncture and disjunction of here and there, of the socially instituted and individually experienced. In recognition of the virtualisation of the art complex that involves the increasingly fluid interrelation between museum, exhibition and artwork, the scenography of *Remote* structures the experience of being dispersed between informatic and physical space.

The range of spatial practices available to art practice and curatorial design far exceed purely architectural factors of gallery space and have come increasingly to include the design of an extended typology of spaces (which today involves digitally-mediated communication spaces, a variety of multimedia modes and the Internet). Exemplified by the works of Nancy Mauro-Flude and Susan Collins, the transmitted image evades containment by maintaining – both literally and figuratively – an active connection between its respective sites of production and exhibition; the exposition of the artwork occurs across an uninterrupted bandwidth that confounds our sense of time, place, proximity and remoteness. As illustrated by the curatorial design of *Remote*, the exhibition form brings together these features into a distributive, aggregative complex of relations. By inducing the exploration of art across this broader 'ecology' of spaces, the artworks that have been assembled through the connective tissue of the exhibition collectively propose how artistic and curatorial practice might negotiate the tension between virtuality and site-specificity.

Notes

1. Facilitating the project's development, an intensive onsite residency supporting preliminary research, content development and exhibition planning took place in June 2005. The aims and objectives of this period of focused curatorial development included refining the articulation of themes and creatively exploring their application to the specificities of the exhibition. Addressing infrastructure and technical requirements was an integral part of this process. As the exhibition was premised on showcasing digital media, the exhibition placed significant demands on computer and digital technologies. Options relating to delivery systems (projectors, monitors, computers and DVD players) and type of technology required (i.e. Internet access and cabling) were explored taking into account local factors and available infrastructure. The exhibition plan forwarded a solution taking relatively limited audio/video and multimedia resources into account.

   Importantly, during this time the inherent potential of the site and available gallery spaces were able to be experienced on a first-hand basis. Through the immediate understanding of the exhibition site, a range of preliminary designs for the installation were explored. Early in the process it was decided that the gallery space *proper* would not be the sole exhibition environment. Within the area of the gallery, the actual installation would be kept exaggeratedly sparse. It was envisaged that the exhibition design would require some reconfiguration of walls to create a narrow corridor or a false entrance that would enable the creation of both naturally lit and 'black box' environments. Ideas entailing further investigation were forwarded and minor fabrication to a number of the spaces was signaled, including options for a rear projection screen solution (to create a large screen 'vista' between the main gallery with the smaller gallery space alongside), covering window surfaces opening onto the garden enclosure with translucent material or film so that it could be used as a projection surface and the option of creating a spatial intervention that will transform one of the gallery entrances into a screen 'portal'.
2. Consultation with local Tasmanian artists working with electronic media was undertaken as part of developing the exhibition inventory. Initial identification and approaches to artists lead to the development of collaborative working relationships. Collaborations involving the development and customising of works by Hobart-based artist Derek Hart and London-based Pete Gomes will be discussed presently.
3. *Littoral Map* is related to a site-specific 'performance drawing' produced by the artist and staged as part of *Node London* in 2006. In this other iteration of the work, titled *Littoral Walk*, Gomes transplanted satellite coordinates of southern Madagascar onto an area in south London in order to draw focus to this area of threatened coastal forest that stretches for 70km approximately on either side of Fort Dauphin. As Gomes relates: 'This London walk is an imagined sense of myself in a specific location; for me, somewhere between future projection, imagination and a dream' [http://www.turbulence.org/blog/archives/002185.html].

   Gomes' combined social and aesthetic engagement with locative media offers a refreshing alternative to the predominant emphasis upon experiencing networked environments through telematic interactions involving immersive formats (for example, see Zapp 2004b).
4. This text was a development of my curator's essay, originally published electronically as part of the exhibition website [http://www.remoteexhibition.com]. This expanded version of the text concentrates most directly on the digital aesthetics associated with the tele-image.
5. Paul Virilio (1994) distinguishes between three logics or 'logistics of perception' involving technologies of visual representation. In summary, the age of what he has referred to as the image's 'formal' logic was the era of pictorial painting, print media and architecture. This era culminated

with the advent of the 'photogram', which introduced the reproductive technologies of photography and the cinema during the nineteenth century. This period was characterised by a 'dialectical' logic of public representation. The close of the twentieth century marked the end of modernism with the inventions of video recording, holography and computer graphics – these infographic and digital technologies heralding the latest phase, which Virilio has termed 'paradoxical':

> *Paradoxical logic* emerges when the real-time image dominates the thing represented, real time subsequently prevailing over real space, virtuality dominating actuality and turning the very concept of reality on its head. Whence the crisis in traditional forms of public representation (graphics, photography, cinema…), to the great advantage of presentation, of a *paradoxical presence*, the long distance telepresence of the object or being which provides their very existence, here and now. (Virilio 1994, p. 63)

6. Extracted from an original letter by Morse published in the New York Observer, 19 April 1839 (quoted in Newhall 1982, p. 16).
7. *Fibreculture Journal* dedicated a full issue to this field of enquiry in 2005. Edited by Lisa Gye, Anna Munster and Ingrid Richardson, this issue proposed that techno-social networks are crucially constitutive of the distributed aesthesia of contemporary networked encounters [http://www.fibreculture.org].

Chapter 10

The Ammonite Order, or Objectiles for an (Un) Natural History

Synopsis

The Ammonite Order, or, Objectiles for an (Un) Natural History was developed as demonstration exhibition exploring a non-deterministic relation between digital mediation and spatial practice that supplants the primacy of real objects present in gallery space. The outcome of a research residency with the Slade Centre for Electronic Media in Fine Arts (SCEMFA) in London, the theme for this work evolved out of imaginatively projecting a fictive correspondence between two local personages: the architect George Dance (the Younger) and naturalist Charles Darwin. Drawing implicitly upon a creative curatorial impulse in order to pursue this narrative *fabula*, the exhibition space was designed to unfold as a multidimensional installation that combined physical elements with an accompanying set of media content. The exhibition promotes a model for a different type of aesthetic experience through defamiliarising how the art object is modulated at the intersection of the exhibition.

Revolving upon notions of coincidence and synchronicity, *The Ammonite Order, or Objectiles for an (Un) Natural History* was an exhibition/artwork that sought to reevaluate the status of objects in the exhibition's evanescent realm. Enamoured with the idea of the museum as a 'haunt of the muses', the exhibit employed the formal languages of ordering and display as means for making the sources of inspiration intelligible.[1] [*Figure 25*] The exhibition's inventory was comprised of a variety of elements categorised as discrete collections of installation 'props' and media 'samples'. Entailing an open conceptual play, these forms gain added force through their recycling and recombination. Collectively, these motifs establish an iconography that operates across the exhibition's interconnected, narrative structure.

The exhibit sends out contradictory signals: the appearance of order and proportion associated with its measured use of architectural space is confounded by the disorientation of its intertextual narrative. While narrative describes the part of a literary work that is concerned with telling the story through the account of a sequence of events in the order which they happened, narratology focuses critical attention on the art or process of telling a story or giving an account of something. For the purpose of this discussion, the qualification between narrative and narratology underpins the translation – and resulting distinction between – exhibition and what might be construed as 'exhibitology' in order to centre on the 'installation as a medium for narrative expression: combining objects in a specific way to make a "story" out of loose "words"' (Bal 2001, p. 162). Mieke Bal has acknowledged the powerful tradition of the narrative mode in 'museal discourse' and how this aspect 'allows for extending from the specific, literalised sense of the role of the museum to a broader partly metaphorical sense, in which the museum postures or exposes' (p. 164). Basing its 'exhibitology' on a non-deterministic relation between digital content and spatial practice, *The Ammonite Order* inverted the conventional expectation placed upon digital mediation in which the interpretive role of the gallery guide is called upon to supplement the primacy of 'real' objects present in gallery space. The more freeform approach adopted in its case contrasts with prevailing museological attitudes and the ideal of reinforcing a coordinated sense of narrative space. Through creating an unpredictable and open-ended aesthetic experience, the viewer was invited to actively participate in meaning-making by intuiting possible associations between the constituent parts of the exhibition left at their disposal.

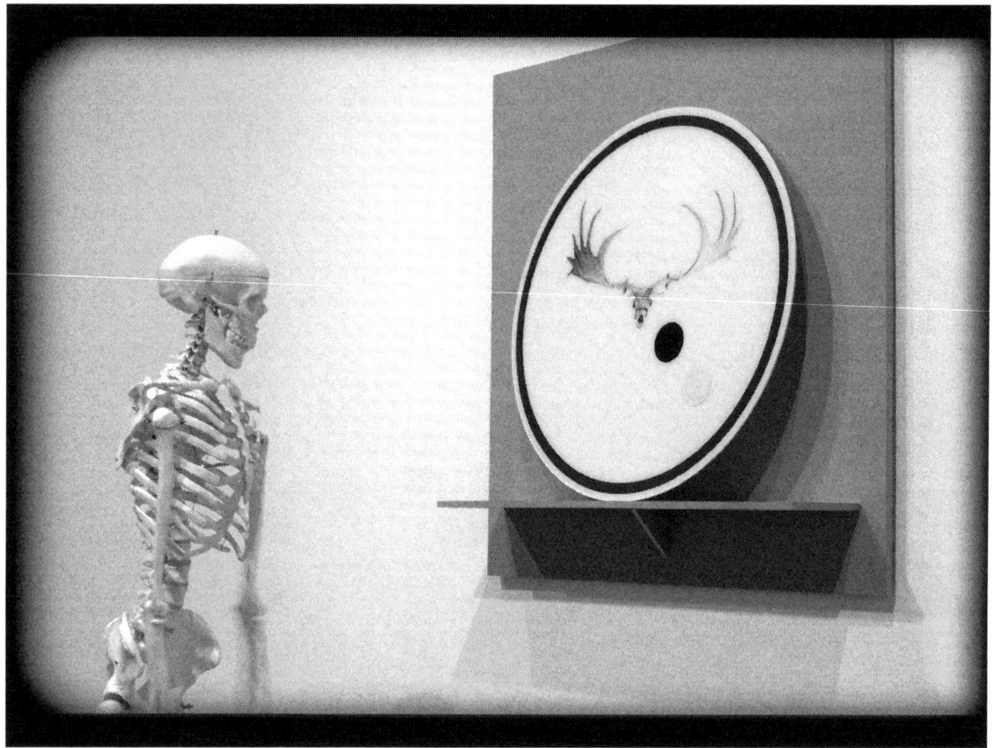

Figure 25: 'Carte-de-visite' documentation from Vince Dziekan, *Demonstration Exhibition – The Ammonite Order, or Objectiles for an (Un) Natural History* (Faculty Gallery: Melbourne, 2008). Digital prints. Laser-cut Perspex. Digital media. Customized iPod interface. Room brochure. Wall-mounted and table display. Variable installation.

Over the pages that follow I will provide a series of notes that offer added insight into considerations related to the creation of the work and themes related to the overarching investigation of virtuality and the art of exhibition.

The resulting demonstration exhibition was the direct product of a research residency, hosted by the Slade School of Fine Art, London, in early 2008. During that time I was provided with a studio at their research centre, based at Woburn Square in the middle of the grounds of the University College London (UCL). Historically, the university itself played an important role in establishing Bloomsbury's reputation as the intellectual centre of London during the nineteenth century. Along with the British Museum – which was founded in 1753 to house the collection of Sir Hans Sloane – the area become notable for its numerous literary and artistic associations. The legacy of the numerous political, scientific, social and cultural contributions made by its residents over time are marked today by plaques that adorn the façades of many of the Georgian brick terraces that front onto the gardens and squares in the area. The genesis of creative ideas for the resulting work was inspired by experiences during this formative period. Most directly, the concept was set in motion by my casual observation of a particular pair of such markers, which I would pass on my regular route to the studio each day. There along Gower Street (the primary thoroughfare connecting the British Museum to the south with the collection of university colleges) I encountered two plaques diametrically facing each other: on the west side, a plaque marking the residence of George Dance (The Younger), and on the east side another commemorating Charles Darwin.[2] Their proximity compelled me to question whether other associations might arise from this coincidental relationship. Subsequent investigation led me to imagine the possibility for a fictive 'correspondence' between these two figures and how that might express something of the spirit of intellectual curiosity and challenge that characterised the age. In Dance's case this *zeitgeist*, or 'spirit of the times', was expressed in architectural form, whereas for Darwin this would draw upon techniques gleaned from his earlier studies in geology, stratigraphy[3] and classification leading up to the revolutionary formulation of his theory of evolution.

The museum itself acts as an expression of this attitude and the prevailing quest of Enlightenment figures to make sense and order of the world through expository techniques that classify, order and arrange. In her overview of shifting cultural attitudes to collecting and exhibiting during the nineteenth century, Celeste Olalquiaga posits that:

The nineteenth century's reification and obsessive collecting of nature was really the culminating point [...] of a cultural process that had started more than four centuries before. Characterised by culture's separation from the organic world (and the latter's ensuing artificialization), this gradual severance established the beginning of the modern era in the broadest sense, distinguishing it from both the classical and the 'dark' ages, where nature and culture were inextricably bound. In most astonishing production, the Renaissance 'wonder chambers' where massive compilations of natural specimens and artificial objects were mixed without care, offered a visual staging of natural history next to which nineteenth-century dioramas pale. Immersed in a perspective of the world that saw in both organic and human creations the physical manifestation of a mysterious cosmic force, the 'age of wonder' anchored all transcendental implications to their earthly correspondents in such a way that, for almost three hundred years, things enjoyed an unprecedented autonomy as purveyors of the enigmas of the universe. (1998, pp. 210–11)

Therefore, my discovery that the site marking where Darwin had lived when he moved to London now housed the university's Grant Museum of Zoology carried with it added resonance. The basis of the collection dates back to its establishment in 1827 by Robert Edmond Grant, whose controversial investigations into the 'unity of plan' of animals exerted an important influence on Darwin's still formative evolutionary views during the latter's prior studies under him at Edinburgh University.[4] [*Figure 26*] From my subsequent ruminations amongst the collection, my imaginative projection of the possible asynchronous relationship between the naturalist and the architect found emblematic expression in the

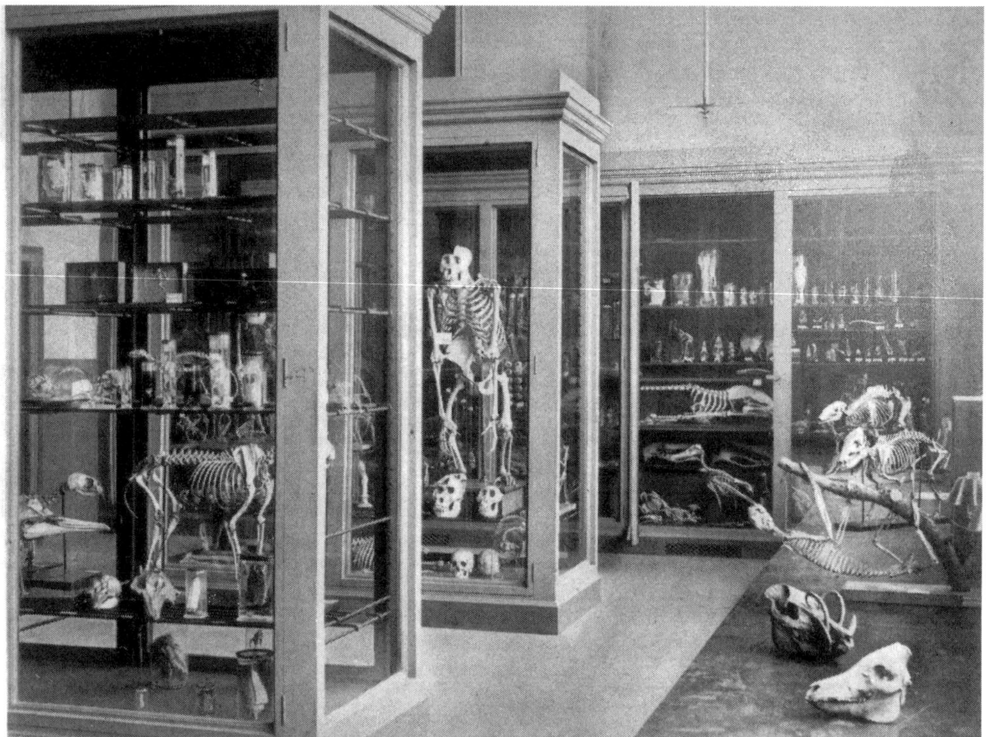

Figure 26: University College London Zoology Museum, c. 1880. © University College London, the Grant Museum of Zoology.

form of ammonite fossils whose distinctive spiral, coiled shape lead to their mythological and symbolic interpretation.[5] Drawing upon this inspiration, Dance was credited with inventing the architectural style known as the 'ammonite order', so described because of its fitting of volutes shaped to resemble fossil ammonites atop fluted columns and capitals.[6]

While not operating properly as a curated exhibition – in the conventional sense of an exhibition involving a selection of works by different artists collected together under an editorial theme or guiding principle – the exhibition/artwork nonetheless draws implicitly on the curatorial impulse in order to creatively pursue this narrative *fabula*[7] and how it would unfold in exhibition space. During my residency period in London in the spring of 2008, a number of exhibitions then taking place proved informative and inspirational on a variety of levels. Collectively, these instances mark out the conceptual and formal extremes of museological practice, ranging from the 'period' displays found in the British Museum's Enlightenment Galleries or the Soane Museum to Doris Salcedo's site-specific transformation of Tate Modern's Turbine Hall. In terms of spatial practice, inspiration was derived from formal principles applied to the design of the exhibition, *The Return of the*

Gods: Neoclassical Sculpture in Britain in the Duveen Galleries of Tate Britain. Also of interest was the integral role that digital mediation played in sustaining the curatorial fiction of *The Martian Museum of Terrestrial Art*, which transformed the galleries of the Barbican Centre into an imaginary museum conceived by and designed for extraterrestrials. As elaborated by its curators:

> Display conventions are used to provide structural order and are supplemented with interpretive materials where the Martian curators consider objects need additional contextualization. While labels, illustrations of objects in their imagined context and an audio guide serve to further explicate the Martians' beliefs about the role and purpose of contemporary art, they also reveal erroneous interpretations and unorthodox readings of the objects on view. (Manacorda and Yee 2008, p. 10)

Of these, the Sir John Soane Museum in London offered the most idiosyncratic example of the synergies that can exist between architectural and curatorial aspirations. Following in the wake of the establishment of the British Museum, Soane – who was an understudy of Dance before becoming a Neoclassical architect of some repute in his own right and Professor of Architecture at the Royal Academy – transformed his private residence on the fringe of Bloomsbury to accommodate his obsessive collection of objects, works of art, models and assorted curios. These suites provided the stage for 'Soane's all-pervading desire to establish a Pantheon of architectural inspiration' (Buzas 1994, p. 8). Conceived to inspire and promote the union of painting, sculpture, architecture, music and poetry, Soane described his encyclopaedic private collection as 'studies for my own mind and being intended similarly to benefit the artist of future generations' (p. 16).[8] Through erecting this labyrinthine monument, Soane's personal quest acts as a museological expression of the spirit of the age.

In one sense, my project developed as something of an *anamorphic* version of Soane's museological expression, as if it were 'formed again' through a distorting mirror.[9] This motivation was reflected in the exhibition's thematic exploration of its own 'medial' nature – its 'inward facing' attitude that playfully explores the manifestation of concepts in material and virtual form – and self-reflexive, even 'mannerist' tendency to its coordination in exhibition form.[10] In so doing, the exhibition was approached as the primary medium through which the artwork assumes shape and form. This inverted relationship to the items displayed in the gallery was betrayed by referring to these components as 'props' and 'samples'.

The resulting exhibition concept operates as a multidimensional, polyphonous installation that combined elements of physical installation with an accompanying set of media content. [*Figure 27*] The *fabula* unfolded as a product of this mixed discourse between objects and media created by their overlapping as part of the distinctive exhibition experience. The prevailing sense involves the viewer actively in forming interpretive meaning from *co-incident* encounters within the exhibition space with these fragments; between the syncronisation of

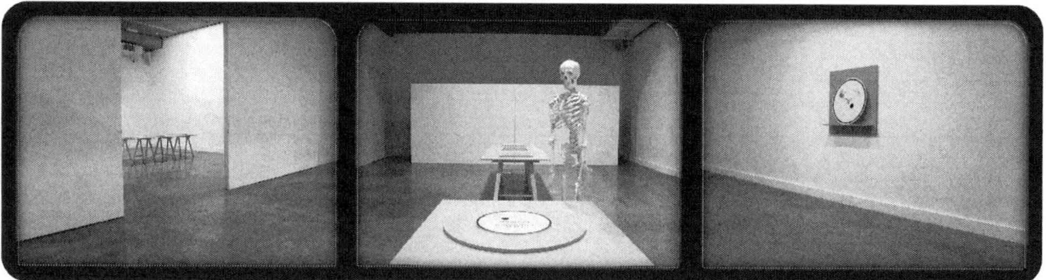

Figure 27: Vince Dziekan, 'Carte-de-visite' documentation from *Demonstration Exhibition – The Ammonite Order, or Objectiles for an (Un) Natural History –* The Dance Room (Faculty Gallery: Melbourne, 2008). Digital prints. Laser cut Perspex. Digital media. Customized iPod interface. Room brochure. Wall mounted and table display. Variable installation.

two events, or two objects made to coexist in the same location. Often linked with claims of psychic phenomena, the psychoanalyst Carl Jung developed his theory of *synchronicity* as a way of accounting for the existence of coincidences and other supposedly anomalous phenomena. The idea of synchronicity, which Jung also described as 'acausal parallelism', is that an underlying relationship between synchronous events can exist that does not adhere to deterministic principles in which a cause precedes an effect. Intriguingly, Jung resorted to an analogy of the *Wunderkammern* to underscore the only relative validity of causality and the bias promoted by a scientific world view when considering the acausal connection between events:

> to grasp these unique or rare events at all, we seem to be dependent on equally 'unique' and individual descriptions. This would result in a chaotic collection of curiosities, rather like those old natural history cabinets where one finds, cheek by jowl with fossils and anatomical monsters in bottles, the horn of a unicorn, a mandragora manikin, and a dried mermaid. (Jung 1969, p. 6)

Structurally, the exhibition's scenographic design proceeded from a series of parallelisms. Twin gallery spaces were set up and formally organised in an identical fashion. [*Figure 28*] Upon entrance into either gallery, the viewer was faced with a small, square, framed panel presenting the detail of an architectural façade. The centre of each image is masked out by a black or white circle. Continuing past this screen, the viewer entered the main body of the gallery. A set of discrete elements were organised in the space. A square framed unit was hung on a side wall perpendicular to a similar unit presented upward and facing on a low plinth. Each of these frames contained a roundel: the wall units presenting an emblematic image of skull and antlers, whereas the sculptural frame presented a disc-shaped print resembling a plaque. This sculptural unit was aligned along the central axis of the gallery with a long table occupying the far end of the space. On its surface a series of panels resembling chessboards were arranged. A narrow opening in the connecting wall

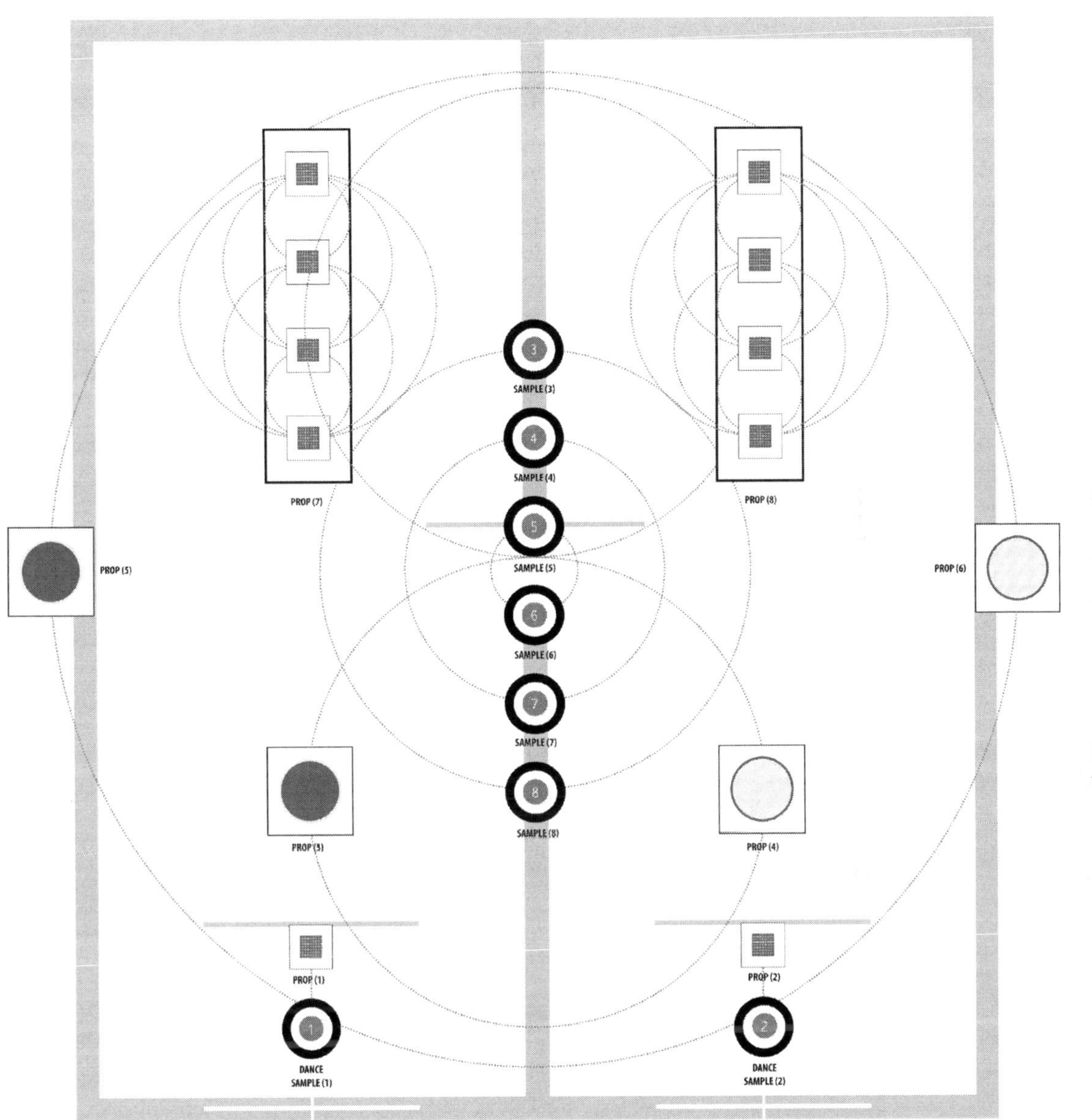

Figure 28: Installation schematic of *Demonstration Exhibition – The Ammonite Order, or Objectiles for an (Un) Natural History* (Faculty Gallery: Melbourne, 2008).

between the two galleries was situated directly opposite the framed prints, their line of sight bisecting the space laterally.

The formality of the display exuded an overwhelming impression of proportionality. The quality of this spatial practice – its highly schematic arrangement alluding to a Neoclassical sense of rationality and geometric simplicity – was confounded by the exhibition's associated digital mediation. It has become increasingly commonplace in conventional museological practice to find physical elements presented in display supplemented by the application of portable media to provide written, audio or multimedia (audio/video) commentary designed to add to the viewer's appreciation and understanding. This approach was indicated with the introductory images first encountered upon entrance to the galleries. Their accompanying wall labels directed the viewer to supplementary information provided on the accompanying iPod media player prepared specifically for the exhibition. But while in this first instance access to this collection of media was predetermined (the media content supplementing the viewer's engagement with the apparent artwork), the relationship of the remaining content was not prescribed. Throughout the rest of the exhibition there were no overt signs announcing the direct correspondence between any given item from the physical inventory with the remaining array of media content – a series of motion graphic pieces creating composite arrangements by superimposing a selection of specimens from the Grant Museum's natural history collection. As a result, the viewer was left with total freedom to access this content how and as they saw fit. The responsibility for making meaningful connections was handed over to the viewer. As a result, the status of objects was undermined and their role as *objectiles* assumed pre-eminence. [*Figures 29* and *30*]

This reconceptualisation of the objectile is derived from architect/philosopher Bernard Cache's critical response to the influence of digital technologies on methods of production and representation. In *Earth Moves: the furnishing of territories*, he proposes a shift from the understanding of the architectural image derived from the pictorial arts to a problematic of dynamics and variability. Cache theorised the idea of a technologically integrated, quasi-object open to the possibility of unpredictable variation from drawing upon the possibilities offered by parametric modelling for nonstandard production of forms through computer-aided design. In recognizing how these systems enable unique objects to be fabricated by modifying the parameters of their calculation, Cache determined that 'objects, which are those solid parts of our actions, are but a moment of densification in the folds of our behaviour that is itself fluctuating' (1995, p. 96). With the advent of digital technologies, 'from the mould we move towards modulation. We no longer apply a preset form on inert matter, but lay out parameters of a surface' (p. 96). According to Boyman, Cache has envisaged: 'a universe where objects are not stable but may undergo variations, giving rise to new possibilities of seeing' (Boyman 1995, p. ix). Accordingly, images 'are connected through a logic where the whole is not given but always open to variation, as new things are added or new relations made, creating new continuities out of such intervals or disparities' (p. viii).

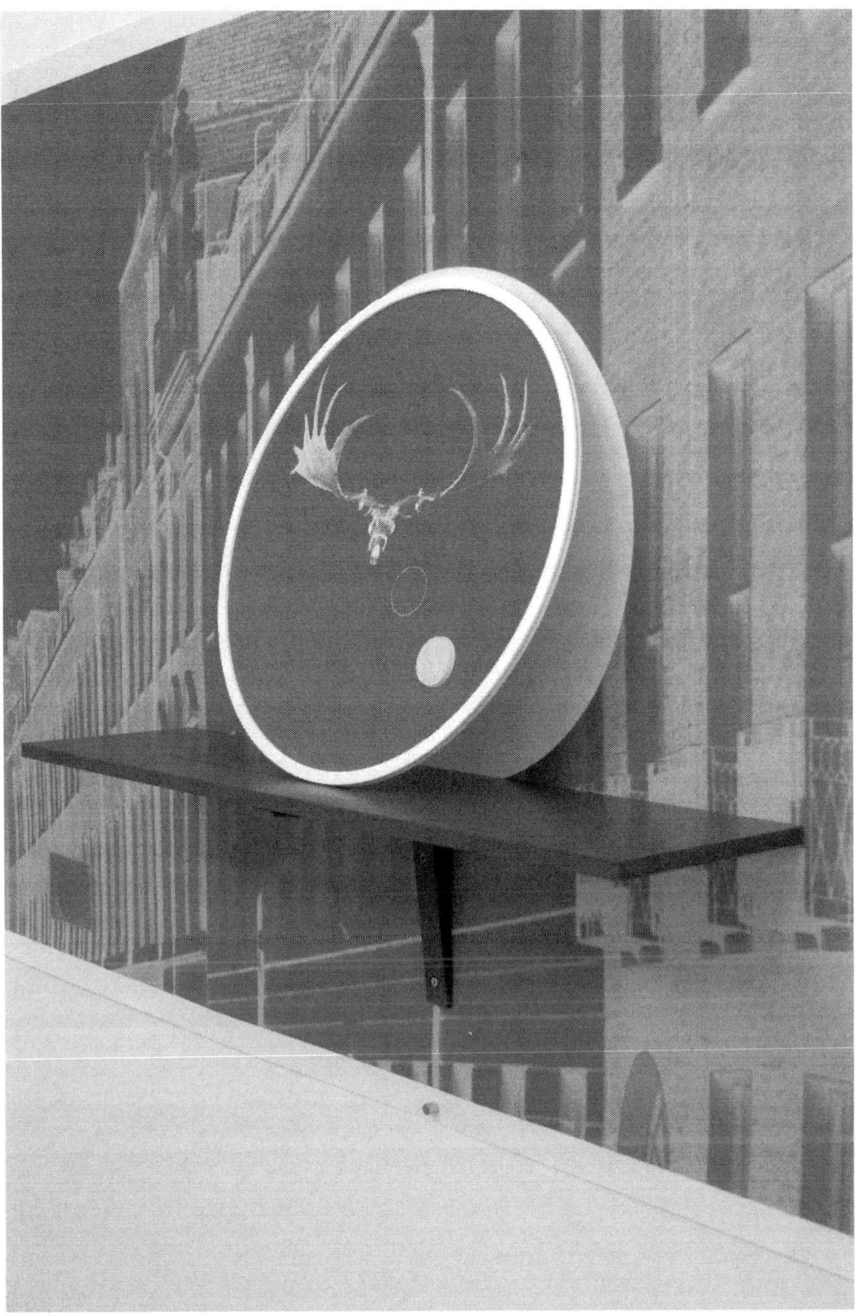

Figure 29: Vince Dziekan, Installation view of *The Ammonite Order, or, Objectiles for an (Un) Natural History – Darwin Roundel* (ISEA: Belfast, 2009). Digital print (40cm/c). Laser-cut Perspex. Wall-mounted display. Variable dimensions.

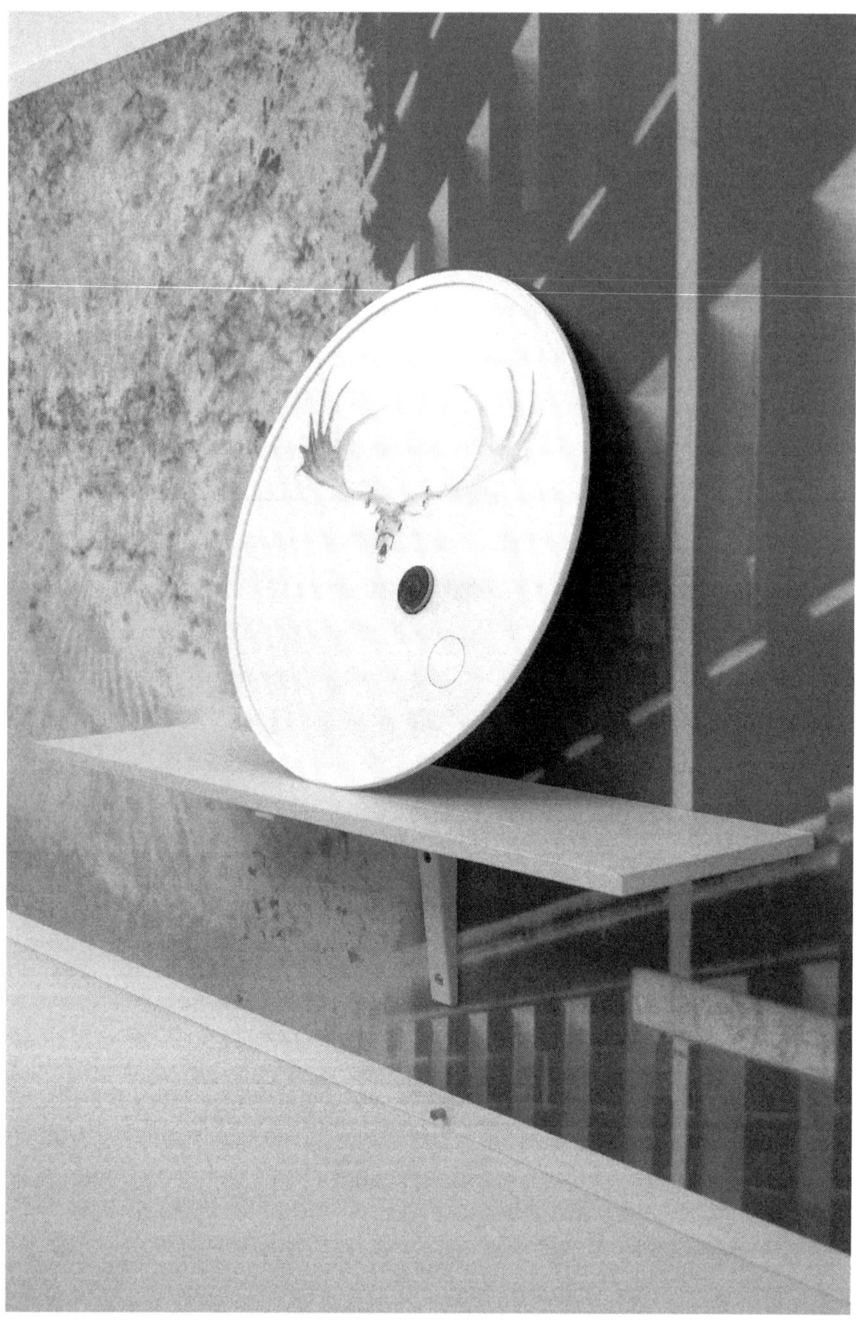

Figure 30: Vince Dziekan, Installation view of *The Ammonite Order, or, Objectiles for an (Un) Natural History – Dance Roundel* (ISEA: Belfast, 2009). Digital print (40cm/c). Laser-cut Perspex. Wall-mounted display. Variable dimensions.

My subsequent application of this concept in curatorial design emphasised how the art object is modulated at the intersection of the exhibition. The exhibition acted as the surface or plane of coincidence that governed the parameters for the viewer's interaction and subsequent interpretation with the objectile as a non-standardised object (precipitating a new kind of objectivity from the interrelation of the virtual artwork with the subjectivities, intuition and imagination of its viewer).

Serving to open up further interpretative license by inducing the viewer's active involvement in meaning-making, the exhibition's construction placed added emphasis upon how syntax and discourse occurs across its physical and virtual dimensions. Mieke Bal has articulated museal discourse as a 'set of semiotic and epistemological habits that enables and prescribes ways of communicating and thinking that may be of use to others participating in the discourse' (2001, p. 164), while syntax operates through meaningful juxtapositions that 'impel the subject to connect the presence of the object to the past of its making, functioning and meaning' (p. 166). The exhibitology demonstrated by this exhibition could best be described as polyphonous. In terms of its scenography, the exhibition design was characterised by the presentation of discrete elements existing on physical and virtual dimensions simultaneously. Exposition was developed through the coordination of space and time. The installation strategy was intent upon creating formal and thematic 'mirrorings' that provide bridges between the works collected within each self-contained gallery, or by extension across the identically set out rooms. Further, the viewer's decision-making was involved in creating composite arrangements, as their synchronous viewing of any of the given 'props' present in the gallery space was overlayed by media content being viewed on the handheld device. This juxtapositonal form of 'split-screen' viewing had a disorientating effect where whatever degree of undivided concentration that is lost, is compensated by imaginative projection.

Increasingly sophisticated strategies around presentation have undoubtedly transformed the contemporary museum. Changes to techniques of exhibition practice impact on the character of aesthetic experience. The exhibition provides the arena for this dynamic to be explored. In closing, this demonstration exhibition was approached as a model that promotes a different type of aesthetic experience through defamiliarising the relationship that presently exists – for the most part – between spatial practice and digital mediation. Russian formalist Viktor Shklovsky introduced his essay 'Art as Technique' (writing in 1916) by asserting that as perception becomes habitual, it becomes automatic. He would go on to champion the rejection of traditional culture and how artistic forms associated with those conditions turn seeing and thinking into conventional exercises:

The purpose of art is to impart the sensation of things as they are perceived and not as they are known. The technique of art is to make objects 'unfamiliar', to make forms difficult, to increase the difficulty and length of perception because the process of perception is an aesthetic end in itself and must be prolonged. Art is a way of experiencing the artfulness of an object; the object is not important. (Shklovsky 2004, p. 16)

By exercising the liberty afforded by its conceptualisation as an exhibition/artwork that blurs the distinction between fact and fiction, *The Ammonite Order* raises the proposition that the integration of real and virtual through the art of exhibition offers a demonstration of how the nature of aesthetic experience associated with the multimedial museum might take shape.

Notes

1. The use of the term 'museum' (derived from the Greek *mouseion* – as shrine, seat or haunt of the muses) to refer to a place designed for the public display of knowledge is closely associated with the Enlightenment movement and came to prominence in the eighteenth century.

   The 'Age of Enlightenment' was characterised by intellectual and philosophical developments based on the belief in the power of human reason. The Enlightenment acted as a central model for many movements that emerged in the modern period, including the founding of the discipline of art history by Johann Joachim Winckelmann. Reductionism and rationality are recognised as distinctive modes of Enlightenment thinking that stand in stark contrast to attitudes espousing irrationality and emotionalism. Represented in design terms, geometric order, proportionality and restraint are seen as expressions of these virtues.

2. The architect George Dance (1741–1825) lived at 91 Gower Street, while Charles Darwin (1809–1882) lived at 12 Upper Gower Street, now the site of the Darwin Building, which houses UCL's Department of Genetics, Environment and Evolution and the Grant Museum of Zoology. Somewhat fortuitously, the presentation of this work as part of the ISEA2009 exhibition in Belfast, Northern Ireland, coincided with bicentenary celebrations marking the birth of Charles Darwin.

3. The term *stratigraphy* refers to the processes by which sedimentary deposits form on the Earth's surface and how those deposits change over time. This particular field of geological study was pioneered by Nicholas Steno in the seventeenth century. Steno's 'Law of Superimposition' provided a theoretical basis for this field by describing how sedimentary layers are deposited as a time sequence by observing two principles: Original Horizontality (which describes the way in which layers of sediment are initially deposited) and Lateral Continuity (which recognizes that sedimentary deposits initially extend laterally in all directions). Reference to Steno's Law added an intertextual 'dimension' to the resulting exhibition.

4. Robert Edmond Grant (1793–1874) was the first professor of Zoology and Comparative Anatomy in England. Upon taking up the chair at the University of London in 1827 he began to amass skeletons, mounted animals and specimens preserved in fluid as a teaching collection. Including many extinct species (including the Tasmanian tiger or thylacine, the quagga, and the dodo), Grant's original specimens as well as those of the comparative anatomist Thomas Henry Huxley (who became an energetic advocate of Darwinian evolution) form the basis of the current collection of the Grant Museum of Zoology and Comparative Anatomy. Through his work on marine invertebrates, including sea sponges and mollusks, Grant established homology between these simple creatures and mammals, controversially suggesting that all life shared a 'unity of plan', thereby supporting the radical ideas by his French contemporaries, the zoologists Jean-Baptiste Lamarck and the Etienne Saint-Hilaire.

5. Ammonites are an extinct group of marine animals of the subclass *Ammonoidea* in the class *Cephalopoda*, phylum *Mollusca*. While outwardly resembling the *Nautilus*, ammonites are more closely related to the subclass *Coleoidea*, which includes octopus and squid.

6. In the Classical architectural tradition, orders establish a visual language or lexicon likened to the grammar or rhetoric of literary or musical compositions. Influencing other Neoclassical architects in England, including most notably John Nash, Dance applied the 'ammonite order' to his celebrated design for London's Shakespeare Gallery in 1789.

7. According to Umberto Eco, *fabula* are 'narrative isotopies' (1979, p. 28) or manifestations of the discursive structure of a text. Derived from the textual analyses of Russian Formalist literary critics (including Viktor Shklovsky and Roman Jakobson), *fabula* relate to the elements that make up a story such as the 'logic of actions or the syntax of characters, the time-honoured course of events. It need not necessarily be a sequence of human actions (physical or not), but can also concern a temporal transformation of ideas or a series of events concerning inanimate objects' (p. 27).

8. In early 2001, contemporary architect Daniel Libeskind produced a personal exhibition that drew inspiration from the idiosyncratic character of the Soane Museum. Evoking something of the same spirit that compelled Soane earlier, Libeskind is quoted as stating: 'I believe that the connection between drawing and building, between models of the mind and materials in space, between tradition and the future, is the core of the practice of architecture' ('Libeskind at the Soane: *Drawing a New Architecture*', Sir John Soane's Museum website, available at: [http://www.soane.org/exhibitions/libeskind_at_the_soane_drawing_a_new_architecture [20 September 2011]). Libeskind used the exhibition, titled *Drawing a New Architecture*, as an opportunity to install a series of conceptual drawings and miniature models arranged in response to Soane's own collection, scattering them throughout like the architectural fragments found elsewhere in the museum. Libeskind's decision to exhibit his work at the Soane Museum attests to a shared interest of how display and exhibition space is mediated through design.

9. Anamorphosis relates to distortions that require the viewer to use special devices or occupy a specific vantage point to reconstitute the image. There are two main types of anamorphosis: perspectival (or oblique), with examples dating from the early Renaissance, and mirror (or catoptric) anamorphosis, which is more commonly associated with the Baroque period. Etymologically, *ana-morphosis* comes from the Greek words meaning 'formed again'.

10. Mannerism describes a period of European painting, sculpture, architecture and decorative arts encompassing most of the sixteenth century. Stylistically, it reacted to the harmonious ideals associated with the naturalism of Italian High Renaissance. In contrast, the early Mannerists – exemplified by Parmigianino's *Self-portrait in a Convex Mirror* of 1524 – employed exaggerated forms, manipulated irrational space and unnatural lighting to heighten the artificiality of their representations.

    In relating this Mannerist tendency to the exhibition, I am inferring to an equivalent kind of knowing distortion of techniques and tropes associated with museological display. The most influential proponent of the exhibition as art form was the Belgian artist Marcel Broodthaers. Employing the eagle as the symbol of his fictional *Musée d'Art Moderne*, Broodthaers wrote:

> There is a mirror decorated with an eagle – a late eighteenth-century antique – which belongs to a museum association in Ghent. An official mirror, if that's the phrase, which reflects the virtual image of those eagles whose multiple heads recount the history of arms as an aspect of art. This is a mirror of misunderstanding. Even though Jupiter's messenger perches on top, it's a trick mirror. (Broodthaers 1988, p. 47)

Conclusion

> Museums are houses that only shelter thoughts. Even the visitor least able to penetrate such thoughts know that what he sees in those paintings hanging next to each other are thoughts, that those paintings are beautiful, but the canvas, the paint that has dried on it and the gilded wood that frames it aren't.
>
> – Marcel Proust

The primary objective of this book has been directed at developing a conceptual framework for digitally-informed creative production with a focus on exhibition-based practices. As an outcome of its collected interdisciplinary investigations, I have attempted to articulate a proposition for *curatorial design*, which has been developed in response to the emergence of what I have described as the *multimedial museum*.

Over the course of its writing, my investigation of *virtuality* has lead beyond it being approached as a limited technological issue. Instead, the focus of my enquiry was drawn inexorably towards a recognition of the effect that various processes involving digitalisation have had on the way the art system operates at a more generalisable level. As a result, in selecting exhibitions and works for close examination in this book I have purposefully gravitated towards cases and examples that do not all categorically address new media art, genres of electronic art or issues specific to the digital curation of online forms. Instead, I have broached the idea that virtuality, more broadly, as a cultural concept that, being articulated through the *art of exhibition*, has come to describe the character of aesthetic experience under contemporary conditions. This orientation to the enquiry opens onto significant opportunities for further exploration and application, as the implications of virtuality begin to affect how cultural organisations function in the face of combined social, cultural and technological factors.[1] How individual institutions chose to respond to these challenges will mark a significant next phase in the evolution of the museum concept.

By combining critical enquiry and creative application, this book has evolved in response to the current state of adoption of digital media across a range of museum-based cultural practices in order to speculate upon the interrelationship of *digital mediation* with *spatial practice*. In it I have tried to describe how the exhibition mediates interaction between cultural processes (encompassing both artistic and curatorial forms of creative practice) and the aesthetic experience of the viewer. The exhibition form itself acts at the interface between media forms and viewing conditions designed through exhibition space. Highlighted by the role that exhibition plays in these theoretical and practical investigations, I have sought to reveal the fundamental interdependence between art objects, gallery space and processes of museological framing. This perception has lead to my critical formulation of the *exhibition complex*, while further refinement of the concept was made possible by its direct practice-based application through curatorial design. I have been able to explore a number of creative inflections on this construct – involving relevant themes, range of methods, types of installation and rhetorical modes or tropes – through the series of projects documented as case studies in the Exhibitions section of the book. As spatial practice and digital mediation become increasingly integrated, new *programme architectures* will be needed to promote alternative ways that the multimedial museum might come to take shape. In this regard, critiquing the exhibition as a cultural form – drawing upon both historical and practice-based methodologies – is particularly important, given the contentions inherent to this particular cultural moment, which has seen the maturation of mixed-art form venues and dedicated media arts organisations. At this juncture, these specialist organisations face a particular challenge in terms of how to best function in order to capitalise on their combined physical and digital 'footprints'. Their contentious place within the creative sector has been summarised by Tom Fleming (whose observations were directed principally towards cross-art form and media venues in the UK, such as the Foundation for Art and Creative Technology (FACT) in Liverpool, Cornerhouse in Manchester and Watershed in Bristol):

> The venues are currently positioned at a crucial juncture between their analogue past and the digital present and future. Their 'analogue' past, represented in their heritage as hybrids of independent cinema, media, education and business centres, interdisciplinary galleries and more, still has considerable currency and attends to a wide value range. However, it no longer adequately describes the role and functions that the organisations can and should have. Their 'digital' future lies in the way in which they are evolving as multi-channel, connected, open, cross-sector and cross-disciplinary facilitators and providers of personalised content, experiences, learning, research and services for the creative economy. (Fleming 2008, p. 90)

This observation points to larger implications faced by public institutions today, namely, the place of common cultural heritage and the role of shared experience in a time where technology is enabling forms of aesthetic experiences that are centred increasingly on the personalisation of content.

In order to meaningfully address the experience of digital media in exhibition space it is necessary to recognise form as a relational property – moving from passive form to active formation. Developing this perspective entails rethinking the nature of media. The question of media-specificity raises the important issue of the united, organic constitution of a particular media form versus how to account for the distributive organisation of hybridised formations. Addressing this problematic holds relevance not only for a digital aesthetics but also more broadly for contemporary art and curating practices in general, particularly in response to what has been posited as a post-medium paradigm shift (Krauss 2000). Rosalind Krauss (2000) has identified the dawning of a *post-medium condition* in late-Modernist art. In modernist aesthetics, the dominant hierarchical mode holds that each media has its own distinct qualities and that the undeterred pursuit of these innate qualities is the calling of the highest aesthetic order. However, with the emergence of 'intermedia', as exemplified in practices associated with conceptualism, mixed media and pluralistic practices of the 1960s and 1970s, a reappraisal of this aesthetic order follows which signals the waning of media-specificity. As part of this re-evaluation, site comes to be recognised as material support – and in its way, site-specificity opens up a multiplicity of situations in which art can operate and finds its form of exposition. The paradigmatic shift announced by this post-medium condition replaces the specific formal traits and properties conventionally used to define media traditionally with an accommodation to the composite operations of an apparatus. The medium, previously consigned to being condensed as a form of material substance, is reconfigured as an aggregative, compound of material support that is interdependent with the viewer and the trajectory of their encounter in, and across, spaces.

The artwork as pure, aesthetic unity has become a less and less tenable proposition under these conditions. Unlike traditional mediums of painting or sculpture, for instance, with multi-media – resorting to this term in order to encompass a wide range of digital technologies – 'media' is fundamentally constituted by data streams (Cubitt 2000). The transformative qualities of the 'zeros' and 'ones' of code that underwrite any digital object, and the variability that is possible across input and output forms is reflected in the characteristic of convergence. Reflected in convergence media, where no singular, essential form need assume primacy, formation becomes the active principle. Henri Bergson, whose thoughts on movement took shape during the time of cinema's invention at the closing of the nineteenth century, perceived that the division of matter into independent bodies with absolutely determined outlines is an artificial division. From the outset of the new millennium what might be called a transitional state has taken precedence, entailing a shift from a concentration on form, unity and media-specificity to an aesthetic based on formation, multiplicity and distribution. Nicolas Bourriaud has noted how 'transivity', taken as a dialogic principle, 'is the tangible property of the artwork' (2002, p. 26). Form, he continues, arises from this 'lasting encounter'. Lending this distinction to the situation of an artwork in exhibition space involves contrasting its exposition as an intrusive 'alien' to a more fluid and distributed interrelationship with the space in which it is encountered. This latter depiction, representative of the multimedial character of the contemporary museum, describes how elements emerge out of material procedures, rather than as pre-existing 'presets'.[2] If the prevailing adoption of digital mediation in museums has conformed to the dictates of a hierarchical order, this is based in large part on how this new situation has been approached from an established media-centric point of view. The hierarchical mode adopts a stance that might be described as hard design, in its adherence to a unidirectional, authoritative point of view that privileges a predetermined, fixed and bounded constitution or outcome. Alternatives to this 'broadcast' attitude have at various times been signalled as demonstrating dialectical and/or dialogical processes. The orientation of these modes involve the user more integrally and tends towards embracing the ephemeral qualities of interactive content in the mixed-reality setting of the multimedial museum. New tropes for curatorial design, capable of integrating forms of interaction, flexibility and feedback as part of the art of exhibition bring these active dimensions of behaviour and material process to the aesthetic experience of contemporary exhibition space.

It is not surprising then that to date, the creative production involved in exhibition forms has found itself largely consigned to the margins of art critique, with most concentrated attention being paid to more formalised and individuated components, such as the artefact, art object or installation artwork. While attention is increasingly being paid to the figure of the curator, particularly those curators who have been responsible for global biennales, the material practice of curatorial design in museums remains a largely under-theorised area. The pluralistic attitude of recent anthologies such as *Curating Subjects* (O'Neill 2007), *New Media in the White Cube and Beyond: curatorial models for digital art* (Paul 2008) and *Rethinking Curating: art after new media* (Graham and Cook, 2010) offer indications of the inter-dependent relationships involved in both the practice of curation today, as well as how critical engagement with contemporary curation might proceed. As Bruce Altshuler has pointed out previously, when discussing the exaggeration of art's social characteristics and how these characteristics were brought to the fore-front of advanced practices in his study of the historical avant-garde:

> Art is made by individuals, and working alone, individuals can create radical pieces that subvert cultural and political assumptions. Yet without a community of acceptance – or rejection – such art remains irrelevant to the history of the avant-garde. The story of the avant-garde is that of mutual support amongst a community and reception of art by a public, all participants enmeshed in a system of personal and economic relations. Its manifestos were those of movements, and its force depended on confrontation with a complex social world. (1994, p. 8)

Belying its relatively peripheral positioning, the exhibition was duly acknowledged as 'the central node of that confrontation' (Altshuler 1994, p. 8). The need to recognise the centrality of the exhibition within art's field has become even more pronounced today as digital technologies have begun to exert a significant impact on the sustainability of art's 'eco-system'.

In the electronic era, the structure of reality is influenced by mass media. Interested in distributive models of cultural practice, anthropologist Ulf Hannerz has used the term 'perspective' to denote the individual's situational involvement within the field: 'perspective exists in a tension zone between culture and social structure' (1992, p. 65). He provides a definition of culture as a 'flow' occurring across three distinct dimensions: modes of thought (ideas), forms of externalisation and their social distribution. 'Cultural process', he states, 'takes place in their ongoing interrelation' (p. 4).[3] Our perception of reality, so considered, is composed from perceptions drawn from many mediated spaces (visual, acoustic, physical, virtual). Such an interpretation is inspired by the thinking of Marshall McLuhan, whose canon of writings relate to how the evolving relationship between media and culture transforms our sense of constructed reality. McLuhan viewed media not simply as tools but as part of the environment.[4] In effect, the medium is the milieu (Strate and Wachtel 2005). From this perspective, a technology can only be properly understood as a medium when it enters into a network of relations with other media and becomes part of the larger socio-cultural fabric. Exerting influence while also being influenced by material practices, Bolter and Grusin have described this interdependency between formal and cultural dimensions of media as 'remediation'. Accordingly, underpinning an understanding of digital technologies today: 'A medium in our culture can never operate in isolation' (Bolter and Grusin 1999, p. 65).

Personally, I have come to find that the term 'ecology' resonates particularly well when attempting to describe such a complex arrangement, particularly in an effort to emphasise an organisational perspective to curatorial design. Matthew Fuller has distinguished between the more humanistic emphasis implied by an environmentalist worldview in contrast to a more ecological focus on dynamic systems. The latter perspective is more interested in how 'any one part is always multiply connected, acting by virtue of those connections, and always variable, such that it can be regarded as a pattern than simply as an object' (Fuller 2005, p. 4). For me, conceptualising such an ecology of exhibition has proven particularly useful because it implies a relational basis to the various processes and interactions involved in the exposition of artworks, as well as alluding to the basis of meaning through a museological arrangement of elements taking place in the spatial sphere of the gallery or site of exhibition. In an expanded sense, this spatialisation also involves temporality, sequencing and the designed arrangement of discrete events across both time and place through digital mediation.[5]

In his formulation of an ecology of communication, David Altheide has discussed how the techniques and information technologies associated with communicative acts are joined interactively with social activities within an enveloping communication environment. Social life is composed through communicated experiences that assert the 'symbolic dimensions of the culture stream' (Altheide 1995, p. 7). Experience is increasingly mediated by an ever-expanding array of information technologies and formats involved with the transfer of meaning.[6] Identifying the resulting set of complex relations as part of an ecology of communication recognises the centrality of the contextual dimension of the communication process to the organisation of information technologies, communication formats and social activity into 'effective environments' (p. 9). Supported this observation, Lance Strate and Edward Wachtel have pointed out that 'in the study of media environments, or media ecology, the first step is to make the invisible milieu visible, to move the background into the foreground, to foster awareness by exchanging the figure and the ground' (2005, p. 3).

While the collected investigations brought together in this book have aimed to present a distinctive set of theoretical and practice-based perspectives that hope to broaden understanding of the influence of digital technologies on exhibition-based cultural production, inevitably, there are limitations to its scope and coverage. While the design of new museums has provided an inspirational backdrop, the liminal zone between museum architecture and exhibition design (as a professionally-defined discipline in large-scale cultural organisations) has not been critically negotiated. Nor for that matter have practices of particular relevance (such as experience design) been thoroughly explored, although innovative exhibition design solutions by NOX, for example, have certainly had an indirect influence on ideas developed at the design stage of my curatorial projects. For that matter, temporary exhibitions and events involving the presentation or performance of media in public space have not been directly focused upon either. While site-specificity has been a central line of enquiry, attention has been limited to the staging of exhibitions that are situated within the context of the museum itself. Particularly as mobile and pervasive media become more ubiquitous, I will be keen to focus in the future on aspects of framing cultural experiences designed to extend aesthetic engagement beyond the museum.

This book brings together a 'constellation' of interrelating concerns. In conceiving this interdisciplinary investigation of virtuality and the art of exhibition, I have tried to remain mindful of an observation made by media theorist Regis Debray in his book *Media Manifestoes*:

> The error of futurologists and disappointment of futurists commonly arise from overestimating the medium's effect by underestimating the milieu's weighty plots. As a general rule, usage is more archaic than the tool. The explanation is self-evident: if the medium is 'new', the milieu is 'old', by definition. It is a stratification of memories and narrative associations, a palimpsest of gestures and legends continuously prone to reactivation, the repertory we rapidly leaf through of representational structures and symbols from all preceding ages. (1996, pp. 16–17)

It is becoming the default situation today, that the aesthetic experience of art is taking place under increasingly virtualised conditions of the multimedial museum. It is undeniable that digitally-based practices, encompassing artistic production as well as a myriad of institutional applications, are beginning to impact more broadly on what this research has described as the art's exhibition complex. As this book's collected critical investigation and practice-based applications attest, by examining the role, function and forms of exhibition, curatorial design proposes a distinctive way of exploring the relationship that resiliently continues to connect art to the institutionalised space of the contemporary museum.

Notes

1. As an indirect outcome of this course of enquiry, I have had the opportunity to engage with these larger issues in association with leading cultural institutions that have recognised such an eventuality. In 2008, I undertook a consultation project with the Foundation for Art and Creative

Technology (FACT) in Liverpool. 'Future FACT' was designed to act as a conceptual 'blueprint' for the organisation to initiate the possibility of conceiving an integrated public programme in response to what might be termed 'Web 2.0 Thinking'. As a by-product, the research and development aspirations of the organisation were articulated by setting the foundations for the establishment of the 'FACT Atelier'. Additionally, in 2009, I was appointed to the steering committee of 'Virtual NGV'. Identified as a priority project as part of the strategic plan of the National Gallery of Victoria, this initiative involved the review and reimplementation of an integrated website architecture centred on exhibition and collection support, audience engagement and service delivery. Subsequently, as this project has evolved, its focus has turned to implementing cultural change and facilitating different types of coordinated communication exchanges between the museum and its audience via digitally-mediated channels.

2. During a public lecture delivered at the National Gallery of Victoria International, Melbourne, on 9 November 2004, Dr. Richard Kurin of the Smithsonian Institution, spoke of the epistemological shift from conservation of material artefacts to material 'work' facing contemporary museology. In that context, Kurin asserted that museums needed to respond to this sort of methodological challenge in order to address the increasingly vital problem of making intangible cultural heritage, tangible.

3. Ulf Hannerz has recognised the role that electronic media has come to play in shaping the complexity of contemporary cultures. By reconceiving culture as process, a rethinking of mediated spaces (physical and virtual) in which culture is 'practiced', and in which individuals filter this experience, is called for. According to Hannerz:

> media relate(s) to all three dimensions of culture [...] [T]hey carry meanings; much media research is occupied in one way or another with content analysis. They entail a range of different modes of externalisation, as technologies variously constrain and make possible particular symbol systems. Clearly, too, they have an impact on the distribution of meanings and meaningful forms over people and relationships. (1992, p. 27)

4. Marshall McLuhan forwarded his own thesis of how electric process transform the arts and sciences into 'anti-environments', which, in turn, through this mediation revises our understanding of the world into art forms. This particular view of media, according to one McLuhan commentator, recognises these 'anti-environments' as 'artistic probes for training perception to reveal new meanings and new roles for us and to enable us to see the world as a "museum without walls" – full of art, being art itself' (Zingrone 2005, p. 45).

5. In an interview with Ross Gibson (1998) that predated the establishment of the Australian Centre for the Moving Image, Gary Warner discussed the idea of 'electronic ecology' in relation to the inadequacy of standard information technology approaches to the deployment of multimedia systems in museums and other 'interpreted' public spaces.

6. David Altheide has singled out interdependence, mutuality and coexistence as the basic elements of ecology (1995, p. 10). Information technology is defined broadly as any externalisable media or procedure used in the creation, processing, transmission and storage of information content, while formats involve the selection, organisation and presentation of media into normative patterns and shapes that structure the form of interaction with the audience or receiver of information.

List of Illustrations

Cover image. 'Carte-de-visite' documentation from Vince Dziekan, *Demonstration Exhibition – The Ammonite Order, or, Objectiles for an (Un) Natural History* (Faculty Gallery: Melbourne, 2008). Digital prints. Laser-cut Perspex. Digital media. Customized iPod interface. Room brochure. Wall-mounted and table display. Variable installation.

Part I: Expositions

Chapter 1: Virtuality
Figure 1. Installation view of Pipilotti Rist, *Gravity Be My Friend* (2007). Audio video installation (FACT: Liverpool, 2008).

Chapter 2: The Art of Exhibition
Figure 2. Installation view of Carsten Holler, *Test Site* (2006). Slide Installation *(Unilever Series*, Tate Modern: London, 2006–7). Photo credit: Attilio Maranzano.

Chapter 3: Spatial Practice
Figure 3. Installation documentation of Marcel Duchamp, *A Mile of String* (1942). String installation (*First Papers of Surrealism*: New York, 1942). © Marcel Duchamp/ADAGP. Licensed by Viscopy, 2011.

Chapter 4: Digital Mediation
Figure 4. Screen documentation of Susan Collins, *Tate in Space* (2002). Website (Tate Online: London, 2002).

Chapter 5: The Multimedial Museum
Figure 5. Installation view of Yinka Shonibare, *Un Ballo in Maschera / A Masked Ball* (2004). Video presented in the context of European painting galleries of the 17th and 18th centuries (NGVI: Melbourne, 2008). Photo credit: Vince Dziekan.

Chapter 6: Curatorial Design

Figure 6. Installation view of Ryoji Ikeda, *data.spectra* (2005). Video installation with multiple projectors, mirrors and four-channel sound. The work was commissioned by the Australian Centre for the Moving Image. Produced by forma. Supported by the Arts Council England and the Japan Foundation (*White Noise*, ACMI: Melbourne, 2005). Photo credit: Christian Capurro.

Part II: Exhibitions

Chapter 7: The Synthetic Image: Digital Technologies and the Image

Figure 7. Installation schematic of *The Synthetic Image* (Faculty Gallery: Melbourne, 2002).

Figure 8. Installation view of Vince Dziekan, *From Catalogue-Museum* (*The Synthetic Image*: Melbourne, 2002). Mixed media, 6 units, 300 × 370 × 100 mm each. Variable installation.

Figure 9. Installation documentation of Marcel Broodthaers, *Musée d'Art Moderne, Département des Aigles, Section XIXe siecle* (1968). Installation at 30, Rue de la Pepiniere, Brussels, 1968. Photo credit: Maria Glissen. © Marcel Louis Broodthaers/SABAM. Licensed by Viscopy, 2011.

Figure 10. Patricia Piccinini, *Lumpland* (1995). Computer-generated digiprint, 1270 × 2300 mm. Edition of 3. Monash University Collection.

Figure 11. Installation view of *The Synthetic Image – Light Room* (Faculty Gallery: Melbourne, 2002). Featured works by Marcus Bunyan, Murray McKeich, Lynne Roberts-Goodwin and Daniel Von Sturmer.

Figure 12. Installation view of *The Synthetic Image – Dark Room* (Faculty Gallery: Melbourne, 2002). Featured works by Megan Evans, Troy Innocent, Gerard Minogue, Matthew Perkins and Vince Dziekan.

Chapter 8: Small Worlds: A Romance

Figure 13. Installation schematic of *Small Worlds: A Romance* (UTS Gallery: Sydney, 2003).

Figure 14. Frames from Richard Brown, *Mimesia* (2003). Wall-mounted 'interactive painting'. Media/software: PowerRender (a games engine). Interactivity: VisualMouse. Collection of the artist.

Figure 15. Storyboard version of Vince Dziekan, *Nature-History (ii. Writing with Light)* (2003). Digital animation. 5.00 min (loop).

Figure 16. Installation views of Vince Dziekan, *Nature-History (ii. Writing with Light)* (*Small Worlds: A Romance*: Sydney, 2003). Digital animation. 5.00 min (loop). Variable installation (projection, viewable from front and rear).

Figure 17. Installation view of *Small Worlds: A Romance* (UTS Gallery: Sydney, 2003). Featured works by Richard Brown, Csaba Czamosy, Bruce Mowson, Joel Zika and Vince Dziekan.

Chapter 9: Remote

Figure 18. Transposition for Pete Gomes, *Littoral Map (Tasmania)* (Plimsoll Gallery: Hobart, 2006).

Figure 19. Interface designs for Vince Dziekan, *V. Travels in the Netherworld* (1890–2006). Digital imaging. Interface design: 320 × 240 pixels.

Figure 20. Installation view of Vince Dziekan, *V. Travels in the Netherworld* (*Remote*: Hobart, 2006). Mixed/locative media: PDA, digital content, graphic markers. Variable/site-specific installation.

Figure 21. Vince Dziekan, *V. Travels in the Netherworld – GirlStar* (1890–2006). Digital animation, 2.00 min (loop), 320 × 240 pixels.

Figure 22. Installation schematic of *Remote* – Plaza and Plimsoll Gallery level (Plimsoll Gallery: Hobart, 2006).

Figure 23. Installation schematic of *Remote* – first floor, Centre for the Arts (Plimsoll Gallery: Hobart, 2006).

Figure 24. Susan Collins, *Glenlandia* (Live and online from 10 September 2005 until 10 September 2006). Web transmission. Projection. Variable dimensions. Collection of the artist.

Chapter 10: The Ammonite Order, or Objectiles for an (Un) Natural History

Figure 25. 'Carte-de-visite' documentation from Vince Dziekan, *Demonstration Exhibition – The Ammonite Order, or Objectiles for an (Un) Natural History* (Faculty Gallery: Melbourne, 2008). Digital prints. Laser-cut Perspex. Digital media. Customized iPod interface. Room brochure. Wall-mounted and table display. Variable installation.

Figure 26. University College London Zoology Museum, c. 1880. © University College London, the Grant Museum of Zoology.

Figure 27. Vince Dziekan, 'Carte-de-visite' documentation from *Demonstration Exhibition – The Ammonite Order, or Objectiles for an (Un) Natural History – The Dance Room* (Faculty Gallery: Melbourne, 2008). Digital prints. Laser cut Perspex. Digital media. Customized iPod interface. Room brochure. Wall mounted and table display. Variable installation.

Figure 28. Installation schematic of *Demonstration Exhibition – The Ammonite Order, or Objectiles for an (Un) Natural History* (Faculty Gallery: Melbourne, 2008).

Figure 29. Vince Dziekan, Installation view of *The Ammonite Order, or, Objectiles for an (Un) Natural History – Darwin Roundel* (ISEA: Belfast, 2009). Digital print (40cm/c). Laser-cut Perspex. Wall-mounted display. Variable dimensions.

Figure 30. Vince Dziekan, Installation view of *The Ammonite Order, or, Objectiles for an (Un) Natural History – Dance Roundel* (ISEA: Belfast, 2009). Digital print (40cm/c). Laser-cut Perspex. Wall-mounted display. Variable dimensions.

Bibliography

ALTHEIDE, D., 1995. *An Ecology of Communication*. New York: Aldine De Gruyter.

ALTSHULER, B., 1994. *The Avant-garde in Exhibition: new art in the 20th century*. New York: Abrams.

APPADURAI, A., 1996. *Modernity at Large: cultural dimensions of globalization*. Minneapolis: University of Minnesota Press.

ÁRNASON, G.J., 2004. Olafur Eliasson – mobile vision. *Arken Bulletin*, Vol. 2.

BAL, M., 1996a. *Double Exposures: the subject of cultural analysis*. New York: Routledge.

—— 1996b. The Discourse of the Museum. *In:* R. Greenberg, et al. (eds.). *Thinking about Exhibitions*. London and New York: Routledge.

—— 2001, *Looking In: the art of viewing*. Amsterdam: G+B Arts International.

—— 2002. *Travelling Concepts in the Humanities: a rough guide*. Toronto: University of Toronto Press.

BANN, S., 1995. Shrines, Curiosities and the Rhetoric of Display. *In:* L. Cooke and P. Wollen (eds.). *Visual Display: culture beyond appearances*. Seattle: Bay Press.

BARTHES, R., 1981. *Camera Lucida: reflections on photography*. New York: Hill & Wang.

BEARMAN, D. and TRANT, J., 2008. Technologies, like Museums, are Social. *In:* J. Trant and D. Bearman (eds.). *Museums and the Web 2008, 8–12 April 2008, Montreal*. Toronto: Archives & Museum Informatics.

BENJAMIN, W., 1979, A Small History of Photography. *In: One-Way Street and Other Writings*. Transl. E. Jephcott, et al. London and New York: Verso.

—— 1992. The Work of Art in the Age of Mechanical Reproduction. *In: Illuminations*. Transl. H. Zohn. London: Fontana Press.

—— 1999. *The Arcades Project*. Transl. H. Eiland and K. McLaughlin. London: Belnap Press.

BENNETT, T., 1995, *The Birth of the Museum: history, theory, politics*. London and New York: Routledge.

BERGSON, H., 2004. *Matter and Memory*. Transl. N.M. Paul and W.S. Palmer. Mineola, NY: Dover Publications.

BLAZWICK, I. and WILSON, S., 2000. *Tate Modern: the handbook*. London: Tate Publishing.

BOLTER, J.D. and GRUSIN, R., 1999. *Remediation: understanding new media*. Cambridge, MA and London, UK: MIT Press.

BONEVENTURA, P., 2002. *Floating Worlds* [online]. Available from: http://www.tate.org.uk/intermediaart/entry15469.shtm [26 June 2008].

BONK, E., 1989. *Marcel Duchamp: the portable museum*. Transl. D. Britt. London: Thames & Hudson.

BORGEMEISTER, R., 1988. Section des Figures: the eagle from the oligocene to the present. *In:* B.H.D. Buchloh (ed.). *Broodthaers: writings, interviews, photographs*. Cambridge, MA: The MIT Press.

BOURDIEU, P., 1993. The Field of Cultural Production, or: the economic world reversed. *In:* R. Johnson (ed.). *The Field of Cultural Production: essays on art and literature.* Oxford, UK and Cambridge, MA: Polity Press.

BOURRIAUD, N., 2002. *Relational Aesthetic.* Transl. S. Pleasance and F. Woods. France: les presses du reel.

BOYMAN, A., 1995. Translator's Preface. In B. Cache. *Earth Moves: the furnishing of territories.* Transl. A. Boyman. M. Speaks (ed.). Cambridge, MA: The MIT Press.

BROODTHAERS, M. 1988. Ten Thousand Francs Reward. *In:* B.H.D. Buchloh (ed.). *Broodthaers: writings, interviews, photographs.* Cambridge, MA: The MIT Press.

BROWN, N., DEL FAVERO, D., SHAW, J. and WEIBEL, P., 2003. Interactive Narrative as a Multi-temporal Agency. *In:* J. Shaw and P. Weibel (eds.). *Future Cinema.* Cambridge, MA: MIT Press.

BROWN, R., 2003. Alchemy, Mimetics, Immersion and Consciousness. Presented at the 5th International Digital Arts and Culture (DAC) conference, 19–23 May 2003, Melbourne, Australia.

BUCHANEN, M., 2002. *Small World: uncovering nature's hidden networks.* London: Weidenfield & Nicolson.

BUCHLOH, B.H.D., 1988. Open Letters, Industrial Poems. *In:* B.H.D. Buchloh (ed.). *Broodthaers: writings, interviews, photographs.* Cambridge, MA: The MIT Press.

BUCK-MORSS, S., 1997. Aesthetics and Anaesthetics: Walter Benjamin's artwork essay reconsidered. *In:* R. Krauss, et al. (eds.). *October: the second decade, 1986–1996.* Cambridge, MA: The MIT Press.

BURNETT, R., 1995. *Cultures of Vision, Images, Media, and the Imaginary.* Bloomington and Indianapolis: University of Indiana Press.

BUZAS, S., 1994. *Sir John Soane's Museum, London.* Berlin: Ernst Wasmuth Verlag.

CACHE, B., 1995. *Earth Moves: the furnishing of territories.* Transl. A. Boyman. M. Speaks (ed.). Cambridge, MA: The MIT Press.

CADAVA, E., 1997. *Words of Light – theses on the photography of history.* Princeton, NJ: Princeton University Press.

COLLINS, S., 2005. Interview with C. Zanni. Unpublished transcript.

—— 2004. The Actual and the Imagined. *In:* A. Zapp (ed.). *Networked Narrative Environments as Imaginary Spaces of Being.* Manchester: MIRIAD.

CONLEY, T., 2000. Introduction. *In:* G. Ward (ed.). *The Certeau Reader.* Oxford and Malden, MA: Blackwell Publishing.

CRARY, J., 1999. *Suspensions of Perception, Attention, Spectacle, and Modern Culture.* Cambridge, MA and London: The MIT Press.

—— 1990. *Techniques of the Observer: on vision and modernity in the nineteenth century.* Cambridge, MA: The MIT Press.

CRIQUI, J-P., 2007. The World According to Christian Marclay. *In:* J-P. Criqui (ed.), *Christian Marclay: Replay.* Zurich: JRP|Ringier.

CRIMMINGS, E., 2001. Luc Courchesne, The Visitor: Living by Number. *In:* V. Lynn (ed.). *Space Odysseys: Sensation & Immersion.* Sydney: Art Gallery of New South Wales.

CRIMP, D., 1993a. The Art of Exhibition. In: *On the Museum's Ruins.* Cambridge, MA and London: The MIT Press.

—— 1993b. On the Museum's Ruins. In: *On the Museum's Ruins.* Cambridge, MA and London: The MIT Press.

CUBITT, S., 2000. Multimedia. *In:* T. Swiss and A. Herman (eds.). *The Web Unspun.* New York: New York University Press.

DAWSON, B., MCDONALD, F. and TREPANIER, G., 2008. Social Presence: new values for museums and networked audiences. *In:* J. Trant and D. Bearman (eds.). *Museums and the Web 2008, 8–12 April 2008, Montreal.* Toronto: Archives & Museum Informatics.

DCITA, 2002. *Myer Report.* Canberra: Commonwealth Department of Communications, Information Technology and the Arts.

DE BOTTON, A., 2002. *The Art of Travel.* London: Hamish Hamilton.

DEBRAY, R., 1996. *Media Manifestoes: on the technological transmission of cultural forms,* Transl. E. Rauth. London and New York: Verso.

DE LANDA, M., 1997. *A Thousand Years of Nonlinear History.* New York: Zone Books.

DELANY, M. and HAMMOND, K. (eds.), 2005. *Extra-Aesthetic.* Melbourne: Monash University Museum of Art.

DELEUZE, G., 1992. Mediators. *In:* J. Crary and S. Kwinter (eds.). *Incorporations.* New York: Zone.

DEPOCAS, A., IPPOLITO, J. and JONES, C. (eds.). 2003. *Permanence Through Change: the variable media approach.* New York and Montreal: Guggenheim Museum Publications and the Daniel Langlois Foundation for Art, Science, and Technology.

DERRIDA. J., 1987. The Parergon. *In:* J. Derrida. *The Truth in Painting.* Transl. J. Bennington and I. McLeod. Chicago: University of Chicago Press.

DE SALVO, D., 2005. Where WE Begin: opening the system, c.1970. *In:* D. De Salvo (ed.). *Open Systems – rethinking art, c.1970.* London, UK: Tate Publishing.

DIETZ, S. 1998. Curating on the Web: the museum in an interface culture. Presented at Museums and the Web: An International Conference, 22–25 April 1998, Toronto [abstract online]. Available from: http://www.archimuse.com/mw98/abstracts/dietz.html [19 September 2011].

DIPPLE, K., (ed.) 2005. Liquid Architectures. Online Discussion Forum [online]. Tate. Available from: http://www.tate.org.uk/forums/thread.jspa?threadID=4453 [26 June 2008].

DONATO, E., 1980. The Museum's Furnace: notes towards a contextual reading of Bouvard and Pecuchet. *In:* J. Harari (ed.). *Textual Strategies: perspectives in post-structuralist criticism.* London: Methuen.

DZIEKAN, V., 1997. Work-in-progress: the influence of photography on the production of representation in the age of mechanical reproduction (1912–1928), with a view towards the development of post-photographic practice and critique. Thesis (MA). Monash University.

DRUCKREY, T., 1993. Revisioning Technology. *In:* T. Druckery (ed.). *Iterations: the new image.* Cambridge, MA: International Center of Photography and the MIT Press.

ECO, U., 1979. *The Role of the Reader: explorations in the semiotics of texts.* Bloomington: Indiana University Press.

FLEMING, T., 2008. *Crossing Boundaries: the role of cross-art-form and media venues in the age of 'clicks' not 'bricks'.* London: UK Film Council (in association with Arts Council England and the Arts and Humanities Research Council).

FREUD, S., 1965. The Unconscious and Consciousness-Reality (1900). *In:* S. Freud. *The Interpretation of Dreams,* New York: Avon.

FULLER, M., 2005. *Media Ecologies: materialist energies in art and technoculture.* Cambridge, MA and London, UK: The MIT Press.

GIBSON, R., 1998. Ecologies of meaning. *Media International Australia, Incorporating Culture and Policy,* No. 89, November (Gary Warner interviewed by Ross Gibson).

GOAD, P., 2003. *The Building: National Gallery of Victoria.* Melbourne: National Gallery of Victoria.

GODFREY, M., 2005. From Box to Street and Back Again – an inadequate descriptive system for the seventies. *In:* D. De Salvo (ed.). *Open Systems – rethinking art, c.1970.* London, UK: Tate Publishing.

GRAHAM, B. and COOK, S. (eds.), 2010. *Rethinking Curating: art after new media*. Cambridge, MA: The MIT Press.

GRAU, O., 2003. *Virtual Art, from Illusion to Immersion*. Transl. G. Custance. Cambridge, MA: The MIT Press.

GROYS, B., 2005. The Mimesis of Thinking. *In*: D. De Salvo (ed.). *Open Systems – rethinking art, c.1970*. London, UK: Tate Publishing.

HANHARDT, J.G., 2003. Case Studies: Nam June Paik, TV Garden. *In*: A. Depocas, et al. (eds.). *Permanence Through Change: The Variable Media Approach*. New York and Montreal: Guggenheim Museum Publications and the Daniel Langlois Foundation for Art, Science, and Technology.

HANNERZ, U., 1992. *Cultural Complexity: studies in the social organization of meaning*. New York: Columbia University Press.

HAUENSCHILD, A., 1998. Claims and reality of New Museology: case studies in Canada, the United States and Mexico. Thesis (PhD). Center for Museum Studies, Smithsonian Institution.

HAYLES, N.K., 2000. The Condition of Virtuality. *In*: P. Lunenfeld (ed.). *The Digital Dialectic*. Cambridge, MA and London: The MIT Press.

HEMMENT, D., 2004. Locative Arts [online]. Available from: http://www.drewhemment.com/pdf/locativearts.pdf [19 September 2011].

HILL, P., 2006. True Lies and Superfictions. Presented at the Sorbonne Conference, 24–25 November 2006, Paris [online]. Available at: http://www.superfictions.com/sorbonne/intro.html [19 September 2011].

HIRST, P.Q., 2003. Power/Knowledge – constructed space and the subject. *In*: D. Preziosi and C. Farago (eds.). *Grasping the World: the idea of the museum*. Hants, UK and Burlington, VT: Ashgate.

HUHTAMO, E., 2002. On the Origins of the Virtual Museum. Presented at the Nobel Symposium on Virtual Museums and Public Understanding of Science and Culture, 26–29 May 2002, Stockholm [online]. Available at: http://www.nobelprize.org/nobel_organizations/nobelfoundation/symposia/interdisciplinary/ns120/lectures/huhtamo.pdf [19 September 2011].

JOHNSON, S., 1997. *Interface Culture: how new technology transforms the way we create and communicate*. New York: Harper Collins.

JUNG, C.G. 1969. *Synchronicity: an acausal connecting principle*. Transl. R.F.C Hull. Bollingen Series. Princeton, NJ: Princeton University Press.

KAYE, N., 2000. *Site-Specific Art: performance, place and documentation*. London and New York: Routledge.

KIESLER, F., 2001. Manifeste du Correalisme (facsimile). *In*: D. Bogner and P. Noever. *Frederick J. Kiesler: endless space*. Ostfildern-Ruit: Hatje Cantz Publishers.

KOCKELKOREN, P., 2002. *Technology: art, fairground and theatre*. Fascinations Series. Rotterdam: Nai Publishers.

KRAUSS, R., 2000. *A Voyage on the North Sea: art in the age of the post-medium condition*. London: Thames & Hudson.

—— 1996. Postmodernism's Museum Without Walls. *In*: R. Greenberg, et al. (eds.). *Thinking about Exhibitions*. London and New York: Routledge.

—— 1990. The Cultural Logic of the Late Capitalist Museum. *October*, No. 54.

KWON, M., 1997. One Place after Another: notes on site-specificity. *October*, No. 80.

LANDOW, G.P., 2000. Hypertext as Collage-writing. *In*: P. Lunenfeld (ed.). *The Digital Dialectic*. Cambridge, MA and London: The MIT Press.

LANHAM, R., 1993. *The Electronic Word: democracy, technology and the arts*. Chicago and London: The University of Chicago Press.

LAVIGNE, E., 2007. A Walk on the Wild Side: fragments for a punk aesthetic. *In:* J-P. Criqui (ed.), *Christian Marclay: replay*. Zurich: JRP|Ringier.

LEFEBVRE, H., 1991. *The Production of Space*. Transl. D. Nicolson-Smith. Oxford, UK and Cambridge, MA: Blackwell.

LUDOVICO, A., 2004. Fenlandia, slow pixels. *Neural.it*, 09/07/2004 [online]. Available from: http://www.neural.it/nnews/fenlandiae.htm [19 September 2011].

LYNN, V., 2001. *Space Odysseys: sensation & immersion*. Sydney: Art Gallery of New South Wales.

MAEDA, J., 2000. *Maeda Media*. London: Thames & Hudson.

MALRAUX, A., 1974. The Museum Without Walls. *In:* A. Malraux. *Voices of Silence*. Herts, UK: Paladin.

MANACORDA, F. and YEE, L., 2008. Introduction. *In: Encyclopedia of Terrestrial Life: Martian Museum of Terrestrial Art*, Vol. VIII. London: Barbican Art Gallery.

MASSUMI, B., 2002. *Parables for the Virtual: movement, affect, sensation*. Durham, NC and London: Duke University Press.

MEADOWS, M., 2003. *Pause & Effect: the art of interactive narrative*. Indianapolis, IN: New Riders.

MILES, R. and ZAVALA, L., 1994. *Towards the Museum of the Future: new European perspectives*. London and New York: Routledge.

MITCHELL, P. and RINTEL, E.S., 2002. Editorial. *M/C: A Journal of Media and Culture*, Vol. 5, No. 4 [online]. Available from: http://journal.media-culture.org.au/0208/editorial.php [19 September 2011].

MORRIS, R., 1993. Notes on Sculpture, Part 1. *In: Continuous Project Altered Daily: the writings of Robert Morris*. Cambridge, MA: The MIT Press.

MORRIS, S., 2001. *Museums & New Media Art*. New York: The Rockefeller Foundation.

MORSE, M., 1998. *Virtualities: television, media art, and cyberculture*. Bloomington and Indianapolis: Indiana University Press.

MUNSTER, A. and LOVINK, G., 2005. Theses on Distributed Aesthetics. Or, What a Network is Not. *Fibreculture Journal*, No. 7 (Distributed Aesthetics) [online]. Available from: http://journal.fibreculture.org/issue7/issue7_munster_lovink.html [19 September 2011].

MURRAY, K., 2003. Revelation in the new cathedral. *Realtime*, No. 55 (June-July) [online]. Available from: http://www.realtimearts.net/article.php?id=7101 [19 September 2011].

NEWHALL, B., 1982. *The History of Photography*. New York: The Museum of Modern Art.

O'DOHERTY, B., 1986. *Inside the White Cube: the ideology of the gallery space*. Berkeley and Los Angeles: University of California Press.

OLALQUIAGA, C., 1998. *The Artificial Kingdom*. New York: Pantheon Books.

OLKOWSKI, D., 1999. The Continuum of Interiority and Exteriority in the Thought of Merleau-Ponty. *In:* D. Olkowski and J. Morley (eds.), *Merleau-Ponty: interiority and exteriority, psychic life and the world*. Albany, NY: SUNY Press.

O'NEILL, P. (ed.), 2007. *Curating Subjects*. London: Open Editions.

PAUL, C. (ed.), 2008. *New Media in the White Cube and Beyond: curatorial models for digital art*. Berkeley: University of California Press.

PUTS, H., 1991. El Lissitzky (1890–1941): his life and work. *In:* C. De Bie, et al. (eds.). *El Lissitzky (1890–1941): architect painter photographer typographer*. Eindhoven: Municipal Van Abbemuseum.

RICE, C. 2004. Rethinking histories of the interior. *The Journal of Architecture*, Vol. 9, No. 4 (Autumn).

ROTZER, F., 1993. Images Within Images, or, from the Image to the Virtual World. *In:* T. Druckery. *Iterations: the new image*. Cambridge, MA: International Center of Photography and the MIT Press.

SAMIS, P., 2008. Who Has the responsibility for Saying What We See? Mashing up museum, artist, and visitor voices, on-site and on-line. *In:* J. Trant and D. Bearman (eds.). *Museums and the Web 2008, 8–12 April 2008, Montreal.* Toronto: Archives & Museum Informatics.

SAUMAREZ SMITH, C., 1989. Museums, Artefacts, and Meanings. *In:* P. Vergo (ed.). *The New Museology.* London: Reaktion Books.

SERMON, P., 2004. The Emergence of User- and Performer-determined Narratives in Telematic Environments. *In:* A. Zapp (ed.). *Networked Narrative Environments as Imaginary Spaces of Being.* Manchester: MIRIAD.

SCHUBERT, K., 2000. *The Curator's Egg: the evolution of the museum concept from the French Revolution to the present day.* London: One-Off Press.

SCHWARTZ, H.P, 1999. Net Art in the Museum [online]. Net_condition. ZKM Online. Available from: http://on1.zkm.de/netcondition/curators/schwarz/default_e [19 September 2011].

SCHWARZ, D., 1988. 'Look! Books in Plaster!': on the first phase of the work of Marcel Broodthaers. *In:* B.H.D. Buchloh (ed.). *Broodthaers: writings, interviews, photographs.* Cambridge, MA: The MIT Press.

SHKLOVSKY, V., 2004. Art as Technique. *In:* J. Rivkin and M. Ryan (eds). *Literary Theory: an anthology.* 2nd ed. Malden, MA: Blackwell.

STANISZEWSKI, M., 2003. An Interpretation/Translation of Muntadas' Projects. *In:* O. Rofes (ed.). *On Translation.* Barcelona: Actar/MACBA.

STRATE, L. and WACHTEL, E., 2005. Introduction. *In:* L. Strate and E. Wachtel (eds.). *The Legacy of McLuhan.* Creskill, NJ: Hampton Press.

STUBBS, M., 2005. A Leap into the Light. In: E. Edmonds and M. Stubbs (eds.). *White Noise.* Melbourne: The Australian Centre for the Moving Image.

SUMMERS, D., 2003. *Real Spaces: world art history and the rise of Western modernism.* London: Phaidon.

TIDEMANN, R., 1999. Dialectics at a Standstill: Approaches to the Passagen-Werk. *In:* W. Benjamin. *The Arcades Project.* Transl. H. Eiland and K. McLaughlin. London: Belnap Press.

TOFTS, D., 2005. Tsk tsk tsk & beyond: anticipating distributed aesthetics. *Fibreculture Journal*, No. 7 (Distributed Aesthetics) [online]. Available from: http://journal.fibreculture.org/issue7/issue7_tofts.html [19 September 2011].

ULMER, G., 1994. The Heuretics of Deconstruction. *In:* P. Brunette and D. Wills (eds.). *Deconstruction and the Visual Arts.* New York: Cambridge University Press.

VERGO, P., 1994. The Rhetoric of Display. In: R. Miles and L. Zavala (eds.). *Towards the museum of the future: new European perspectives.* London and New York: Routledge.

—— 1989a. Introduction. *In:* P. Vergo (ed.). *The New Museology.* London: Reaktion Books.

—— 1989b. The Reticent Object. *In:* P. Vergo (ed.). *The New Museology.* London: Reaktion Books.

VIRILIO, P., 1997. *Open Sky.* London and New York: Verso.

—— 1994. *The Vision Machine.* London and Bloomington: BFI and Indiana University Press.

WEBSTER, D. (ed.), 2000. *The New National Gallery of Victoria – One Vision, Two Galleries.* Melbourne: National Gallery of Victoria.

WEIL, S., 1990. *Rethinking the Museum, and Other Meditations.* Washington, DC and London: Smithsonian Institution Press.

WOLLEN, P., 1995. Introduction. *In:* L. Cooke and P. Wollen (eds.). *Visual Display: culture beyond appearances.* Seattle: Bay Press.

WRIGHT, P., 1989. The Quality of Visitors' Experience in Art Museums. *In:* P. Vergo (ed.). *The New Museology.* London: Reaktion Books.

ZAPP, A., 2004a. Introduction. *In:* A. Zapp (ed.). *Networked Narrative Environments as Imaginary Spaces of Being*. Manchester: MIRIAD.

—— (ed.) 2004b. *Networked Narrative Environments as Imaginary Spaces of Being*. Manchester: MIRIAD.

ZINGRONE, F., 2005. Virtuality and McLuhan's 'World as Art Form'. *In:* L. Strate and E. Wachtel (eds.). *The Legacy of McLuhan*. Creskill, NJ: Hampton Press.